THE VIENNA I KNEW

THE VIENNA
I KNEW

Memories of a European
Childhood

JOSEPH WECHSBERG

Doubleday & Company, Inc., Garden City, New York
1979

Library of Congress Cataloging in Publication Data

Wechsberg, Joseph, 1907–
  The Vienna I knew.

    1. Wechsberg, Joseph, 1907–   2. Vienna—Biography.
I. Title.
DB844.W4A38   787'.1'0924 [B]
ISBN: 0-385-12674-3
Library of Congress Catalog Card Number 78-22540

To the Memory of My Parents

THE VIENNA I KNEW

1.

I DON'T KNOW exactly when it was that I saw my father's cuff links again after all these years. I had opened a drawer in the baroque chest where I keep old photographs, clippings, pseudo-gold medals of bizarre awards, and other memorabilia, some of them now meaningless. Most of us keep far too many things. But the cuff links belong there.

They are the only things of my father's that I still have. He went away one day in September 1914 and was killed two months later, in the First World War. The cuff links are made of silver, showing the profile of a baroque angel. Actually it is my mother's profile as a young girl when she met my father. She looks, on the cuff links, as she does in her early photographs. I don't know whose idea the cuff links were, but it is tender and affectionate, and tells a lot about my parents and their happy life together. It had to be happy because it was so short.

My father had other cuff links, some for formal wear, in gold, but they have disappeared, as so many people and things disappear, one doesn't know how or where. Shortly after my mother was officially notified of my father's death two of his brothers claimed some of his things, saying that "dear Siegfried promised them to us before he went away." Perhaps it was true; she was too sad to care. Later on an acquaintance claimed something else that had been "promised" to him. By that time my mother knew

it wasn't true but she didn't refuse. She didn't want to keep the
things that reminded her intimately of her husband. And so his
personal belongings disappeared one after another.

Only the silver cuff links with my mother's picture remained.
Perhaps no one wanted them. Perhaps they were too personal
and not really valuable. But my mother told me later that my father had liked these cuff links best. I believe it now. I paid no attention when she said she was going to keep the cuff links for
me. I was seven years old when my younger brother Max and I
lost our father. At the age of seven one doesn't think of cuff
links.

I don't know who made them, perhaps a silversmith in
Vienna who specialized in baroque art work. My mother looks
like a painting by an Italian *seicento* master. The silver has
darkened and the cuff links have the dark gray shade of the candlesticks we had on our table on Friday evenings and the high
holidays. Such cuff links are hard to find nowadays; even the an-
tique stores no longer have them. Not long ago I asked an old
man, one of the last remaining silversmiths in Vienna, whether
he could still make them. He shook his head, regretfully. It
wasn't that he lacked skill, for he and a few others might be able
to reproduce them, but they would be prohibitively expensive.

"No one would want to pay that kind of money now," he
said. "People would rather buy something shiny and golden,
something that 'projects an image.' That's what they call it, isn't
it?"

Yes, I said. My father's cuff links project no image. No one
notices them—which was exactly the idea. No one was supposed
to notice them. Yet in a way they were the beginning of my
search for my father, of whom I had known so little when he
went away.

Now I can see him clearly. I believe that I really remember
the day when I saw him for the last time. For many years I

didn't remember but lately my memories have become sharply focused. In 1914 my father was forty-one. He was tall and erect in his light blue tunic and dark blue pants, with saber and shako. The k. & k.—*kaiserlich & königliche* (imperial & royal)—Austrian army was a superb peacetime army, and, while no one knew how good it would be in battle, the officers wore beautiful uniforms. Nowadays such uniforms are seen in operettas and in films with a Merry Old Vienna background. In Vienna they often provoke outbursts of nostalgia and enthusiasm, especially among older people who glorify the monarchy, but also among younger ones who saw the olive-drab, not particularly glamorous uniforms which we American G.I.s wore in the Second World War.

For many years, every time I saw the widely reproduced picture of Emperor Franz Joseph I, I was secretly pleased that he wore "my father's uniform," as I thought of it. The Kaiser wore a general officer's red stripes on his pants, and he had a beautifully embroidered gold collar. After all, he was the Emperor. My father had only the two gold stars of an *Oberleutenant* but his uniform projected for me the magic that—I know now—is more effective on the operetta stage than in action.

I think of my father more often now than I did when I was young. I am trying to create a composite picture of him, which is difficult. The people who knew him have died, and there is no one to talk to. And I want to see him as he really was, not to idealize him. When he went away to die "for God, Kaiser, and Fatherland," I clearly perceived his presence. What I've learned since makes the impression only more true, almost three-dimensional; nothing has changed it. He was quiet and gentle. He lived in an era when a man could afford to be quiet and gentle. Today he might be sadly out of place.

The decade prior to the First World War was perhaps the best time for the comfortably off Jewish middle class in Moravia, one of the oldest parts of Austria-Hungary, where my family lived. (It is now part of Czechoslovakia.) The Habsburg Empire was breaking up—my father sensed it instinctively and talked to my mother about it, in the resigned way of those who are convinced they cannot change the inexorable course of history. Yet Austria-Hungary in its years of deepening decay and gradual breakup was a glittering, fascinating phenomenon. My father became a banker, which was always a strange word and is now a dirty word in my home town of Mährisch-Ostrau* (or Ostrava, as it is called today).

I was known as "the banker's son" long after the family bank had disappeared in the aftermath of the First World War. Not only people and their possessions but banks and fortunes too disappeared. Like plumbers and dentists, bankers will always be needed, but they lead precarious lives, close to the abyss of their credibility. My father was a junior partner in the family bank which *his* father had founded, but he was not a banker at heart. He did his job to please his father (just as I later became a lawyer to please my mother). I was glad to discover, first from vague hints and later from detailed reports by my mother and elderly cousins, that my father had run away from home when he was thirteen. In 1886 he went all the way from Ostrau to Trieste, then the great harbor of the Habsburg monarchy. There he managed to get himself hired as either an apprentice seaman or a cabin boy on an oceangoing vessel before his father found him, just in time, and brought him back home. Yes, "just in time," it was said. In time for what?

❖   ❖

* In this memoir I call my home town both Ostrau, its German name, and Ostrava, the Czech name, depending on whether I mean the place of my childhood and youth, in the early years of the century, or the town after 1918, at the end of World War I, when its name was changed.

I remember my father, his warm brown eyes, his dark brown hair, the longish nose and big ears that I'm said to have inherited, the fine oval face. Above all, I well remember the sense of peacefulness he seemed to radiate. My father had learned early that life is often dramatic, and it is useless to dramatize the drama. I felt tranquil and secure near him. I hear the sound of his voice, a lyric baritone voice. I never heard him raise it; he liked to speak softly. And I remember that he often smiled but rarely laughed. After 1914 my mother, then a widow, would say, "He never shouted. Sometimes he was really angry, usually with good reason. Even in such moments he wouldn't shout. He might look at me in his quietly expressive way. I well understood, though I wouldn't admit it at the moment. He would walk out of the room and leave me alone for a while. It was much worse than if he had shouted. Other people get noisy when they quarrel. We became very quiet."

My mother laughed a lot; she loved to laugh, and she could laugh and cry in the same breath. She and my father were well matched because they were so different. He was tall, perhaps six feet two, and she was rather short. When he extended his right arm horizontally my mother could walk under it without hurting her ambitious coiffure. She wore her hair up in an opulent crown. At family parties her performance, walking under her husband's outstretched arm, never failed to amuse some and impress others. They thought it was "symbolic." In the street, when they walked together and she took his arm, either she had to wear high heels or he had to bend down slightly.

I cannot remember that my father ever shouted at me or slapped my face, and I was certainly a spoiled brat. For the first five years of my life I was my parents' only child, the apple of their eyes. In some circles I am now known as a man who is serious about eating. (I dislike being called a "gourmet" as much as I dislike being called "Doctor.") As a child, my "gourmet" inclinations were limited to *Würstel*—small sausages, a pair of hot dogs—and to hot cocoa. At the same time. I had *Würstel* and cocoa, or cocoa and *Würstel*, for breakfast, at noon, at night. Idiotic—and it may shock people who nowadays compliment me on my "gastronomic" writings, but it is true. It wasn't so much the components—*Würstel* and cocoa are good, taken separately—but the combination that seemed to irritate people.

My silly, steady diet of protein and ground cocoa butter had a deplorable effect on my appearance. Some dear friends of my parents would hint that the poor child perhaps didn't get enough to eat. This would upset my mother, but my father would just smile because he knew the truth. My aunts said I was too thin, too pale, too green in the face, while other kids were robust and normal. No one went so far as to suggest I was "abnormal." But I was always sniffling and coughing and running a temperature. My poor mother would get worried and call Dr. Himmelblau, the family doctor. For the benefit of younger readers who may not know that expression, I'd like to state that Dr. Himmelblau knew something about everything, from appendix to depression to "stones." He understood that the women in the family meant diamonds when they mentioned stones and that the men meant kidney stones. Best of all, Dr. Himmelblau would come to the house whenever he was asked, day or night. *He* was a family doctor.

He would look at me and know the shabby truth, of course. But then he would turn around and see the worried expression in the eyes of my father and mother, and he would give an invisible shrug. No use telling them that all I needed was a good spanking, and nothing to eat for a couple of days, not a single *Würstel*. In no time I would be as hungry and normal as other kids. Goodness, I might even eat spinach and look pink-cheeked and healthy, not pale or green. But he understood how my parents felt, and so he uttered some meaningless words that would make them feel better. And he would prescribe a small tea-spoonful of cod-liver oil. That was his way of getting even with me. No child, even a normal one, if such exists, likes cod-liver oil, and I was no exception. Dr. Himmelblau knew it would be a major undertaking to make me swallow the teaspoonful of oil. It had to be inserted quickly between a bite of *Würstel* and a swallow of cocoa.

Sometimes I wouldn't take it and sometimes I would—not from "the women," only when my father gave it to me. "The women" were my mother; Marie, the cook, my maternal grandmother's "wedding present" to my mother after she got married; and Fräulein Gertrud, our *Kinderfräulein* from Upper Silesia whose job was vague. I suppose we had a *Kinderfräulein* because many well-to-do families had one. It must have been a status symbol, like a swimming pool in Hollywood in the 1930s. In moments of a cod-liver oil crisis my mother would call my father, explaining that the women had tried everything and that I resisted. Only *he* could do it.

My father would approach me, smiling. He did not hide the spoon behind his back like those silly women; he displayed it prominently. And he did not foolishly promise me a chocolate candy—I didn't refuse good Swiss chocolate, which is made of cocoa butter—if I swallowed the disgusting liquid. Instead he explained matter-of-factly, man to man, that it might be "sensible" to swallow the cod-liver oil "and get it over with."

I was so surprised to be accepted almost as an adult that I nodded and swallowed. My mother and Fräulein Gertrud broke into hosannas. My father seemed rather embarrassed by what the women considered his "achievement." He was also sad because he knew they didn't treat me right. And he was proud of me because I had acted "sensibly." I was his son.

Obviously Dr. Himmelblau knew his business. He also knew the use of the ambiguous phrase when he wanted to calm the worries of anxious parents. He had quite a few "patients" who were spoiled brats, not sick at all. Much later I found out that he had once been in love with my mother—before she met the man who became my father. He had hoped to marry her but he had never proposed.

To me it seemed absurd that my mother might have married Dr. Himmelblau. In appearance he was the very opposite of my father; short, with a completely bald head, a billiard-ball head, and a healthy reddish face. He spent his Sundays hiking in the mountains and believed in fresh air and long walks. My father liked to sit and meditate. Dr. Himmelblau remained a devoted friend of my mother and our family doctor after she became a widow. When things were getting bad for a while he sent her no bills.

Soon after my mother and father were married in 1906, he married another woman. His wife was smiling when she met my mother, then a widow: *she* still had her husband. In some moments, when Frau Dr. Himmelblau thought she wasn't being watched, she would give my mother what even I, a naïve teen-ager, recognized as a dirty look. She had no sympathy for my mother's and Dr. Himmelblau's not so secret wish that one day I might marry Gerda, the older of the two Himmelblau daughters. Gerda knew it. We had great fun when we went to Herr Exner's dancing school together and our mothers were present. Once we even pretended to be in love, for their benefit (or irritation). But of course we were not in love. We agreed that we would certainly never get married.

We were good friends until I left my homeland in 1938 and went to America. When I came back to Ostrava as an American soldier at the end of the war, trying to find my mother and many others, the Himmelblau daughters had "disappeared"—as had almost everybody else I had known.

❖   ❖

I am ahead of myself, as I'll often be in this memoir. Memories and thoughts are not like the logical lines of geometric drawings. They are more like the artfully intertwined arabesques of art nouveau ornaments. Or like the small marble pebbles on the paths of the Jewish cemetery in the South Tyrolean town of Merano, one of the few places on earth where I feel at peace with myself. The cemetery has dark old trees and is surrounded by vineyards and mountains. One is called Monte Giuseppe, Joseph's Mountain. For a while I had the silly notion that the mountain might have been named after me; it never occurred to me that it might be the other way around. (Actually I was named after Great-uncle Joseph.) The road leading to the cemeteries—one Jewish, the other Catholic—is called St. Joseph's Street. Now that cannot be an accident.

The cemetery is a short walk from the Merano railroad station where I usually arrive. I no longer drive a car. I've always been fond of trains and trees, of vineyards and mountains. When I move there permanently I shall have them all. A pleasant prospect for a man whose father was buried in an anonymous mass grave and whose mother has no grave at all.

❖   ❖

My father was the youngest of nine children—six boys and three girls. I scarcely remember his sisters, my aunts. They seemed to be always ailing and old, as though they had been born that way. I have only a vague memory of Uncle Rudolph, a high-ranking official of the Austrian railroads. His only claim to fame was having been in charge of two special trains carrying archdukes and minor members of the House of Habsburg.

Grandfather Albert Wechsberg had been born in 1827, "three years before the Kaiser was born," they said in our family. The Kaiser was Franz Joseph I. Naturally. He wasn't an emperor when he was born, only an archduke, though he became emperor at the tender age of eighteen. Grandfather Wechsberg was eighty-six when he died in 1913, again three years before Emperor Franz Joseph I died. My mother never failed to mention the mysterious relationship between Grandfather and the Kaiser. All important dates in the family were related to the Kaiser. No one bothered to remember that Beethoven had still been alive—though barely—when Grandfather Wechsberg was born, and Goethe as well.

As the youngest child, my father was often criticized and rarely spoiled by his parents. In Jewish families it's usually the first-born son who is pampered—the dynastic principle has been the rule since Abraham. Grandfather Wechsberg was mainly interested in his sons—the girls were married off as quickly as could be conveniently arranged. And it was his sons who gave him trouble. Uncle Hugo, the oldest, "lived with that woman," as my aunts would say. "That woman" was Aunt Alma, and her sin was not that she was living in concubinage with an unmarried man—*that* they might have forgiven—but that she was not Jewish. She was a Protestant and, to make matters worse, she was "from elsewhere," from Hamburg. The way the aunts talked about Hamburg, it must have been the modern incarnation of Sodom and Gomorrah, a Protestant branch, to be sure. I didn't understand what a Protestant was but I began to wonder why even Fräulein Gertrud joined in the anti-Protestant chorus of my aunts. Fräulein Gertrud was a Catholic from Gleiwitz, Upper Silesia. Why would a Catholic be on the side of my Jewish aunts whenever Aunt Alma from Hamburg was mentioned?

I met Aunt Alma eventually. I was then a teen-ager traveling to Hamburg and the North Sea. That was during the early 1920s, the time of the astronomic inflation in Germany, and very inexpensive since my mother had given me some good Czech crowns. A distant relative in America had sent me a few dollar bills for my *bar mitzvah*, when I was thirteen and became a man, in the Orthodox Jewish sense of the word. The distant relative, whom I never met and whose name I have forgotten, had suggested I might change the dollar bills in Germany, where they were worth a fortune, and buy myself the collected works of Friedrich von Schiller. But I already had two Schillers and so I bought myself an early Leica. It had a low number and is still quite good, after all these years, better than the newer Leicas that my fellow soldiers in the American army got in Germany after the Second World War, when a dollar was again worth a fortune and a Leica an object of widespread greed. Economic history goes in cycles but basically never changes.

By the time I met her, Aunt Alma was married to Uncle Hugo. They lived in a spacious apartment overlooking the Binnenalster in Hamburg. Uncle Hugo, whom I had not known, looked exactly what he was, an important scholar of chemistry. Aunt Alma was what my father would have called "sensible," making no fuss, practical and kindhearted, especially when she talked to Uncle Hugo, who had "a bad heart." They seemed to adore each other. I instantly and permanently revised my ideas about Protestants from elsewhere, no matter where.

Uncle Hugo gave me a long, sad look when he saw me. He said he had not seen me since I was a baby. I already knew that sort of look. Some people who had known my father and saw me for the first time looked at me that way. Shock mixed with delight.

Uncle Hugo said, "Pepi, you look *exactly* like Siegfried." (At home and in school I was called Pepi, the Czech nickname for Joseph, and my few classmates who have survived still call me that. My brother Max, an American since the Second World War, no longer calls me Pepi but Joe.)

Uncle Hugo was staring at me. Then he hesitated and walked toward the large window and looked out, standing with his back to us, turned around and came back, and I noticed, with a sinking heart, that he was crying. It was terrible to see a grown-up man crying. Aunt Alma was deeply worried. She put her hand around his shoulder and said, "Hugo, *please,* you know you mustn't upset yourself."

He nodded at her and lightly touched her cheek with his fingers, an affectionate gesture that I remembered so well. My father had often done it to my mother. Uncle Hugo put his arms around me and all the time he was crying.

"I'm all right, Alma," he said. And speaking toward the window, he said, as though to himself, "I was *very* fond of my youngest brother." He looked down at me with great warmth. "Of your dear father."

Aunt Alma broke up the sentimental scene by suggesting, in her brusque Hamburg dialect, that we'd better go into the other room and have "*Ka*ffe," with the accent on the first syllable, as in English, with a short *e* at the end. At home we pronounced it the Viennese way, "Kaf*fee,*" as the French say "*café.*" Aunt Alma was moved too, though she tried not to show it. Before I left Hamburg she told me that my mother was the only one who had been kind to her, and that she had once come to Hamburg to see her and Uncle Hugo, while my father's sisters had consistently ignored her.

"We were not married then," Aunt Alma said. She wasn't apologetic at all, just told me the fact. I liked her.

❖   ❖

That was not the first time that someone who had been close to my father compared me to him, but it was the first time I remember. It has happened many times in the years since. The resemblance was noticed by people who had been fond of my father and were now fond of me. My cousin Martha, for instance, who was my mother's age.

"It's not so much that you look like him," Martha said. "It's the way you speak and are suddenly silent. It's very strange." She shook her head, dumfounded. "I hope you will always be like him. Uncle Siegfried was really a wonderful man."

Gradually the picture of my father emerged more clearly, in focus, with many details. Several years had passed since his death, and my mother no longer broke into tears at the mere mention of her husband. People began to talk about my father at some distance, objectively, with no sentimentality. They would say he had been kindhearted and decent, "a good man." The way they said it, I understood that there were not too many good men around. Friends would tell my mother, "Siegfried was the best of the Wechsberg brothers," perhaps implying that the others were not so terribly good. Then they and my mother would nod, matter-of-factly, as though they knew exactly what they meant. I didn't.

"He trusted people," my mother said. "Strange because, after all, he was a banker by profession." I didn't know as I do today that a banker is not supposed to trust people, that he's trained to distrust them. Though, having met quite a few bankers, I believe the best of them are those who trust people. Perhaps good bankers know instinctively whom to trust and whom to distrust.

The friends shook their heads; they agreed that dear Siegfried had been a remarkably trusting person. Once somebody said that my father may have inherited his "sixth sense, the banker's sense," from *his* father, Grandfather Wechsberg, the founder of the family bank. Grandfather Wechsberg was said to have looked at a would-be creditor and decided, instantly, yes or no. When he decided yes, the man got his credit, and often he wasn't even asked for collateral security. And when Grandfather Wechsberg decided no, it was no, and there was no way of making him change his mind, though some customers had tried very hard. People said my father had been exactly like that, in a more withdrawn, quiet manner. He would shake his head regretfully, and that was that. No credit, sorry.

At that point my mother would say, "He always trusted *me*," and I was getting bored because I knew what was coming: the story I had so often heard of how my father would take her to a ball though he hated balls and noise and crowds. He took her because he knew she loved to dance. He would dance with her three or four times. Paradoxically, my mother said, he was a very good dancer though he didn't like to dance. After the third or fourth dance my father would kiss his wife on the eyes, and she would ask, "Wouldn't you stay at least for another hour?" My father would shake his head, gently but firmly, as with the would-be creditors. He would get his coat and opera hat and the doeskin gloves, and he would walk home, leaving his wife at the ball.

"And why not?" my mother would finish her story, almost belligerently, though no one had provoked the question. "Because he knew he could trust me."

They all nodded; they knew what she was hinting at. I didn't, not then. I understood a few years later when I secretly got hold of a copy of Arthur Schnitzler's *Reigen* (*La Ronde*) and read the dialogue between the married woman, the one wearing a veil, and the young man who secretly meet to make love in the afternoon. My father and Arthur Schnitzler were of the same generation—my father was born in 1873—and my mother was perhaps the age of Schnitzler's married woman. My mother was attractive, and she often happened to wear a veil, though there the resemblance to Schnitzler's heroine ended. I began to understand some things. The result was increased respect for my father. He must have known the story of *Reigen*; he had read everything Arthur Schnitzler wrote. In our family, as in many Jewish families, Schnitzler was considered a sort of distant relative. He was a neurologist and a chronicler, and above all the poet of his epoch and its society. He knew so much; and he knew everybody. And my father, knowing the risk, had left my mother at the ball, just making sure that someone would accompany her home.

"Maybe Siegfried knew you were a good credit risk," a friend would tell my mother, and everybody would laugh. A while ago my mother had been on the verge of crying, and now she was laughing. She was beginning to see herself as a famous actress playing the part of Frau Wechsberg. My mother admired the Vienna Burgtheater, now called the "Burg," and I am sure she saw herself in the role of the attractive *Salondame* at the ball, surrounded by admirers with more or less doubtful designs though she would "just dance" and have fun. And then she would go home. The next morning she would tell my father everything: with whom she had danced and what some awful women had said about him, leaving his attractive young wife alone at the ball. My father would just listen, and he might smile.

"He didn't care about silly gossip and what some people said about him, but he was amused," my mother would say. "Sometimes I got very angry. In his place I would have been concerned, not amused."

More pieces of the puzzle fell into place. My father had trusted his wife. He even trusted her about money, when many husbands didn't trust their wives, and vice versa. He didn't ask her to keep a record of the household expenses. I learned from him that it pays to trust people.

"He was *generous*," my mother said, with feeling. I thought I understood. I already knew that a great many people are not generous. Later my cousin Martha told me a few stories about my father's generosity.

The oldest daughter of my father's oldest sister, Martha could have been my aunt, so far as her age was concerned. But when she reminisced about my father she would call him "Uncle Siegfried," which never failed to surprise me. But of course he *had* been her uncle.

When Martha was sixteen she had been sent to Grandfather's home in Ostrau to keep house for him. That was around 1900. Grandfather had lost his wife Fanny, my paternal grandmother. My maternal grandmother, my mother's mother, was also named Fanny. It was confusing and I was secretly relieved that Grandmother Fanny Wechsberg had died before I was born. She remains remote to me, just a character in the family history.

Martha had lived with her family in Trieste. Her father had been *Marine-Ingenieur,* a builder working for the imperial Austrian navy. Why did she have to come to Ostrau? It seems that Grandfather Wechsberg, one of the richest men in town, "who could have afforded a first-rate housekeeper and all the personnel he wanted" (I quote my mother), hated the idea of having "people" around the house. Servants, employees. Grandfather, who trusted his clients at the bank, didn't trust "people" at home. Poor Martha, sixteen and skinny and frightened, was sent from sunny Trieste to Ostrau with its gray skies and there had to run Grandfather's large house. Today most girls at her age would have refused, rebelled. She went. My father soon became her favorite uncle, and later she transferred her affection to me, because I reminded her of him. I know many things about him from her.

The three sons of Grandfather Wechsberg who lived in Ostrau and were his junior partners at the family bank had to take turns visiting their father. They took their wives along. Grandfather Wechsberg didn't care about his daughters-in-law, and he cared even less about his own daughters; they didn't have to visit. But he insisted upon seeing his three resident sons—Eugen, Alfred, Siegfried, according to age—who lived at the house he had built at Brückenstrasse 8 where I spent my formative years.

The sons had to go to Grandfather's villa once a week, whether they liked it or not. I don't think they did, but my mother said it was their duty, and she sighed. My uncles often went there alone, but my father always took his wife along. Grandfather Wechsberg liked her because she laughed a lot and cheered him up.

He was then known as a patriarch and a sage. The arrangements he had made at our house in Brückenstrasse seemed to prove it. The bank's counters and the cashier, my cousin Nelli with the incredibly nimble fingers, were on the street floor. The offices of the three junior partners were above, on the second floor, from which two spiral staircases led down into the public rooms. Over the bank were the apartments of the three junior partners, one apartment on each floor. The house had five floors, which, just after the turn of the century, when it was built, made it one of the highest in town.

Unfortunately there was no elevator. Grandfather Wechsberg considered an elevator a luxury and bad for the health. "Walking up and down the steps will do you a lot of good," he told his sons. The apartments were allocated according to seniority. Uncle Eugen, the oldest of the three, was just above the bank. One floor higher up was Uncle Alfred. Our apartment was on the top floor, the fifth. Going down, I had to walk or jump 134 steps, and coming back I had to walk up 134 steps. I didn't mind, though it was a lot of steps when one walked them four or five times a day, but some older people complained and refused to visit us. After one of my father's elderly sisters had complained that she couldn't walk up there, he smiled and said that was one advantage of living on the fifth floor.

Martha told me that the ritual visits to Grandfather's villa were regulated by seniority. The older brothers went during the week. On weekends they made excursions to the nearby mountains or went to the Radfahrverein, the Bicycle Club, which locally had the status and the minor intrigues of a country club in a middle-sized town in America. Meanwhile my father and mother were "on duty" at Grandfather's home on Saturday and Sunday. Poor skinny Martha was responsible for dinner and refreshments. Many years later she told me that Uncle Siegfried and Aunt Minka (my mother's name was Hermine but everybody called her Minka) were the only visitors Grandfather had enjoyed.

"There was no trouble when they came. Grandfather laughed more on these two nights than during the rest of the week. He wasn't easy to get along with as he got old. He could be quite stubborn."

After my parents had cheered up Grandfather on their weekend visits my father would call Martha aside and ask her whether she needed a little extra money to pay all the bills. He knew that Grandfather was getting quite stingy, even saving the backs of used envelopes to write imperious memos to his sons at the bank.

"I never had enough money," Martha remembered. "Everybody knew it but Uncle Siegfried was the only one who did something about it. He always told me not to mention it to anybody."

❖   ❖

Martha also told me what happened in Trieste when my father, then a teen-ager, had run away to work on a ship and see the world. 1886. Martha was a baby then, but years later she was told about all the excitement my father had caused.

"Maybe Uncle Siegfried read Joseph Conrad and that gave him the idea," she said. Ostrau was a thousand kilometers from the nearest coast, and no one at home thought of ships or going to sea.

"Exactly what *you* did when you ran away to America,"

Martha said. "I tried to explain it to your mother. But she cried and wouldn't listen to me."

I hadn't read Conrad, though; that came later. I had gotten bored at the Paris Sorbonne, not a cheerful place on a dark winter morning, when the yellow lights were on in the auditoriums named after great French scientists. I began to play the fiddle in cafés and obscure night clubs and eventually I became second violinist on a small French Line steamer that went from Bordeaux to New York, by way of Vigo and Santander in Spain, and Halifax, Nova Scotia. I didn't tell this to anybody at home because they wouldn't have understood it. Today it would hardly matter, everybody is running away from something, but in 1928 it was different. It was an interesting life, good food and little work, not at all Joseph Conrad-style, except for the rats in the corridors. Even some very elegant ships had rats.

"You caused a family scandal, just like your father," Martha said warmly, looking pleased. "I was happy." She didn't say what she'd been happy about but I had a good idea. I asked her what happened to the boy in Trieste, in 1886, and how they had traced him all the way from Ostrau. Trieste seemed farther away than the Seychelles or Fiji Islands are today.

"I believe it was my father who found the boy on that ship," Martha said. Engineer Goldoni, who worked at the harbor, knew a lot of people and when he was notified by Grandfather that the boy might be around Trieste he had started to look for him.

"Trieste was the logical place," Martha said. "The big Austrian harbor. Ships going out almost every day. If a boy was serious about running away he would go to Trieste. Well, that ship was due to leave in forty-eight hours for the Far East. My father sent a telegram to Ostrau, and Grandfather arrived, just in time. It cost him a lot of money to straighten things out but, if Grandfather wanted something, nothing would stop him. He took

Siegfried home and put him right back into the *Realschule* though Uncle Siegfried hated algebra and geometry. Many years later he told me that he was sorry they had found him. He wanted so much to see the Far East."

I was glad to know "the secret." It made my father more real and human to me. He seemed a paragon of virtue in the memories of my mother, of other people. I felt better knowing that he had tried to run away; that he didn't want to be a banker; that he became a banker because he didn't want to hurt his father.

"The secret," also called "the Trieste affair," had for a long time been closely guarded; knowing it helped me to explain to myself why I had run away from home at the age of twenty-one, in 1928, and played the fiddle on ocean liners all over the world: perhaps the heritage of wanderlust and revolt, of nonconformism and unrestricted individualism.

"Uncle Siegfried wasn't even Grandfather's favorite son," Martha said. "That was Uncle Max, the family's black sheep, but such a charming black sheep." She smiled and was almost pretty though she wasn't a handsome woman, with her tall, bony figure and her aquiline nose. But there was so much goodness in her eyes.

The fascinating Uncle Max remains a dim, vague figure in my memory. He always came to see my parents on his annual visits from Vienna, and I must have seen him, but perhaps I was too young; I don't remember. He was fond of my parents and they were devoted to him. In earlier years, when Uncle Max had been in trouble, Grandfather Wechsberg would go to Vienna. Later my father got the delicate assignment. Tact as well as strength was needed. Uncle Max was almost always in debt.

He must have been a character straight out of Schnitzler, who had known Uncle Max and may for all I know have used him in one of his composite characters. No one can tell; even the

playwright himself might not have known. Uncle Max had
been a noted physician, just like Schnitzler. He was a successful
gynecologist, which, according to my mother, "explained his
success with all those women." The way she pronounced "those"
opened up a whole new world, especially after I'd read *Reigen*.
I had never been in Vienna but I thought I had an idea of what
had been going on there around the turn of the century.

And Uncle Max had been right in the middle of it. A bachelor, dashing and elegant, who needed only "three or four hours
of sleep." Again, I quote my mother. And he was a wonderful
dancer. The most exciting balls in my mother's memory were
those when Uncle Max happened to be in town. Maybe my
mother had asked him to come. He would dance with her and
he would bring her home.

"You can imagine what 'those' women were whispering when
my husband's brother took me home," my mother said happily. I
was pleased that "those" women existed not only in Vienna but
in our provincial town too. Perhaps they were everywhere.

He played the piano beautifully and was a friend of Alfred
Grünfeld, the celebrated Viennese pianist. Grünfeld took Uncle
Max to the house of Johann Strauss in Vienna's Fourth District.
Strauss had long been a national hero because of his great
waltzes and *Die Fledermaus,* first performed in 1874. On his
visits to Ostrau, Uncle Max regaled my parents with many details of evenings *chez* Strauss. The food wasn't important, and
dinner was rarely a formal affair. In his old age Strauss and his
friends liked simple, good things. *Würstel,* the gastronomic fascination of my early life, and good wine from nearby Gum-
poldskirchen. But there were always expensive cigars—my father, who knew about cigars, would nod approvingly—while
Strauss smoked his Meerschaum pipe. The men played *Tarock,*
whist, or billiards, and sometimes Strauss would sit down at the
piano and improvise. Or one of the friends might play. Theodor

Leschetizky, or Karl Goldmark, famous after his recent success with *The Queen of Sheba*. Or Grünfeld and Uncle Max would play four-handed. I wished I had been there.

I asked my mother whether Uncle Max had mentioned Johannes Brahms, who had often called on Johann Strauss. She didn't know. Strauss was certainly more popular than Brahms. According to a poll taken in 1890, the "most popular" people in Europe were Queen Victoria, Bismarck, and Johann Strauss. And my mother remembered only the things she had liked. She didn't like the music of Johannes Brahms but she loved the waltzes of Johann Strauss.

In our dining room we had a very early gramophone, with a big brass horn, like the one on His Master's Voice labels with the little dog. My mother said it had been the first such gramophone in town and had caused a sensation. The brass horn soon became a source of weekly irritation for Marie, our elderly cook, who cleaned it every Saturday afternoon with a white liquid and several dustcloths. She worked hard to make it nice and shiny, and then somebody would use the gramophone and his fingerprints were seen all over the freshly cleaned brass horn. Probably my fingerprints.

On one of the records I loved Alfred Grünfeld played his brilliant concert version of Johann Strauss's *Frühlingstimmen* waltz. I never tired of listening to the virtuoso runs and fast cascades. They sounded miraculous though this was an acoustical recording made before the turn of the century. Uncle Max had received the record from Grünfeld and later gave it to my parents. Somehow my mother felt that the record established a direct relationship between her and Johann Strauss, who had died in 1899.

All these wonderful stories and sounds, the records and photographs were brought to our home by Uncle Max. My mother loved Vienna, and Uncle Max was the ambassador from Vienna,

always surrounded by a haze of miraculous Blue Danube perfume. The only flaw was that Uncle Max had never been introduced to the Emperor. His Majesty had no need for a prominent
gynecologist. But Uncle Max knew some archduchesses, "professionally and personally," my mother said, with some pique.
All was not lost however: there was another famous relative in
Vienna, Dr. Friedrich Wechsberg, a cousin of my father and a
noted specialist in internal medicine. *He* had been presented to
Emperor Franz Joseph I. The trouble with him was (and you
can guess whom I quote again) that he moved in a remote
world, didn't care about his lowly relations, and never visited
Ostrau, a "provincial" town.

Uncle Max was not so "serious." He worked all day long
and spent his nights talking with his friends, dancing with
"those" ladies, and playing the piano. "The women were crazy
about him," my mother remembered, with a wistful look in her
eyes. No doubt she too had been very fond of Uncle Max. And
then he had started giving himself morphine injections when he
had spells of depression.

Spells of depression? Uncle Max? It made no sense to me.

"It does to me," my mother said sadly. "Long, dark spells after
he'd lived through many hectic days and exciting nights. Your
father never had them though." She didn't want me to worry
about hereditary depression. In those days I wouldn't have
worried anyway. That came much later.

One night in 1913 my parents came home from the theater
and found Uncle Max on the sofa. He often lay down for a
while when he was tired. He could sleep anywhere and any
time. He seemed to be asleep and they didn't worry. But then
they found the syringe. And Uncle Max didn't wake up any
more.

"He wanted to die in a place where he felt at home," my

mother would end the story. It made no sense to me then, but it does now.

❖   ❖

A little genealogy is needed to make this report clearer. As I have said, my father had five brothers and three sisters. To me that meant five uncles and three aunts. On my mother's side the situation was even worse. Grandmother Krieger, my mother's mother, was a widow with thirteen children. Six more uncles and six more aunts. I had never known Grandmother Krieger's husband. He died before I was born. His portrait in an oval Biedermeier frame in her living room, underneath the old pendulum clock, showed a bearded, serious man with severe eyes who seemed to have laughed rarely in his life. My mother never talked about her father; he remains a vague figure. Grandmother always wore black after his death. She was a formidable dowager who ran her family the way a tough captain runs his battleship. Once she slapped the face of Uncle Leo, then forty, for having made what my mother called an impertinent remark.

Between the Kriegers and the Wechsbergs there were personal, social, and economic tensions, particularly between Grandmother Krieger, the widow, and Grandfather Wechsberg, the widower. "He always thought the Wechsbergs were better than we," my mother said. It had started with the grain business. Grandfather Wechsberg occasionally liked to forget that he had grown up on a farm and made his first money by selling grain. Later, when he became prosperous and bought "the mill," he became a "financier" and finally had his own bank. By that time he was almost a public person in our town, and there was much dispute about him. People liked or disliked him, depending on whether he gave a man credit or turned him down. Some called him a usurer though he never demanded more than five per cent interest. Some said his abrasive manner often offended them.

Could be. I'd often heard that he would walk up and down in

front of "Frau Krieger's wholesale grain store," muttering to himself. He had not been pleased when his son Eugen married a Krieger girl, Aunt Irma, a sister of my mother. From Grandfather Wechsberg's point of view it was a mésalliance. He was, after all, a "financier." He was pleased when some people in town who urgently needed his help called him "our own Rothschild." It was said that such people could get personal loans at less than five per cent but that was hearsay and I doubt it. As Grandfather Wechsberg got richer, he also got stingier. There was strict discipline in his family though on a more sophisticated level. He would not slap the face of a forty-year-old son for making an impertinent remark. After the incident he said that Frau Krieger couldn't help herself, she hadn't "progressed," she was still in the grain business, figuratively speaking, though she had given it up. In short, he was angry because she had become the mother-in-law of one of his sons.

Grandfather Wechsberg became really upset when his son Siegfried informed him, respectfully but firmly, that he was going to marry another of the Krieger girls. There must have been a lot of bad feeling on all sides. My mother never spoke about it. Grandfather Wechsberg at first ruled out another "mésalliance" but was informed by his youngest son that he was going to marry the Krieger girl, with or without his father's consent. He was aware of the possible "consequences" and willing to face them. The consequences were being "disinherited" and thrown out of the bank. He told his father, quietly and seriously, that he was ready to go away with Minka and start all over again.

I don't know what happened exactly but from vague hints of my cousin Martha's I gathered that "after some struggle with himself" Grandfather Wechsberg gave his consent. Very reluctantly. He may have remembered that his youngest son had already run away from home once, and he didn't want this to hap-

pen again. Grandfather Wechsberg was then in his late seventies.
Perhaps he was getting mellow.

So the young couple were married in a simple ceremony and
went away on a short honeymoon. The next morning Grandfather Wechsberg was seen walking up and down at the corner of
Johannygasse and our street, watching both his bank and Grandmother Krieger's house. He looked dandy that morning. The
story has been told often in the family with slight variations but
it is true. Grandfather wore a black suit and his black derby, a
gold chain across his waistcoat, and an elegant cane with a silver
handle. Our own Rothschild. The cane is an important requisite
of the story. Grandfather Wechsberg played with it joyfully. He
was smiling, very pleased with himself. That in itself was unusual. His detractors said that "Albert the Benevolent" smiled
only when the stock market could not be the source of his con-
tentment. Either his presence was reported to Grandmother
Krieger or she may have seen him from the window. The
sources don't agree. At any rate, she got so curious that she came
down and stood in front of her house. She later admitted to my
mother that had been a mistake, but now it was too late.

Grandfather Wechsberg, still promenading on the other side
of the street, elegantly doffed his derby, smiling and playing
with his cane. He looked like the local version of a white-haired,
bearded Beau Brummell. Grandmother Krieger was very angry
and made mistake number two.

"You look very happy this morning, Herr Wechsberg," she
said, from her side of the street. They used the formal *Sie* when
talking to each other though one would have expected a certain
rapprochement after two Wechsberg men had married two
Krieger girls.

"I *am* happy, Frau Krieger," he shouted across the street. "Because you still have two unmarried daughters, and I have no
more unmarried sons." He doffed his derby again, bowed for-

mally from the waist, and marched off toward his bank, leaving Frau Krieger in a state of mixed emotions.

❖   ❖

This indicates some of the problems I had to cope with when I grew up. I resembled my father and was known as "a Wechsberg." I was reminded of this several years later by Herr Feiner, the family barber. He had his shop in our street, across from our house. He would come up every morning to our apartment on the top floor to shave my father. He had already been on the two floors below, shaving Uncle Eugen and Uncle Alfred. (Herr Feiner, a confidant of our family for many years, respected Grandfather Wechsberg's seniority arrangements.) He finished and while he was cleaning his razor—I never looked at him while he did it—my father put on a small white net which he fastened at the back of his head. The white net kept his small mustache in place. Not long ago, after I had shaved in the morning, I absent-mindedly covered the spot above my upper lip with a piece of Kleenex, narrowly folded. All of a sudden I saw my father wearing his mustache net as I looked at myself in the mirror.

Around 1915 Herr Feiner stopped coming up. The stairs were too much for him; he was getting old. Uncle Alfred—the only one of the Wechsberg brothers still in the house—shaved himself alone. When I needed a haircut my mother told me to go into the barbershop down in the street. Some men were always sitting there. I didn't know them. They needed no haircut, no shave. They sat there talking or they read the local newspaper that was folded in a bamboo frame, as at the coffeehouse. Herr Feiner often sat with them, talking, but when I came in he got up and held the chair for me and cut my hair himself. He insisted, though he had two employees. "You are a Wechsberg," he once said to me. I was the connection with the past. He took no money from me. I had already learned, though, that nothing is free in

life. Herr Feiner put the amount on the bill. Once in a while
my mother would pay it.

❖   ❖

I am waking up in the brass bed in our children's room. It is
still dark but my brother Max is stirring in his small bed with
the net curtains, to my left. Max is always up early in the morning. Max is four, so I am nine years old. 1916. So much has happened in the past two years. My father has gone and will never
come back. I find it impossible to believe. I still say that he will
come back one day. Suddenly he will be here.

Our children's room is cold. In a while the graying winter
dawn will creep in, and I'll see the ice flowers on the windows.
When the room gets warm I'll be up, and I'll breathe against the
ice flowers until a small hole forms on the pane and I'll be able
to look out. There isn't much to see though. The window of the
children's room has bars.

I love the beautiful ice flowers, like fairy-tale designs in a nice
dream. They completely cover the windowpanes and turn the
children's room into a dream cave. No way out, only that small
hole through which I can see the two cupolas of our synagogue,
the roof of the low Mannaberg house below, and across the
street the Savings Bank.

Lying there in the large brass bed, I enjoy the dreamy half
hour between waking and getting up. The pendulum clock on
the wall makes reassuring tick-tack sounds. The rhythm of life.
(Later when the clock is older—clocks are almost living things
and they age, like people—it will sometimes stop at fifteen minutes past three, with the two hands lying on top of each other.
At the jeweler's shop the clocks always show times like ten minutes past ten or five:forty. Never three:fifteen, with the minute
hand covering the hour hand.)

The children's room is all white. The stove is made of white
Dutch tiles. Underneath the pendulum clock is the flat table,

white, where Fräulein Gertrud places Max to put fresh diapers around him. She has told me I used to lie there too, but I don't believe it; diapers were not for me, I say. There is the white chest where our shirts and clothes are kept. A small white shelf with our children's books. A round white table in the middle, and five white chairs. The only non-white piece of furniture in the room is my brass bed with two brass bowls at the lower end. Many years later I will see a similar brass bed at the Ritz in Paris and immediately feel at home there though the Ritz is not exactly the kind of place where I would normally feel at home.

The white children's room, and a white day, a holiday. It must be a holiday, since Marie, the cook, hasn't told me to get ready for school. The couch on the right side of my bed is empty. When I was younger Fräulein Gertrud would sleep there. But a year ago things began to change at home, and my mother was obliged to let Fräulein Gertrud go; she could no longer afford her. Fräulein Gertrud understood, and both cried. Even Marie cried a little though she had never liked Fräulein Gertrud. For one thing, no one ever called Marie "Fräulein" though she had as much right; she had never been married. There must have been a sort of romantic attachment, when I was very young. I remember walking into the kitchen and there was a man sitting, and Marie had served him coffee and a piece of *Striezel.* He had a very large pocket watch and I was told that he was a locomotive engineer in one of the mines, one of my glamorous professions. He took his watch off the heavy silver chain and let me hold it. I was afraid I might drop it and reluctantly gave it back. When the war came the locomotive engineer didn't come any more, and Marie sometimes cried, and one day she said that he too had been killed in the war, like my father.

Letting Fräulein go was only the first step my mother had to take "to save money." That was the first time the word "money" was mentioned at home. I had never heard it while my father was alive. Then my mother was forced to rent the *Herren-zimmer,* the gentlemen's room, which had been my father's private domain. My mother was unhappy about it, and she left the room unchanged. His desk was there, three comfortable leather armchairs, books on shelves in a glassed-in bookcase, a table and several chairs, and a sofa. Everything dark and old and very pleasant. During the week my parents used to have their black coffee there after lunch. It wasn't really black, both put a little cream into their demitasse, but it was called "the black coffee." On Sundays I was permitted to join them, feeling much older than my six or seven years, though I wouldn't get coffee.

Sundays were wonderful, always special occasions. In the morning while "the women" stayed at home getting ready for the noonday meal, my father would take me on the streetcar that went from the street in front of our house to the suburb of Schönbrunn. Our Schönbrunn had no connection with Vienna's, where the Kaiser had his summer palace, except the name. The Czechs disrespectfully called Schönbrunn "Svinov," possibly because it sounded like *svině,* the sow. The Czechs had no use for the Kaiser and called him "Proháska," a common Czech name, especially when telling jokes about "Proháska" with the Austrian police around.

During the half-hour streetcar ride to Schönbrunn I was permitted to stand on the front platform, next to the motorman. My father stood next to me, because I might fall out. He tipped the motorman and I was permitted to press the bell down with my foot. That was the climax of the whole Sunday. On the way back we got out at the Ring and walked over to Wollgart, the best pastry shop in town. My father would select a few things for dessert, such as *Indianer, Creme-schnitten,* or a fresh *Linzertorte.* I was not permitted to eat anything there before lunch; my father had promised my mother. But I didn't really care. The

Wollgart things were delicious, but they couldn't compare with the thrill of the streetcar bell.

The *Herrenzimmer* was located at the end of the hall, with a door leading directly into it. It was somehow separated from the other rooms but my mother was bothered by the presence of a "stranger" in her apartment. After a while, toward the end of the war, when things didn't get better but instead much worse and my mother had no more income from the bank because "the papers no longer paid interest," whatever that meant, she also had to rent the children's room. That was even worse because the children's room was next to what had been my parents' bedroom. Afterward Max slept on the sofa in the bedroom, as we called it, and I slept in the twin bed next to my mother, where my father had slept.

In the morning my mother would complain. The roomer in the children's room, a Herr Dr. Michalitschke, was an editor of the local newspaper who usually came home late and woke her up. She said she shouldn't have taken a newspaperman who kept "irregular hours." She should have taken someone who led "a more normal life" and would be at home before 10 P.M.

That was later though. Now I am still in the children's room. Max is stirring next to me. Marie comes in with a pail of coal. On top are pieces of firewood and some of yesterday's newspaper. Marie kneels down and opens the two doors of the white-tiled stove. Dawn has crept in, and there is just enough light in the room to see her. She removes yesterday's ashes with a small shovel and puts them into the paper bag that she placed down there last night. I turn on my left side to watch her; I always enjoy the ritual of Marie's building a fire. After the ashes are removed she puts in two newspaper pages, rolled into small balls. On top of the paper she places the kindling, first the small pieces that she has split in the kitchen, and above them the larger ones. Then comes an exciting moment. Marie strikes a match, sets fire to the newspapers, and closes the inner door. She gets up and stands, waiting. In a few seconds there will be the crackling sounds of burning wood and the scent I like so much. Marie takes her time. She knows she must wait until the fire is really going. Only then will she open the inner door and put in a few pieces of black coal from the pail.

Our town is a coal town, with anthracite coal mines all around, each with a pit tower, and with subterranean galleries running deep underneath the streets and the houses. I like to imagine that one gallery might be located exactly below our house, that we have a shaft going down there into the ground, and that we get the pitch-black pieces of coal from our private gallery below. A nice fantasy. Now Marie is about to place the coal pieces on top of the brightly burning wood and then she closes both doors, gets up, and leaves the room. I lie there, listening and waiting. Any moment now the crackling sounds of burning wood will turn into darker sounds. The coal pieces take fire. In a few minutes a delicious breath of warmth will drift from the stove into the cold room. No real heat yet but the white tiles are getting warm. I think I'll get out of bed and touch the white tiles.

Almost all my adult life I've lived in places with central heating. Very comfortable, you just turn it on; and in Southern California the thermostat would even do that. There might be a few knocking sounds as steam went through the radiators, and I would remember wistfully the capricious noises in the white-tiled stove of my childhood, the cozy warmth that filled the children's room, after the windows had been opened for a while "to let in fresh air." The women at home had a theory that the cold fresh air from the outside would "warm up faster than the bad air inside." It was no good telling them that it was just getting colder inside. All I know is that the dry, anonymous heat that I have become used to is worlds apart from the warmth of the tile that was alive, almost living. That sort of warmth has become a luxury, to be found nowadays only in old-fashioned peasants' homes.

Later I had some second thoughts about the tiled stoves consuming so much coal. (Only in the dining room did we have a gas stove, in a "modern" brass setting. It caused as much excitement as the gramophone with the brass horn but it was rarely used. My mother said gas was very expensive and, anyway, one didn't need much heat during the meal. "Eat your soup, that will warm you up," she would say.) Aside from the cold dining room, there was a tiled stove in each of the other rooms, and Marie had to bring up all these buckets of coal, walking down the stairs into the cellar and coming back again. On each trip she could carry only two buckets of coal, hardly enough for one stove a day. Then down again and back with two more heavy buckets. On the back of the house there was a primitive windlass installed above our kitchen balcony. The empty buckets were lowered down, and someone standing there—I suppose it was the cook who worked for Uncle Eugen or Uncle Alfred—would replace the empty bucket with one that was full. Then Marie would pull up the bucket. It was hard work but she said it was better than having to walk all those stairs, carrying the buckets. But the windlass was often out of order and then somebody said it was not "safe," the police might come, so Marie preferred to walk down and up again, though her legs hurt her. And eventually she had to quit. My mother helped her to get a small room in a Catholic home for retired women in the suburb of Přívoz. Marie would come up occasionally for a visit and to pray at the Old Church which she called "my church." She said the nuns were nice and took good care of the pensioners. The Přívoz church was nearby but it wasn't old and mystical. It was just an ordinary church.

For a while we had no servant. I had to carry up the coal

buckets and didn't like it but then Tonka came. Franzl, the new tenant of the *Herrenzimmer,* an employee at the Länderbank, called her Tonka *šibenice,* "the gallows Tonka," which was the title of a macabre story about a prostitute in Prague, written by Egon Erwin Kisch. But Tonka was nothing of the kind, naturally, and that was the joke. Tonka didn't even have a boy friend. Her father was a coal miner. The family lived in a small apartment, if you could call it that, just a kitchen and a small room for four people in one of the miners' houses in the "colonies." I went there once with Tonka. The "colonies" were rows of dark, grimy houses belonging to the mines. Most mining towns in Europe had these dark brick houses that looked alike, but that was no consolation for the people living there. It was said that the mines and the houses belonged to very rich people who had big houses in Vienna and on the Riviera and had never seen the "colonies" they owned. There was always the smell of wet mortar, even on hot summer days, said Tonka, and of warmed-over food.

"You always know what the other people in the house are cooking," Tonka said, and laughed. It must have been terrible because she considered the tiny "maid's room" behind our kitchen a great improvement. It was just large enough, more exactly small enough, for a bed and one chair. The small window faced a dark, dirty wall. No light, no air ever came into that room, which was the architect's idea of a "maid's room" at the turn of the century. Tonka didn't mind though. She said she spent most of her time in the kitchen, and she liked our kitchen, which had Dutch tiles, white ones with a blue windmill, very bright and cheerful. I saw such tiles later in Holland but I don't think ours came from there. Tonka wasn't perfect though; she couldn't cook, and Marie's soups and warm desserts were soon remembered by my mother, usually with a wistful sigh; but then she would give a shrug and say, "You cannot have everything."

She was right. You cannot have both cheese dumplings and lots of coal for the tiled stoves.

I asked Tonka to show me how to build a fire. She did but I was impatient and didn't wait long enough until the wood was burning, or I hadn't taken out all the ashes, or I had dumped too much coal dust on top of the wood, which smothered the flames. People complained that the miners were mining "more dust than coal." I thought it was the miners' revenge for having to live in the "colonies," but I didn't say that, the adults wouldn't listen to me anyway. I never managed to build a fire in one of the tiled stoves, and after a while I gave up trying.

Today I miss the warmth of our white-tiled stove in the white children's room. I miss the ice flowers on the windows with their fairy-tale patterns. It was cold in our room before Marie came in to build the fire but I don't remember that I was really cold when I was a child. One gets cold only later, and then one feels cold for a long, long time.

2.

I MUST HAVE become conscious of Wien (Vienna) and its strange magic long before I went to school, even before my brother was born. It may have been around 1911; I was four years old. I still tyrannized the entire household with my bizarre eating habits. I would suddenly stop chewing the food, holding it in my mouth, thinking up ways of extortion. I promised to chew if I didn't have to go to bed at seven, if I were taken to the circus on Sunday, or if my mother would "tell me about Vienna."

The Vienna demand was my most sophisticated method of blackmail. My mother's stories about Vienna seemed more fascinating to me than Fräulein Gertrud's silly fairy tales, especially those ending, "And if they didn't die, they live happily ever after." This I simply refused to believe; I already knew that no one lives forever.

When my mother talked about Wien, she would repeat herself, but I didn't mind. She would never tell a story exactly the same way twice. Perhaps she had learned from the Viennese, many of them born storytellers who know that a good story must have elements of fact *and* fancy. Even before my mother got married in 1906, when she was twenty-three, she would spend *the* week in Vienna, as the house guest of Aunt Bertha, her mother's sister-in-law. That made Aunt Bertha my great-

aunt but she would have been angry to be called a great-aunt.
She looked like the Empress Maria Theresia—more distinguished, perhaps, more like the Hungarian Princess Metternich,
Pauline Metternich-Sándor. Aunt Bertha was, my mother
said, "typically Viennese," with a still elegant figure called
vollschlank, "full-slim," and her hair done up in an impressive
crown by a hairdresser who came up to her apartment every
morning. That alone was an indication of Aunt Bertha's big-city
sophistication. My mother said, with a trace of bitterness, that
she knew no one in Ostrau who had the hairdresser at home
every morning.

My mother was very fond of Aunt Bertha, who was not a
member of the family, strictly speaking, and different. Her husband, Uncle Emil Storch, a brother of my maternal grandmother, had these awful spells of "the family sickness." Today
one might call them depressions or psychoneuroses or God
knows what. Aunt Bertha was cheerful, often laughing; no wonder she loved my mother, who also liked to laugh, sometimes
even for no evident reason. I suppose that was how *the* week in
Vienna had started. My mother was the only one among her
twelve brothers and sisters who was invited to Vienna.

The week in Vienna was never seven days but two or three
weeks. It ended when my mother received strict orders to come
back home. But she always called it "the week in Vienna." She
would spend months looking forward to it and after her return
she would spend months telling us about it. Aunt Bertha lived
with her husband and their three daughters in a spacious, comfortable apartment at the corner of Mariahilferstrasse and Neubaugasse, then and now one of the liveliest street crossings in
Vienna. Uncle Emil was "at the stock exchange." A tycoon,
powerful and genial, very hearty and always jovial, except when
he had these spells of "the family sickness." Thinking of the frequent depressions in the families of both my mother and my fa-

ther, it is surprising that I haven't jumped out a window yet. My mother would angrily deny, though, that there was any "sickness" in *her* family.

"Look at the Wechsbergs," she would say. "Grandfather Wechsberg married his first cousin. Anything might have happened. Incest." I was shaken. At the local Gymnasium we had studied the Greek tragedies, and I knew what incest could do to people. Compared to the ancient Greeks, though, there was astonishingly little degeneration in the Wechsberg family.

It was more amusing to talk about Aunt Bertha, whose only sickness was her morbid fear of gaining weight. I knew all about her apartment long before I ever saw it. You came into the large hall. There you sat "before lunch" or "before dinner," and there you had "the coffee afterward." That was a ritual in Vienna. One must not have the black coffee in the dining room. There was also the large drawing room, "in oak" (I didn't know what that meant), which occasionally was referred to as Aunt Bertha's "salon." It seemed that people who came for a visit would sit in the "salon" and they would talk.

"What do they talk about?" I asked my mother.

She gave an impatient shrug. A silly question. I was too young to understand. Perhaps talking for the sake of talking was an important pastime in Vienna, upper-class Vienna. The pleasure of conversation. People would listen to one another. It was a civilized age. A lot of gossip was very involved then in Vienna, and there was some name-dropping, but the people would wait, out of habit or mere politeness, until the other person had finished speaking, and only then would they talk. Much of the gossip was about friends who were not present, but there was also that specific Viennese upper-middle-class *Klatsch* about theater and opera—not the artistic events, but the actors and singers, the personal intrigues and specific scandals, and the best of them were those that involved someone who was well known to them but not present.

My mother registered those conversations in Aunt Bertha's salon with considerable accuracy. I found them later all over again in the books and plays of Arthur Schnitzler. He had the true poet's ability to trace feelings and express emotions in sensitive, often exquisite prose. He was often misunderstood; he is still widely misunderstood outside of Vienna. But he wrote the truth about these people. When I now read one of his plays, I have a strange sense of *déjà entendu,* as though he had been there in Aunt Bertha's salon, listening to the erotic gossip, the social complications, the little comedies and tragedies that fascinated my mother and made Vienna so interesting to her. I believe she must have instinctively sensed that the end was near. But it is always fascinating to dance at the rim of the volcano.

I knew many details. From the window on the left side of the drawing room one could see Mariahilferstrasse making a slight turn on the way down toward Ringstrasse. In spring and summer, on a nice morning, one might look out, waiting for the Emperor's coach on the way to Schönbrunn. Aunt Bertha may have had a secret connection with someone at the Hofburg. Every time she told my mother they were going to see "him" tomorrow morning, they did see him. The Kaiser.

The house in Neubaugasse was "a real Viennese house," with its patrician façade and the red rug on the stairway fastened by horizontal brass bars "that were cleaned twice a week." The house is still there. The façade has been modernized and the red rug on the stairway has disappeared. They say it is more functional now. For many years the Austrian headquarters of Metro-Goldwyn-Mayer was among the house's corporate tenants. MGM is no longer the antechamber to heaven which it was in the early 1940s when I was a struggling writer in Hollywood, where they talked about Louis B. Mayer the way they talk in the Vatican City about God, but things could be worse. At least Aunt Bertha's former "salon" is not used by an obscure real estate firm or a doubtful finance company.

❖   ❖

Grandmother Krieger also had a "salon," but it wasn't the same as those in Vienna. Grandmother's salon was the large corner room in her apartment which remained always locked, except on religious and family holidays. On such days Grandmother Krieger would unlock the salon with a key which she gave to no one. The windows were opened and the dust covers were taken off the armchairs. But my mother said the room had been locked for so long that "fresh air didn't have time to come in and stay in." She was right; there was always a musty smell of dust and old flowers. Down on the street floor there had been the large store with the "family enterprise," the wholesale grain business, but that was before my time, and later the premises were rented by a textile firm with which, my grandmother said pointedly, she had no connection. Grain was all right, textiles were out. After the sudden death of her husband Grandmother Krieger had carried on "a man's business" and had done quite well. And she had found the time and energy to bring up thirteen children, each of them having "learned something." My mother had helped her mother in the store.

Grandmother Krieger's birthday happened to be the first of May. In our town it was better known as Labor Day, an important holiday in a mining town. The large salon was opened, and Grandmother would be installed in almost regal fashion in the best fauteuil. Tall and imperial, dressed in her best black, with the white hair artfully fastened in a crown, she would accept the congratulations of her large family and a wide circle of friends. I think it was this strict birthday protocol that made her known as "our Maria Theresia," though the late Austrian Empress had had sixteen children, not just thirteen.

Grandmother's salon looked as though it had been furnished by the curator of a second-rate museum. It was cool even on warm days. The waxed parquet floor was as slippery as an ice rink. There were small Persian rugs lying around because Grandmother claimed that several small rugs reflected better taste than one pretentious large one. We grandchildren loved the small rugs because you could slide on them all over the floor. Since the rugs were costly and "should have hung on the walls," as my mother said, large strips of gray canvas were laid on them —perhaps not very good taste, though on Grandmother's birthday the canvas strips were removed. There was a heavy sideboard, dark and ugly, said to be "older than Biedermeier," and on the heavy table was a decorative silver bowl, also ugly, but popular with the children because it was filled with fresh fruit when the salon was opened. The pièce de résistance was the Bösendorfer piano, which seemed as unused and unfriendly as the rest of the room. Grandmother Krieger refused to have a piano tuner come in because once upon a time a tuner was said to have departed with a silver plate, though Uncle Bruno, my "musical" uncle, said the theft had never been proved. Now the piano was badly out of tune and this drove Uncle Bruno into fits of despondency.

The climax of the annual birthday celebration was the performance of a trio, the only possible combination. Aunt Grete played the piano, Uncle Bruno the viola, and I the violin. The literature for this combination is not large. Neither Aunt Grete, a mediocre pianist, nor I, a beginning fiddler, was up to the almost professional standards of Uncle Bruno. He was a tragic figure. He loved music and let himself be persuaded by Grandmother and his brothers that "one cannot become a musician," that it was as bad as being a professional pickpocket or working for the circus. Poor Uncle Bruno had had several "respectable" commercial jobs but he always failed and went back to his beloved music. Eventually he played, with more or less skill, the violin, the viola, the cello, the clarinet and flute, and the piano. By temperament he was a viola player; he didn't like to speak up and preferred staying in the background. But there was a dearth of first violinists in Ostrau and he had to play first fiddle in his own string quartet, to which I was admitted as second fiddler at the age of eleven.

For one of Grandmother's birthdays (I believe it was in 1918) he had selected Mozart's "Kegelstatt" trio, K.498, originally written for clarinet, viola, and piano. I played the clarinet part transcribed for violin. The whole thing was an ordeal from beginning to end. Uncle Bruno insisted on rehearsals. His idea of rehearsing was to shout at Aunt Grete and me when we did something wrong, which happened frequently. He would beat time when he wasn't playing by tapping the stick of his viola bow against my right collarbone. God knows what he would have done to Aunt Grete if he had sat closer to her. She had no sense of rhythm at all. Rehearsals took place at the salon, with Grandmother pretending she wasn't there, but listening. Officially the salon was locked and the dust covers were on the armchairs, but she had opened it with her key. At last there was the day of the performance, and Grandmother considered it the most important item on her birthday program.

It was terrible. Uncle Bruno wouldn't count aloud but he *would* tap his right foot, especially during the soft phrases. When Aunt Grete missed a run that no one might have noticed, he cursed her, and then they all knew. Grandmother cried "because it was so nice." Aunt Irma cried because she saw her mother crying. My mother cried because she wished that "dear Siegfried could have listened." Uncle Hugo yawned and Uncle Jacques had the hiccups. Uncle Leo quietly drank up all the *Schnaps* he could find. We played the whole trio but it was a disservice to Mozart. For three successive years we played it on

Grandmother's birthday but our performance didn't improve. The fourth year we played Dvořák's "Důmky" trio, with Uncle Bruno playing the cello part. It is a sad piece and there was more crying than before.

❖   ❖

I came to know *the* week in Vienna as well as if I had been there with my mother. On the first day Aunt Bertha would take her to Zwieback's, the best department store. There she would buy my mother a complete wardrobe, dresses and hats and gloves and handbags and shoes—everything. This created some consternation among her sisters at home when she returned with the Viennese wardrobe. Aunt Bertha disapproved of the things worn in Ostrau; she disliked the "provincial" taste there. That was also the official reason why she never came to visit us. Personally, my mother admitted that Aunt Bertha didn't like her in-laws. She liked my mother. "But not because I was her niece," my mother said.

Aunt Bertha failed to understand that Grandmother Krieger couldn't afford to buy new clothes for her thirteen children every year. Aunt Bertha had only three daughters, and she was rich. In my mother's tales, Zwieback's became a veritable treasure house where brocades and silks were sold. Even ordinary dresses were called *robes,* and a fur coat was *une fourrure.* Several salesladies spoke good French. There were deep rugs everywhere. The P.T. (*pleno titulo*) customers were not expected to remain standing while a piece of silk was shown to them. Aunt Bertha and my mother were asked to sit down, please, "even though they didn't know whether we were going to buy anything." Aunt Bertha never paid cash. Money was vulgar; the bill would be sent home; a symbol of class. We in Ostrau certainly had a lot to learn.

Gradually a picture of Vienna at the turn of the century

emerged. Vienna was then perhaps the world's most glittering capital. Nowadays when the historians explain the gradual decay and the "inevitable" downfall of the *Kaiserstadt,* they always stress the inevitability. But how would they feel if they had lived through the epoch, as my mother did, just for a short time every year, so that her impressions were always strong and fresh? Today, looking back, it is relatively easy to see the beginning of the end. "There was a phosphorescent glitter that came from the irrevocable decay of the foundations on which the capital rested," wrote the late Ilsa Barea. Though she managed to keep legend and reality apart, she admitted that she was scarcely aware of the decay while she was growing up there and watching the "glitter." Only the poets had "that secret knowledge" as Sigmund Freud called it in his famous letter to Schnitzler of June 8, 1906.

"I have often asked myself, wonderingly," Freud wrote, "from where you were able to draw that secret knowledge which I have to acquire through laborious investigation of the subject, and in the end I have come to envy the poet whom I had only admired before." Scientists have often "envied" the poets but few have had Freud's greatness and admitted it. Another poet, Stefan Zweig, who was born in 1881, wrote that Vienna was "rich in beauty, rich in talent, and also rich in despair," but he admits that he knew this only after living through the exciting era that he so truthfully called "The World of Yesterday." And my mother was just two years younger than Zweig.

I believe my mother noticed the beauty and the talent but I don't think she noticed the despair. Aunt Bertha's salon was a long way from the despair. So were her husband's stock exchange speculations, and the entire way of life of the Jewish upper-class bourgeoisie at a time when the wealthier Jews were "almost" accepted in Vienna. The delicate interplay of psychological relations between those who were still secure and the "almost" people, who remained aware of their background, is a recurrent theme of Schnitzler.

But my mother was no poet, and the talk in Aunt Bertha's salon only skirted the realities. People knew the score though they didn't talk about it. Certainly Uncle Emil, Aunt Bertha's husband, did. The big businessman and jovial trader must have known "the conditions in the factories," somewhere in the suburbs where the workers—hundreds of thousands of them—labored from seven in the morning to seven at night, for very little money. He knew about the general strike on November 28, 1905, when more than two hundred thousand workers had marched silently down Ringstrasse—the boulevard that an earlier generation had called the *via triumphalis* of the Habsburg Empire. There had been delegations of Czechs, Slovenes, Croats, and Ruthenes who didn't think much of the *via triumphalis*. In 1910, Vienna had more than two million people—more than it has today—and the working-class districts were dominated by people who had not been born there.

Uncle Emil went on playing the game, and so did everybody else, trying not to see certain things. When the end of the First World War extinguished the "phosphorescent glitter" and there was not enough left to continue the nice life they were used to, not enough even to pay one's debts, Uncle Emil faced the consequences. In a moment of depression—"the family disease," they later said apologetically—he walked over to his large office in nearby Kirchengasse and shot himself.

❧ 3. ❧

AFTER MY MOTHER was married and went to Vienna as Frau Wechsberg, she never failed to see Uncle Max. Also on her program was a more formal visit with the only Wechsberg whom His Majesty had honored with the title *Hofrat* (Court Councilor). The noble title survives though the Habsburg court disappeared sixty years ago. Nowadays it is awarded to Austrian citizens working in the civil service who have done a good job, unless a more specific title is available. In Vienna a man with no title has no identity. Deserving employees of the State Opera are named *Hofrat* after retirement. A former director of the Burgtheater is a *Hofrat*. Moreover, the title has subtle shades known only to the bureaucrats. There is a *wirklicher* ("genuine") *Hofrat*, a *vortragender* ("reporting") *Hofrat*, and an ordinary *Hofrat*, who possibly isn't quite genuine. Hofrat Wechsberg was a "genuine" one.

During the monarchy the title was awarded to people who had performed special services for members of the imperial court. My distinguished relative was a famous internist whose patients included the families of some archdukes. He was also a *Dozent* (university lecturer), not quite but almost a *Professor*. He had been assistant to Professor Hermann Nothnagel, himself a pillar of Vienna's celebrated medical school and an early supporter of Sigmund Freud.

Hofrat Dozent Dr. Wechsberg, whom I didn't know, had his

office in Universitätsstrasse, a short walk from the Berggasse office of his colleague Dr. Freud. They had long known and respected one another. My mother once met Dr. Freud at the *Hofrat's* apartment and was totally unimpressed. She said Freud looked "like a typical Viennese professor," serious and bearded. She was not interested. "One *Dozent* in the family was enough for me," she later said.

Unlike Uncle Max, who was fun, the *Hofrat* seemed to be a bore. Like so many Viennese, my mother preferred Uncle Max, on the life-is-short, let's-be-merry theory. The tomorrow-we-die leitmotiv has run through the Viennese culture for a thousand years. It has often proved to be right. Vienna and the Viennese have gone through an improbable chain of disasters and have always bounced back. "Bending, not breaking," is an old Viennese saying.

❖   ❖

My mother once told me she was upset because there was talk that she had married my father "for his money." Such talk is inevitable when one partner has more money than the other. But my mother had never thought of my father's rich family; money was the last thing on her mind when she fell in love with him. And in a small town the differences are never dramatic. No one I knew in Ostrau was very rich and no one was very poor. My mother almost never discussed these matters.

One day my father brought her the engagement ring, with a stone. "Not a large stone, but a beautiful diamond, very pure, almost blue," she said. She never wore it after she had received her wedding ring, a flat band of yellow gold. She put the diamond ring into the small box lined inside with blue velvet and placed it in her laundry closet, beneath the pile of bed sheets "where no one would look for a ring." The sheets were held together by a blue ribbon and tied with a mesh. Sheets, pillowcases, towels, all divided into small stacks, with lots of ribbons and meshes. Sometimes she would take out the engagement ring and look at it for a long while but she wouldn't wear it and always put it back underneath the sheets. As a widow she wore only the golden wedding ring. One day in 1941, when "they" came for her, they must have ransacked the laundry closet and found the ring. They took everything away. I wasn't there and cannot prove it but I have a hunch that's the way it happened.

My father had bought the engagement ring in Vienna. There were good jewelers in Ostrau but he knew my mother's fascination with Vienna and wanted her to have something from there. He himself had lived for some time in Vienna before meeting my mother. His relationship to Vienna was strictly intellectual, not emotional, as my mother's was. Grandfather Wechsberg had sent him there for a couple of years, to work at the Merkur Bank, in various departments, so he would have the best possible training for his job at the family bank. I don't know how my father felt about the job. But having decided he would become a banker to please his father, he decided to learn a lot and be a *good* banker. Everybody envied him the chance to live in Vienna for a while, where, they said, he would have "the best of everything."

My father seems to have felt at ease among the artists, doctors, and other friends he met at the home of his brother Max. He later told my mother that the people he had known in Vienna "talked his language" much more than the people in Ostrau. Again I didn't understand, and now I do. Like so many liberal middle-class Jews, my father was a relaxed monarchist who admired the old Emperor as a living symbol but had no use for the institution of the monarchy. He sensed that the Emperor was a decent man, though often weak. Weakness is the price some decent men pay for their decency. Franz Joseph's private letters prove that he had a violent distaste for men and politicians such as Karl Lueger, the mayor of Vienna, who built his career on the always popular issue of anti-Semitism. My father had given up his dreams of sailing around the world but he remained interested in the world at large and had no doubt that many things were rotten in Austria-Hungary and that, unless something was done quickly, the Habsburg monarchy was finished. But what *could* be done? Wasn't it already too late? He was a cautious pessimist, owing to his training as a banker. Optimistic bankers didn't last long in Central Europe.

My father admired Franz Joseph for his dignity and stoicism when facing tragedy. The emperor's only son, Crown Prince Rudolph, had shot himself in 1889, after killing the young woman who was in love with him. Nine years later the Emperor's wife was murdered by an anarchist near Geneva. "The Old Gentleman," as he was later called, was hurt—he had never ceased to love his beautiful, capricious wife—but he was the ruler of an empire, His Apostolic Majesty, and wouldn't permit himself the luxury of private emotions, certainly not before other people. He was conscious of his duties but had lost hope. After the death of the Empress, even his great friend Katharina Schratt didn't, or wouldn't, comfort him. "At a time when Franz Joseph needed her most, she let him down," they said in Vienna.

My father understood that the Emperor's stereotyped way of talking concealed his true feelings. He respected the Emperor's stubborn attitude and his views of the future. Franz Joseph foresaw the breakup of his empire, as the centrifugal forces of nationalism grew stronger, but he was unable to do anything about it. He had become a prisoner of his own court. My father had no use for the court, the pompous dignitaries, the young aristocrats he met at Uncle Max's. He once told my mother, "They are educated, have good manners, and are often brilliant in expressing themselves but the trouble is they have little to say."

My father had a special contempt for the imperial bureaucrats. He knew that many of them were unable to face the risks of a private career and had settled for slow but steady promotion, security-first, with an old-age pension and perhaps a title at the end. "Meanwhile," he would say, "they are thinking up ways to harass the population." He had no use for the military bureaucrats either. He had served in the k. & k. 34th Infantry Regiment in Hranice (Mährisch-Weisskirchen), a small town an hour away from Ostrau, with a military academy as its only distinction. He'd been there as an *einjährig-Freiwilliger* (a one-year volunteer); at the end of the year he became a young lieutenant. The military academy was for professional soldiers, with a special section to train the one-year volunteers. The best graduates, the ones who had shown ability and had the good manners "indispensable for a professional officer," were invited to remain in the army as professional officers, which meant prestige and promotion. My father had been asked to stay and become a member of this exclusive club. He politely thanked his superiors for the honor and turned down their offer. He didn't want to be a member of any club.

He returned to Hranice every year to attend the autumn maneuvers. A generation of librettists and operetta composers in Vienna made careers and comfortable lives out of the *Herbstmanöver*. It was the sort of warfare in which the Austrian army excelled. Bizarre sham battles, much noise made with blank cartridges, elegant evenings in the maneuver towns, the wife of the mayor or notary sleeping with a dashing officer, and finally a splendid parade in front of a field marshal, who was often a Habsburg archduke and had a graceful way of saying silly things.

The disastrous defeat by the Prussians in 1866 at Königgrätz had been forgotten, and new alliances were busily made and often quickly canceled. General Staff officers were widely respected, almost as highly as celebrated actors. It was no secret that there was an influential "war party" at the Emperor's court in Vienna, centered around Archduke Franz Ferdinand, the heir to the throne. The members of the war party were convinced that only war against Russia could solve the monarchy's problems and save the Empire. The Emperor was said to favor peace. He was said to have implored his nephew Franz Ferdinand to give up his dangerous ambitions. All this and the attitudes of many professional officers made a military career impossible for my father. He would go if he had to go. He accepted the inevitability of war as we now accept the unquestionability of the decline of the Western world and the terrible possibility of atomic holocaust. But he remained a civilian at heart. The attitude created conflicts between him and some of his friends.

While working at the Merkur Bank in Vienna, he met some officers he had known at the autumn maneuvers. He was invited to join their circle, but he kept away from them. The 34th Infantry Regiment was not an elite outfit; a Thirty-fourer didn't automatically "belong," as did the members of certain gala regiments. My father preferred to spend his free time with Max, though (here I quote my mother) "he was difficult even with some of Max's friends whom he didn't like." My father was relaxed only among people he was comfortable with, who understood his wry humor. He would become devastatingly silent when somebody he didn't like entered the room, and he made no effort to conceal his dislike. This created unpleasant moments for Max, who once complained to my mother. They agreed, rather unhappily, that nothing could be done about it.

"Your dear father could be *very* difficult when he didn't like someone," my mother once told me, with feeling. "There were so many people he didn't like. Noisy, phony, pretentious people. And especially people who talked only about themselves. He would completely withdraw, saying nothing. He was bored and let them notice it." My mother sighed deeply. Perhaps she had remembered such a moment. "Later he told me he'd counted how many times that man said 'I.' In the end he didn't attend some parties at Max's; he didn't want to spoil the fun. In Vienna they didn't like people who 'spoiled the fun.' " They still don't.

Then what did he do in Vienna when he wasn't at the bank?

"I really don't know," my mother said. She noted my mild astonishment and said, "Someday you'll understand. When we got married we agreed not to ask questions about the past. Why make life difficult by arguing about something that's over and done with? But, my goodness, he was thirty-three when we got married. And he hadn't lived all that time in a Trappist monastery."

I looked that up in Meyer's Konversationslexikon, the encyclopedia we kept at home. The Trappists were monks who had taken a vow of silence. That wasn't much help. But I didn't pursue the matter. Perhaps I didn't want to know too much. According to a silly proverb, knowledge is said to be power, but more often knowledge is danger. I asked my mother whether my father had been jealous.

She smiled, and looked younger than her age.

"I wouldn't have liked it if he hadn't been jealous. The trouble was he didn't show it. He would stop speaking, he wouldn't even talk to me. Then I knew. . . . Sometimes I myself couldn't help wondering though. He wasn't a gambler, but he knew a lot about gambling. I don't mean his playing cards with his brothers and some friends. *Tarock,* but that was more like whist, it wasn't gambling."

I remember the *Tarock* cards at home. They were longer than ordinary playing cards, and they were very good for building a house of cards. *Tarock* was *the* card game in my home town when I grew up but it was a complex game, and I never learned it.

"*Tarock* was all right," my mother said. "But how come he knew so much about roulette? Most people just bet on a number, or on red or black. But he knew all about it—the theory, all the combinations. Maybe he learned about it in Vienna. They had everything in Vienna."

"Perhaps Uncle Max had a small roulette wheel at home?"

She considered the suggestion too childish to react to it, just shook her head, emphatically.

"I didn't ask him, though I often wanted to. But you know what happened when he took me to Monte Carlo."

I had heard the story before but not in this context. My mother had often told it as an anecdote, with varying details. They went to Monte Carlo six or seven months after I was born. I was left at home. My father probably wanted to get away from diapers and a crying baby, and there were "the women," the cook and Fräulein Gertrud. My parents stayed at the Hermitage Hotel, which was smaller, more distinguished, and more anonymous than the luxurious Hotel de Paris where my mother would have liked to stay. The hotels were next to each other; it was only a short walk to the Casino.

My mother had never been in a gambling place; she was overwhelmed. The roulette tables, the women's strong perfumes, people's strained voices and greedy faces, showing avarice and anger, and sometimes triumph. The windows were closed though there was sunshine outside. My father gave her a gold coin and suggested she might try her luck. They had gold coins then, in 1908. My mother asked him whether he didn't want to gamble. He shook his head. He didn't gamble.

"He didn't say 'any more,' but that was the way it sounded," said my mother.

She put the gold coin on number 29 because the twenty-ninth was my birthday. She lost. My father gave her another coin. Again she bet on 29 and lost. She wanted to leave but my father said, "Try once more," and she did. Again on 29, and she lost for the third time.

They turned away from the table, and the croupier said, "*Rien ne va plus.*" My mother stopped and looked back for a moment. Then the croupier said, "*Vingt-neuf, rogue, impair, manque.*" The number 29 had come at last but she hadn't bet. She started crying. My father seemed amused, and that made her cry even more. People began looking at her and some smiled. My father became embarrassed and quickly took her out of the Casino. My mother was still crying. She said that never, never would she gamble again.

"And then he took me to that jeweler just across the street and bought the earrings that I always wore. They were expensive, everything was expensive at that store, and I didn't want them. I had lost so much. But your father shook his head in his quiet way and smiled and said, 'No, no, you didn't lose today. You won because you won't gamble any more.' He was right, too."

I knew the rest of the story. Many years later my mother, then a widow, went with Martha and Martha's husband to Monte Carlo. Martha and her husband gambled, and lost, I suppose, but she didn't step into the Casino. She was cured. My father had accurately predicted that she wouldn't gamble again.

I liked the story, though I knew it by heart and sometimes couldn't stand hearing it once more. But it told me a great deal about my father. He had been no Trappist monk. And he knew a lot about gambling. Perhaps he had gambled in Vienna and lost a lot of money: he was the brother of Uncle Max and everybody knew that Uncle Max was a "passionate" gambler. But if my father had also been a gambler, why would Grandfather Wechsberg later on send *him* to Vienna to bail out Uncle Max? Uncle Max who had lost "more than he could afford"—*that* I had overheard—and needed help badly. Why didn't Grandfather send one of his other sons there who never gambled, maybe Uncle Eugen or Uncle Alfred, who "took a dim view of their brother Max"? That I had also overheard.

Had anything happened that made my father particularly trustworthy in the eyes of *his* father? It was common knowledge that Grandfather Wechsberg was a wise man, a man who understood human beings and knew instinctively whom to trust and whom to distrust. It remained a secret that Grandfather took with him when he died. Even Martha couldn't explain it. I didn't mind. I wanted my father to have *some* secrets, and this was not an unpleasant one.

❦ 4. ❦

To my mother Vienna remained a world of its own. She didn't live in that world but at least she knew it, and the knowledge helped her to bear the realities of life in a provincial town. My father seems to have understood the importance of the annual visit. He encouraged my mother to go enjoy the pleasant ritual with Aunt Bertha. My mother felt guilty about leaving him with "the women" and with me, then a baby, but my father smiled and said he would manage, and I'm sure he managed quite well.

He might join my mother in Vienna at the end of the visit and stay with her for a couple of days at a hotel. When they returned home my mother would talk about Vienna as though she were living there and had come to Ostrau on a short visit. This irritated her brothers and sisters, who never went to Vienna, and I am certain that was her purpose. She didn't like the small town with its silly jealousies and petty rivalries. She admitted that these things existed in Vienna too—they exist everywhere—but she said the intrigues and the gossip in Vienna were "genuine, not bad imitations," as at the Ostrau coffeehouses. She meant bad imitations of what the intrigues might have been in the Imperial City.

"There they do it at least with some *flair*," she said. No one knew what she meant by "flair," but everybody was furious, and my mother was very pleased with herself. She was no snob but *her* values were different from those considered important in our home town. Perhaps she should have lived in a big city. Being married to a banker and feeling secure with him, she didn't care about meeting local financiers and captains of industry. My father naturally had to see them, since he did business with them, but he always kept his business life separated from his private life. He would see his business acquaintances at his office on the second floor. He rarely invited them up to our home on the fifth floor. His home was for his friends and for some relatives, the ones he liked.

The week in Vienna and the influence of Aunt Bertha helped to shape my mother's tastes. Like so many Viennese, she was far more interested in performing artists than in creative ones. The baroque city of Vienna remains a large stage where everybody enjoys himself by playing a part, as in a play. The Viennese is at the same time an actor, his own audience, and his own critic. Often he would be unable to state exactly what he is doing at any given moment—acting, listening, or criticizing.

Life is a gigantic play but no one seems particularly interested in who wrote the play. "He only wrote the play," I've heard them say. After a while the actors become convinced that *they* have written their own parts. There are celebrated professional actors at the Burgtheater who know only those parts of a play in which they appear. The rest doesn't interest them at all. I knew a famous opera singer who got "killed" in the second act of an opera, took off his make-up, and left. He told me, with some pride, that he had never heard the third act, since he wasn't in it.

❖   ❖

Aunt Bertha didn't care for "serious" music, and neither did my mother. During the week in Vienna they went to look at the new paintings at the *Sezession,* and my mother talked about the applied-arts patterns of Josef Hoffmann's *Wiener Werkstätte* long before art deco became famous. She told me that they had met Gustav Klimt, Adolf Loos, and Otto Wagner. Aunt Bertha knew them "quite well." Their names meant nothing to me then. I asked her whether she had known Gustav Mahler, who had been *Direktor* of the Court Opera until 1907. I was already interested in music and it remains one of my great regrets that Mahler died in 1911, when I was just four years old.

My mother shook her head. No, she hadn't met Mahler. She had gone with Aunt Bertha to the Burgtheater where "the people" felt more at home than at the "aristocratic" Hofoper. Didn't I know that it was Prince Montenuovo, the influential high chamberlain at the court of Emperor Franz Joseph I, who in 1897 had negotiated the appointment of Gustav Mahler?

"The Emperor subsidized the Opera but when he wanted to enjoy himself he went to the Burgtheater," my mother said. "It was not an accident that *die* Schratt was a Burgtheater actress, not an opera singer."

Katharina Schratt was pretty—some say she was extremely attractive, though not exactly beautiful—and very popular when the Emperor met her in 1886. He was fifty-six years old, very unhappy with his wife, and he fell in love with Katharina Schratt. That surprised no one in Vienna where actors and actresses were always famous. If the Emperor must fall in love, then of course with a pretty actress, they said. No one except a few intimates knew that the Empress Elisabeth herself had engineered her husband's meeting with the actress. *Die* Schratt— when an artist becomes famous in Vienna, the first name is replaced by *der* or *die,* the English "the"—was then thirty-three and separated from her husband, a Hungarian nobleman. *Die* Schratt was even then a wise woman: she knew what the Emperor needed. Companionship, relaxation, in her small house, from the rigors of "Spanish" court protocol, a good breakfast

with coffee and homemade *Guglhupf* at seven in the morning
when he came to see her. Frau Schratt has since emerged as a
great lady. She never published her memoirs, she never "told
all" about the Emperor and herself. Serious historians are convinced that the friendship which the Emperor so desperately
needed was platonic. The readers of today's popular newspapers,
however, are not. Today both the Old Gentleman (the Emperor) and the Gracious Lady (Frau Schratt) are very much
alive in Vienna.

My mother was not convinced either. She knew all the
details. How Franz Joseph walked through the gardens of
Schönbrunn until he came to the wall, opened the small door,
and found himself in Gloriettegasse, and there was her small
yellow villa. (Yellow was the color of the buildings belonging to
the imperial household.) The breakfast, and the pleasant gossip,
mostly backstage gossip. He loved the Burgtheater and was always interested in the little intrigues that make stage and backstage life so fascinating in Vienna.

❖   ❖

My mother admired *die* Bleibtreu, the Burgtheater actress
Hedwig Bleibtreu who made an occasional appearance in Aunt
Bertha's salon. Every successful Viennese hostess had "her" stable of celebrities. There was a considerable supply of celebrities
in the early years of this century—writers, musicians, painters,
sculptors, architects—but none of them could compete in local
fame with the stars of the stage. It was Aunt Bertha's great
regret that *der* Girardi, the famous comedian, never accepted her
invitation after meeting her and my mother in Kärntnerstrasse
and kissing their hands. But *die* Bleibtreu came, and my mother
met her there.

She also talked often about the unforgettable Josef Kainz, the
great tragic actor, and as I've mentioned, she had met Alexander

Girardi, the celebrated comedian. Nowadays Girardi is called the last of the true Viennese because he wasn't born there. He came to Vienna from "provincial" Graz, the capital of Styria, and eventually became more Viennese than a born and bred one. Today they still differentiate between being born in Vienna and being born elsewhere.

"The way I play a Viennese for them isn't what they are, it's what they'd like to be," Girardi would say. "If I had been born in Vienna, I could never manage it." He was more than a good actor; he had instinct and insight, and some wisdom. His best part was that of the professional Viennese, and he completely immersed himself in it.

"And when Girardi kissed your hand . . ." my mother said wistfully, leaving the sentence unfinished. Though I was young and silly, I knew I must not ask further questions. I could see my mother, pretty and happy, a girl of eighteen or nineteen who dropped her "provincial" manners the moment she put on that new dress from Zwieback's; and there came Girardi, with his light swagger and his charm, a dashing figure as he raised his straw hat—in Vienna it was known as "a Girardi," but not in America where it became fashionable during Prohibition—with his walking stick, and his mannerisms imitated by everybody in Vienna who aspired to be somebody. My mother had a record of Girardi singing the *Fiakerlied*, one of those kitschy, sentimental Viennese songs. And when the disembodied voice from the brass horn sang, "Anyone can become a *Fiaker* but only in Vienna do they know how to drive," my mother would start to cry quietly.

I would leave the room; I couldn't bear to see her crying, and I was angry because she seemed moved by what I considered Girardi's sentimental kitsch. I know better today. It is sentimental but in a strange way it is true, and thus it isn't pure kitsch. My mother didn't cry because Girardi sang the *Fiakerlied*. She cried because she had lost Vienna as she had known it, and Aunt Bertha, the Prater and the dashing young officers walking there who now appear in Viennese operettas and in silly films.

"I didn't know that someday I would marry one of them," she said after the death of my father. Much later I understood what she had meant; by that time my mother was dead too. On the rare occasions when I attend an operetta performance at Vienna's Volksoper I can't help seeing the wistful expression in the eyes of the women. I am no longer surprised. My father certainly looked better in his uniform than I did in my various uniforms, first in the democratic Czechoslovak army, and later in the democratic United States Army. Uniforms in democratic armies are not designed to please the women. Infantry soldiers are not born to live but to blend into the countryside. The smart-looking k. & k. officers of Emperor Franz Joseph didn't blend into the countryside but they impressed the women at the Prater.

❖   ❖

My mother was catholic in her tastes. She didn't mind having missed Gustav Mahler at the Court Opera. She had seen Johann Strauss and later Franz Lehár at the Theater an der Wien. She hadn't heard of Arnold Schönberg but she had seen Alexander Girardi as the carpenter Valentin in Ferdinand Raimund's *Der Verschwender* (*The Spendthrift*). Mahler was Vienna, and Girardi was Vienna. Today, having spent much time in Vienna in the past thirty years, I know that Girardi meant more to more Viennese than Mahler, who fascinated only a small minority with his "revolutionary" treatment of Mozart at the Court Opera, and who profoundly upset his admirers when he conducted one of his own symphonies at the Musikverein on the other side of Ringstrasse. They may have cheered him the night before, after a great performance of *Don Giovanni*, but they would boo him the next morning when he conducted the disturbing, prophetic music he had written himself. Mahler is now being recognized in Vienna—reluctantly; he is still controversial—but even the people who loved and hated him were always a small minority, certainly not the "typical" Viennese who adored Girardi and the imitators who succeeded him.

Perhaps the Viennese are right. Like most people, they don't want to be perturbed; they want to be entertained. For them life remains a continuous fairy tale, an operetta—only much better, without an operetta's sentimental second-act finale. Everything seems lost, for the moment. It isn't lost, of course, and the audience knows it, and that is why so many stay around waiting for the happy end in the third act. Today the Viennese love a certain local comedian (his name shall not be mentioned) who tells them every week in his popular radio and television shows how lovable they are. He pours out the blessings of the "golden" Viennese heart though many listeners suspect, shrewdly and correctly, that their city's heart is made of tinsel, not of gold.

It was always that way. The Viennese built a monument in the Stadtpark to Johann Strauss, who made them forget. "Happy is he who forgets what cannot be changed," is the theme song of Strauss's *Die Fledermaus*. And they put up no monument to Sigmund Freud, who taught them to remember. Who wants to remember the many unpleasant things that happened, that no alibi can wash away?

Yet Johann Strauss, whose music my mother loved—"he makes me so happy," she would say—suffered from frequent depressions. He had a morbid fear of sickness and death. He was afraid to look at a hospital. He wouldn't attend the funerals of his beloved mother and of his first wife, with whom he had been happy. He was afraid of drafts and suffered from neuralgia. Mountains and tunnels made him uncomfortable. He could have used the services of Dr. Sigmund Freud, then living and teaching in Vienna. Freud might have helped him. But the two never met, probably couldn't have met. They were both Viennese, but antipoles of the Viennese character. Strauss overcame his fears to give people moments of joy; Freud overcame his fears but never managed to make people happy; at best he made people able to live with themselves. My mother sensed this instinctively when she rejected Dozent Dr. Freud and accepted Johann Strauss. Even after she had lost her husband she would listen to the waltzes of Strauss; she needed his melodies. Better than Valium, better than Librium. People still listen to Johann Strauss. He has never been out of fashion.

❖   ❖

Similarly, in Vienna today Franz Joseph I remains *the* Emperor, not just one of the Habsburg emperors. More than sixty years after his death the colored postcards showing him, bewhiskered and benevolent, in his uniform—which I still identify with my father's uniform—are best-selling items in souvenir shops. Vienna traditionally has a Socialist majority in its City Council. Naturally the Red city fathers take a dim view of His Majesty's posthumous popularity. They are not pleased to see fresh flowers at the base of *the* Emperor's statue in Burggarten, near the Opera. The statue created so much attention that for a time it was moved to an inconspicuous place near a children's playground. Now *the* Emperor stands with his back to Ringstrasse, Austria's *via triumphalis*, which he ordered built in 1857 to replace the old walls and ramparts around the Inner City.

It doesn't seem to matter. People looking for *the* Emperor always find him. They always place fresh flowers at his feet. On the anniversary of his death they attend mass for him in the early-Gothic St. Augustin's Church near the Imperial Palace. Many of the people are not monarchists, though; to them, "the Old Gentleman" epitomizes the illusion known as the Good Old Days. Some may even be Socialists. In the baroque city of

Vienna some members of the anti-monarchist Socialist Party are not embarrassed to have sentimental feelings about *the* Emperor.

❖   ❖

After 1918 many once "exclusive" stars of the Burgtheater gave guest performances in the regions which they called, condescendingly, "the provinces." No wonder. Vienna was cold and hungry but in these "terrible" places, the provinces, there were warm rooms and plenty of food. Frau Bleibtreu occasionally appeared at the German Theater in Ostrava in one of her famous parts, which my mother called "Burgtheater parts." *Die* Bleibtreu was at least loyal, which cannot be said of many celebrated actresses. When she was in town she always came for lunch, and my mother was happy. Frau Bleibtreu said that Marie's *Topfenknödel* and *Böhmische Dalken* were better than any she'd had in Vienna. A great compliment since the "better" Viennese houses had women cooks from Bohemia and Moravia. Aunt Bertha had a Bohemian woman cook who, according to my mother, "terrorized the entire household."

When Frau Bleibtreu came to our home she and my mother would eat alone, but I was permitted to join them for coffee. Once I brought my album of autographs. *Die* Bleibtreu wrote her name in large letters over a whole page so that no one else would sign there. I knew that many artists liked to have a whole page for themselves. Later, as a member of the State Opera claque, when I studied in Vienna, I had some personal contacts with the stars, and my album continued to grow. Unlike my mother, I preferred the signatures of creative artists who might be remembered longer than singers and actors. Most of them wrote their normal signatures. Many didn't mind sharing a page with someone who had already signed. Strauss ("Dr. Richard Strauss"), Hans Pfitzner, Arthur Schnitzler, John Galsworthy, Hermann Hesse (who signed underneath the signature of

Thomas Mann). When I went to America in the fall of 1938 on what I thought would be only a three-month visit, I left the autograph album in Prague. I returned almost ten years later. The velvet-covered autograph book had disappeared with almost everything else I'd owned. I still regret it though many other things were much more valuable.

Thinking of the album of autographs now, it is more remarkable for the signatures I missed than the ones I got. In Ostrau I missed the great Leoš Janáček. And in Vienna it never occurred to me to get Schönberg and Alban Berg. In Paris I missed Stravinsky and Maurice Ravel, and in Hollywood I missed Bertolt Brecht. Not to mention other painters, artists, poets.

Before joining *die* Bleibtreu and my mother for coffee I had been briefed to watch Frau Bleibtreu's manner of speaking. She spoke the celebrated, immaculate German that the Burgtheater artists used on the stage. In Vienna it was called the best "spoken" German though it was no secret that some artists spoke some terrible dialect off the stage. And now I had a chance to hear the best spoken German as I listened to Frau Bleibtreu. Unfortunately I rarely caught her beautiful diction, since she often had her mouth full, devouring Marie's pastry with her coffee.

❖ ❖

After 1918 my mother would often say that Vienna was "finished." I didn't understand. The big city was still there, wasn't it, the baroque palaces, the churches, the Burgtheater, the great streets? My mother shook her head. I was a child, I didn't understand. I now do. Vienna was only a big city then, no longer a world apart that my mother had found there. Once people had made a pilgrimage to Vienna to see the magic of the *Kaiserstadt,* the Imperial City. Now the magic was gone, the Kaiser was gone. Now people like Frau Bleibtreu came *from* Vienna to spend a week in the once despised provinces.

It must have been almost a personal loss to my mother. She had lost her own world, and suddenly she was thrown back into the harsh reality of small-town life. After the lost war we had become poor—almost everybody I knew was now poor—and it must have been a struggle to bring up two boys, to pay the bills, to endure the indignity of having to take tenants into her once beautiful home.

And there was the new problem of the stationery store that Uncle Heinrich, the husband of one of her sisters, had persuaded her to open. Uncle Heinrich had a successful store in the Moravian town of Olomouc (Olmütz) that had made him rich for the past twenty years. A real gold mine, people said, almost like an apothecary's shop. Uncle Heinrich said he would help her to set up such a shop in Ostrava. It would be a gold mine too.

My mother was unable to do all this alone. It was arranged that Uncle Bruno, my "musical" uncle, should join her as a partner. Poor Uncle Bruno knew the subtle differences between an *allegro con brio,* an *allegro assai,* and a plain *allegro.* But he would never learn to distinguish the various qualities of onionskin paper. He was a musician at heart and not a paper salesman.

It was a luxurious store. Uncle Heinrich had said it must be luxurious to succeed. No sense bothering with a small place selling pencils and paper clips. "The store" was no Tiffany but it was quite elegant for a medium-sized provincial town. As you entered, you were greeted by an atmosphere of refinement, bright lights, arrangements of leather-bound diaries, displays of elegant fountain pens. In the rear was the counter, half hidden, where pencils and paper clips were sold—against Uncle Heinrich's advice, but my mother had insisted. They compromised and placed a couple of screens to hide the plebeian element. People buying a leather-bound diary or an expensive fountain pen were not supposed to know that such lowly things as pencils and paper clips existed.

I still associate beautiful stationery with my mother's store but its elegance was probably the very reason for its eventual failure. Not many people in my home town appreciated beautiful things. They wanted pencils, not fountain pens.

5

My own relationship with Vienna started on a low key. In September 1913, shortly after my sixth birthday, my parents enrolled me as a pupil at the Jewish Public School in Ostrau. My father said that life was now going to be a serious business for me, but as he said it he smiled. Perhaps he was joking. Or perhaps he meant to say, It will be all right, don't worry. Somehow I understood, though. Until then I had taken everything for granted, my parents, my home, Marie and Fräulein Gertrud, my favorite breakfast, lunch, and dinner, always sausages and hot cocoa, Sunday rides on the streetcar to Schönbrunn. I still thought of perhaps becoming a streetcar conductor but that summer I had a new enthusiasm. I wanted to be an elevator operator.

Elevators were unknown in my home town. I had discovered this wonder of the new technological era in the large hotel in Engelberg, Switzerland, to which I went with my parents that summer, before going to public school. The hotel was called Titlis, after the name of the high mountain that we saw from the beautiful alpine valley where we were staying. The Titlis is 3,239 meters high but the scenery didn't impress me, though I had enjoyed the boat ride on the Lake of Lucerne and the train ride from Stans to Engelberg on the narrow-gauge mountain railroad. The region has become one of my favorite vacation spots in Europe. It is very beautiful, truly a magnificent ensemble of dark woods, snow-white glaciers, blue lakes. But when my parents took me there the elevator at the Hotel Titlis fascinated me most. It was large and glass enclosed, with art nouveau decorations made of brass. Inside it had a mirror and two lamps, and it moved majestically up and down in a space surrounded by a large stairway on three sides. The elevator at the Hotel Titlis was a small glass palace. You could look out at the people walking down. Some pretended that elevators were only for going up. In Vienna today there are many houses built around 1900 that have elevators in which it is forbidden to ride down.

My father had bribed the elderly liveried man who ran the elevator. He was a sullen Swiss and spoke an incomprehensible dialect but I didn't care about conversation, only about motion. I couldn't decide whether going up or down was the greatest sensation; anything as long as I was moving. I wonder what a psychiatrist would make of *that*. (I still like elevators and railroads though now I like ships best. Not the small white ones on the Lake of Lucerne but big ocean liners where you have a sense of being out of the world as long as you forget that people can always reach you by radio or shore-to-ship phone.)

But in September the glass-enclosed elevator was already a thing of the past, and now I was being enrolled as a first-grade pupil at the Jewish School. A new satchel, the classroom with a blackboard, writing paper that had that unmarked, white, threatening appearance that as a writer I have come to fear. Fräulein Gertrud had told me, with feeling, on my first school day, "A little discipline will be a good thing for you." She never knew how right she was. I've had plenty of discipline since I stepped into the classroom that September morning in 1913. I wonder whether it has been a good thing, though. The only useful discipline is self-discipline, which they don't teach in school. Not in the many schools I attended.

The Jewish Public School was located next to the Old Church, where Marie went to mass every morning, just around the block from our house. Today my mother would say, "He doesn't have to cross the street," and would feel relieved, but there was no traffic problem then in Ostrau. The convenient location wasn't the reason why my parents sent me to the nearby school. They felt it was their "duty." Ostrau was liberal-minded long before the word "liberal" became suspect, almost dirty. I'm sure few people in my home town had ever heard of King Friedrich II of Prussia, who had decreed that in his state every person should be happy *"nach seiner Fasson* [in his own fashion];" but that was actually the general idea in Ostrau. Czech parents would send their children to the Czech school, German parents theirs to the German school, and Jewish parents theirs to the Jewish school. Why not? A fine solution for a town of thirty-six thousand people, with a Jewish minority. After centuries of religious and national bloodshed, the "historical" Austrian crown lands of Bohemia and Moravia had arrived at a genuinely liberal way of thinking.

The Jewish Public School, financed partly by public money and partly by private donors—Grandfather Wechsberg had been among the prominent ones—had the same curriculum as the Czech and German schools, with special emphasis on Jewish religion and the study of the Hebrew language. Only the primary school existed for Jewish children. The idea was that at the end of the four-class school, when a pupil was ten years old, he would have enough Jewish education to give him a basis for life; afterward he would attend either the Czech or the German secondary school. Consequently the most important member of the teaching staff at the Jewish School, as it was called, was Dr. Spira, the widely admired chief rabbi of our synagogue, who taught religion.

Dr. Spira looked, spoke, and acted like a biblical prophet. He had a luxurious gray beard, a sonorous voice—I still think of it as the voice of doom—and powerful movements of his hands. My uncles and aunts, who rarely agreed on anything or anybody, all admired Dr. Spira for his Talmudic wisdom. He tried to convey some of it to his pupils but we were too silly or maybe too young to perceive it. Only years after I'd finished public school did some of Dr. Spira's wise sayings come to mind and become mottoes for life.

Many Jewish families in our town had come from "the East," the old Jewish communities in Poland, then part of the Habsburg monarchy, and those even farther away in czarist Russia. Grandfather Wechsberg had been born in a small village near Wadowice, not far from Craców, the old city of the Polish kings (Pope John Paul II comes from Wadowice). One of my mother's sisters had married Uncle Bernard and lived in Andrychów, a small town close to Wadowice. Uncle Bernard had gone to school in the town of Bielitz (Bielsko) with a certain Selma Kurz, born there in 1874. He courted her for a while; "courted" was the expression he used. Selma Kurz later became the coloratura prima donna of the Vienna Opera under Gustav Mahler. Her famous trill was said "to have aroused Nellie Melba's jealousy at Covent Garden" where she did *not* appear between 1907 and 1924. Never mind; she sang the part of Zerbinetta in the world premiere of the "Viennese" version of Richard Strauss's *Ariadne auf Naxos* in 1916, which is good enough for me. I met her during my claque days at the Vienna Opera. Madame Kurz was an appreciative client of our claque. I once asked her—foolishly—about Bielitz and Uncle Bernard, and she became distant and evasive. She didn't seem to remember; perhaps it wasn't such a small world after all. She was then the wife of the eminent gynecologist, Professor Halban, luminary of Vienna's medical school.

My mother's family had lived for generations in Ostrau,

though originally they also had come from "the East." The Western trend that later culminated in the mass movement toward the New World created in many Jewish families a tendency to assimilate. Our small-town atmosphere prevented many an assimilant from "going too far," converting to Catholicism and changing his name, if it sounded "too Jewish." I remember how shocked we were in Gymnasium when a classmate named Kohn one day appeared and told us his new name was Kresta. It didn't help him; when he got involved in arguments on the soccer field—he was a first-rate player—he remained Kohn.

❖   ❖

Even by European standards, Ostrau was an old town. A small fishermen's village had been there in the twelfth century but its origins may have gone back to the dawn of the Middle Ages. The almost legendary fishermen had fished in the Oder or in its small tributary, the Ostravica, a scant two hundred meters from the house where I grew up. A legendary secular ruler was said to have had his castle in nearby Hochwald. The Church had been represented by the Bishop of Olmütz. The earliest church had been built in 1276—the Old Church just around the corner from our house; in 1520 it was enlarged and given its onion-shaped tower. Fifty years later two side chapels were added, dedicated to St. Mary and St. Vincent.

Trying to sketch the history of my home town is a thankless job. The available material is spotty and ambiguous. Various sources seem to disagree on the same events, depending on who wrote the history, the Germans or the Czechs. (The Jews never got around to writing their version, which is just as well.) The Czechs ignore the presence of the Germans, and the Germans rarely mention the Czechs; and both Czechs and Germans ignore the cultural contribution of the Jews.

After the Battle of the White Mountain in 1621 the ruling

German classes, supported by the Catholic Habsburgs, relegated the Protestant Czechs in Bohemia and Moravia to the status of unpersons. For three hundred years my home town often reflected the status of a suppressed nation. All orders came from Vienna.

By 1918 the unpersons had overthrown their rulers, but they couldn't change some facts overnight. For almost three centuries the Czechs had been the have-nots and the Germans the haves. The Jews, many of whom spoke German and sided with Vienna, were almost-haves.

Coal mining, which changed the rhythm of the town, began in the late eighteenth century. Empress Maria Theresia was said to have worried about the depletion of her forests. People used too much wood for heating, as they now use too much gasoline for driving. Count Wilczek, a Moravian aristocrat who had a fine palace in Vienna's Herrengasse, just a short walk from the Empress' palace, reported that black (anthracite) coal had been found on his estate in Silesian (later Polish) Ostrau. He was encouraged to go ahead with exploitation. Mining was done in a rather primitive way: strata of fine black coal were found only a few meters below the surface of the earth. The big change came after the invention of the steam piston engine by James Watt in 1769 and the locomotive by James Stephenson in 1814.

In 1845 the first trains from Vienna arrived in Mährisch-Ostrau on the newly built railroad. The locomotives were heated with coal from Ostrava. All historians agree on *that* but that is about all they agree on. Thereafter it is either the abused, exploited Sudeten German miners, or the abused, exploited Czech miners who did much of the coal prospecting and mining. In 1828 the Rothschilds in Vienna had bought a small ironworks in the suburb of Witkowitz (Vítkovice). They expanded the small factory into the largest enterprise of its kind in the Habsburg monarchy and one of the largest in Europe. Gradually the

Rothschilds and their partners, the Wilczeks and other far-sighted, "reckless" enterprisers, bought up the prospecting rights in and around our town. The citizens were surprised to be told that they lived on a subterranean mountain range of anthracite, on mountains of enormous wealth. By that time, most of it belonged to aristocrats and rich people in Vienna.

Around 1920, after the First World War, Ostrava had the aggressive atmosphere of a border town. People would come there from Bohemia and Slovakia, from Poland and Germany, even from Hungary and Austria, with the sole aim of making money. Some citizens from neighboring towns called Ostrava an "American" town, which was not meant to be a compliment. A mini-Pittsburgh, a mini-mini-Chicago. We who lived there also called Ostrava an American town, but it *was* a compliment; we were proud of it. The Moravian Pittsburgh, the poor man's Chicago, had smart wheeler-dealers, elegant coffeehouses, attractive whores, admired embezzlers. The air was said to be polluted with all that coal dust. But the town had a low rate of tuberculosis. Local doctors claimed the coal dust was "healthy for the lungs."

People's projections for the future were clearer than their memories of the past. Admirers and detractors agreed that there was almost never a dull moment. It was a fine place to grow up for a youngster who had no illusions about the past and few about the future. It was understood that life is rarely a bed of roses, that it is a rat race. Ostrava was survival of the fittest, not a place for dreamers.

And today? Everything belongs to "the people," which means that nothing belongs to the people, everything to the State. Ostrava has become the "steel heart" of the Socialist Republic of Czechoslovakia. It is the country's third largest city, with a population of more than 200,000 people, and still growing. Few people hail from the town. But that is a different story—not one for this book.

❖   ❖

At the Jewish School in Ostrau we boys learned to read the Old Testament in the original Hebrew text. At the local synagogue we prayed in Hebrew. All prayers were said in Hebrew but the sermon was delivered by Dr. Spira in archaic German, embroidered with Hebrew quotations and Talmudic wisdom that needed some time to seep through one's untrained brain. We were luckier, however, than our Catholic friends. They prayed in Latin, which they didn't understand at all. And they didn't have the advantage of listening to a biblical prophet. Dr. Spira became so widely admired that some Catholic classmates came to the synagogue to listen to his shattering sermons. Some forgot to bring along a hat, and I had to run upstairs to get something for them, an old hat or a cap.

Delivering his sermon, Dr. Spira had the terrifying manner, a blend of doom and dignity, that he also used when addressing the six-year-old pupils of our class in the Jewish School. During an early lesson he said something I understood only many years later. He said, "One cannot teach religion, one either has religion or one doesn't have it." When I related this bit of wisdom to my parents, my mother looked startled.

"Maybe we shouldn't have sent him to that school," she said to my father, but he shook his head.

"It's all right. Someday he will understand." Yes, someday I did.

My father understood that being taught by Dr. Spira was a distinction though we children didn't know it yet. He also realized that it might create complications. Dr. Spira had given up his fight against the growing trend toward assimilation among the more or less affluent middle classes in my home town. He knew that some Jewish people were, as he said, "beyond hope."

He didn't say they were hopeless. There is more than a semantic difference here, and Dr. Spira expressed himself with great accuracy. The Jewish people in Ostrau were Vienna-oriented, and Vienna was full of converted Jews who were trying hard, but not successfully, to forget their past. My mother once remarked that if Uncle Alfred—my father's older brother, who lived in the apartment underneath ours—were to move to Vienna with his wife, "Aunt Anna might have worked hard to make him a Herr von Wechsberg." Little did I know then how close she came to the bitter truth.

Instead of fighting the "horrors of assimilation," Dr. Spira chose the positive approach. He kept us aware of our Jewish heritage. He would quote from Jewish spiritual history, all the way from Moses in the Old Testament to the philosophers Moses Mendelssohn and Baruch Spinoza. He said that being Jewish "was often a burden but always a distinction." Dr. Spira was a practical-minded sage.

"Boys," he would tell us, "be proud to be Jews. If you are not proud of it, you are still going to be Jews. Why not be proud of it?"

A somewhat arrogant though eminently logical conclusion that has served me well in life. People are respected more for what they are than for what they are trying *not* to be. Sometimes Dr. Spira expressed the same thought with a slight touch of resignation when he said, "Once a Jew, always a Jew." The Germans have an obscure, typically German expression for this state of mind: *Schicksalsgemeinschaft*. It implies passive membership in a group, whether-you-like-it-or-not.

Such statements may not convince anyone on the printed page but they were powerful when uttered by Dr. Spira, with his dark, piercing eyes and his deep, ringing voice. His personality even made his more profane statements strongly alive. When a classmate tried to shut out the voice of doom by surreptitiously reading below his desk a little comic book describing the latest adventure of one Percy Stuart, "member of the Eccentrics' Club," and was caught by Dr. Spira, the Talmudic sage raised both hands and gave the poor sinner a sad smile.

"Look at the fool," he said. "Tomorrow he'll read in the *Kronen Zeitung 'Ein Pferd ist gestürzt* [A horse tumbled]' and he will admire the sentence structure." The target of Dr. Spira's contempt was Vienna's *Kronen Zeitung*, then widely read by the concierges and petty bourgeois, the paper expressing "the soul of the people." Today the *Kronen Zeitung*, sturdy survivor of the past, delights hundreds of thousands of people with its simple sentences and is the most widely read newspaper in Austria. It is read not only by janitors and "the little people" whom the politicians love, but also by the politicians themselves and other men of influence. Dr. Spira would have been amused.

He was a true prophet. "There is a fly on the wall and thirty pairs of eyes are watching it," he said, accurately describing the state of boredom prevailing in our classroom. Such everyday wisdom made Dr. Spira so popular with my classmates later on, when I was at the Gymnasium, the secondary school, that many non-Jewish boys asked us about his latest sermon and discussed it with us. At the synagogue the rabbi was an impressive sight in his gold-embroidered white robes. When he held up the Torah and spoke the Mosaic confession of faith, *"Sh'ma adonoi . . ."* it was very quiet in the large room and I thought I could hear a collective shiver run down the backs of the members of the congregation. Such was the spiritual power of Dr. Spira.

I have less pleasant memories of our first-grade classroom at the Jewish School. There was the smell of wet concrete on the stairway, and the smell of dust in the classroom. The floor was made of wooden boards. During intermission we sometimes played soccer with an old tennis ball, and afterward a cloud of dust settled on the desks. In good weather we were ordered to leave the classroom during intermission and walk down into the courtyard with its old trees. There was no space to play soccer and we preferred bad weather, when at least we could stay indoors. I don't remember much of what we did during the lessons, probably because I didn't like them. Learning to read and write was all right, I could see *some* advantage in it. But simple algebra and the multiplication table gave me a sense of terror which remains to this day. At the Gymnasium the mathematics exercises and the monthly oral examinations were always preceded by sleepless nights. I didn't understand mathematics, I still don't; and at visits to celebrated institutes of fundamental research, such as the Weizmann Institute of Science at Rehovoth, Israel, I have been filled with awe when introduced to a "pure mathematician," a great scientist solving incredible problems in his head or on his blackboard.

Somehow I managed to pass my math examinations. Perhaps my teachers were impressed by my knowledge of languages, literature, and history. Maybe I was just lucky. The only subject I disliked even more than mathematics was gymnastics. I never learned to climb a pole.

❖   ❖

A few months after I'd entered the Jewish School I got a bad cold which developed into pneumonia and was complicated by pleurisy. My mother stubbornly complained for years that it was my dislike of primitive algebra and of poles that had caused my sickness.

"It wasn't ordinary pneumonia," she would say. "The poor child had caught a particularly vicious strain of the virus. His fears in school had lowered his powers of resistance." No one could talk her out of it.

Antibiotics were unknown and people would actually die of pneumonia. "He didn't die," my mother later summed it up, "but he came pretty close to dying."

After the "crisis" of pneumonia, I seem to have made rasping noises in my chest every time I inhaled or exhaled. In fact I vividly remember the noises. I was pleased with them and gladly produced them for my envious classmates who came to visit me and reported the latest utterances of Dr. Spira's wisdom. Dr. Himmelblau listened to the rasping noises through his stethoscope, shook his head meditatively, and suggested that I be taken to Vienna. Dressed warmly, of course, since it was wintertime. In Vienna my illustrious relative, the celebrated internist Hofrat Wechsberg, would examine me. Vienna was still the citadel of internal medicine. Not everybody in Ostrau had such a relative. Why not take advantage of it?

My first impression of Vienna is dim. It was a cold, dark day and I remember standing in a large, wood-paneled room that looked like a library. It wasn't a library, it was the doctor's office. Court Councilor Wechsberg was no ordinary doctor, of course, like Dr. Himmelblau, whose office was white and sterile. The *Hofrat* was a luminary of science, dignified, bearded, and old, like the great professors one now sees on framed pictures in the waiting rooms of elderly, conservative Viennese doctors. I stood in front of the *Hofrat* with my bare torso, and I was cold.

My illustrious cousin, twice removed, cast a professionally doubtful glance at my chest. "You could count the poor boy's ribs," my mother later remembered dramatically. After using his stethoscope, which was cold and tickled me, and after knocking at my chest and ribs, the *Hofrat* shook his head gravely and authoritatively. To return to Ostrau and to school now was out of the question, he said to my mother. It was nothing dangerous, many children had this lung condition. Sunshine and fresh air and plenty of food would fix it in no time. A teaspoonful of cod-liver oil, twice a day.

My mother promptly started to cry. I was overjoyed. I wouldn't have to go back to the multiplication table and high poles. The cod-liver oil business wasn't so good, but I had already learned that nothing in life is perfect. The *Hofrat* tapped my mother gently on her shoulder and said it wasn't serious, there was nothing terribly wrong with me—nothing that time and sunshine, plenty of milk, and lots of sleep couldn't cure. In time—he was careful to give no definitive date—I would become healthy again, a healthy, normal boy. He said "normal," which bothered my mother. Who is normal anyway? Perhaps he had talked too long to his friend down the street.

The *Hofrat* said he knew the place we must go to—the South Tyrol, which had more hours of sunshine in wintertime than the rest of the monarchy. The spa of Meran was just what I needed. He coughed apologetically for suggesting such an expensive convalescence. My mother cried even more bitterly.

But he was right, God bless him. The doctors of two armies, first the peacetime army of (democratic) Czechoslovakia and later the wartime United States Army, agreed with him (though they didn't know he had existed). Twenty and again thirty years later they had to decide whether I was fit for military service. I confess I often wished I would produce the rasping sounds in my chest that had often worried my mother. Alas, my breathing was disgustingly normal. In the American army they even X-rayed my lungs to be scientifically sure.

They were. In both armies I was considered absolutely fit, 1A. The diagnosis which the late Hofrat Wechsberg had made back in 1913 was confirmed, proof of the eminence of the old Viennese medical school. He had made no tests, used no X rays, and there was no computer then. He just knocked his fingers against my chest and then "he thought it over," my mother said. He was a great diagnostician and trusted his sixth sense which, many doctors now tell me, is a poor way of arriving at a diagnosis. They like to be sure now, to be backed up by laboratory tests and computers.

We spent a day at Aunt Bertha's. I had a chance to verify my mother's earlier tales. I was not permitted to leave the house. It was cold outside and I might have a relapse, God forbid. But I *was* shown the window from which they could see the Emperor's coach on its way to Schönbrunn, in good weather. Unfortunately it was cold winter weather then, and His Majesty preferred to stay at the Hofburg in town. Emperors usually inhabit more than one palace.

Still, I liked the comfortable atmosphere of Aunt Bertha's apartment. It was different from our home in Ostrau, from the apartments of my rich classmates. There was a simplicity about it, and bright pastel colors. The carpets were light green and light gray, the furniture was bright. There were light and space. People didn't sit close to one another, they could stretch their legs—though my mother had often warned me not to stretch my legs; she said it was bad manners. Perhaps, if the grownups did it, it wasn't bad manners. There were lamps on the tables and paintings on the walls. The salon had paneled walls. "Oak," my mother said and sighed. In Ostrau they wouldn't know what oak was like.

In the evening my mother and I boarded the sleeping car for the overnight trip to Meran. For a while the excitement of the sleeping car obliterated all other impressions of the Imperial City. Vienna was all right but the sleeper was out of this world. Mahogany walls with inlaid flowers, brass fixtures over the washbasin, cozy lights with *belle époque* lampshades, dark felt blankets in front of the windows to ward off drafts. It was a glorious experience. I was so excited that I didn't sleep all night.

My enthusiasm for sleeping cars remains undiminished though the Compagnie Internationale des Wagons-Lits et des Grands Express Européens has made sad compromises with "progress" and cut down on old-fashioned comfort. One of the last elegant sleepers is on the Red Arrow Express between Moscow and Leningrad. The Russians left everything as it was in 1913. Etched glasses, *belle époque* lampshades, tea served in a silver samovar. The Russians know better than to adapt to the changing times. Let the times adapt to their old sleeping cars.

❖   ❖

The glamorous ride came to an end, and we got off at Meran, as the Austrians then called it (or Merano, as the Italians, the present owners, call it now). For me Meran-Merano remains the end of the line. In every respect. The pleasant, small railroad station hasn't changed since the winter morning in 1913 when I first saw it. In the 1970s it got a darker coat of paint. The Habsburg yellow was replaced by the Italian Republic orange. Fortunately the cemetery remains as I remember it. Nowadays I go there to place a few flowers on the grave of Martha, who is buried there. She liked simple wild flowers and that is what I take her. It is reassuring to know that certain things do not change in this era of continuous change.

I hope that Merano is going to remain the end of the line for me. Most of us go back somewhere as we get older. Not necessarily to the place where we grew up, but to our early thoughts and impressions that helped us to become what we think we are. That is not nostalgia, it is a necessity. We are always in motion, and when we don't walk forward we must walk back. I couldn't go back to the house in Ostrava where I spent my childhood and grew up. The present regime wouldn't exactly welcome me. And it is no longer the place I knew. A place is not houses and streets and squares; it is people. The people I used to know there have gone. Some died peacefully (does anyone die peacefully?) and some "disappeared," as the saying goes.

But when I go to Merano, and once or twice a year I really feel like going back, I almost feel like coming home. It seems to be *my* place. Perhaps because I arrived there the first time that winter morning with my mother and spent the following months on the open terrace of the Lamberg villa, lying on a comfortable chair and wrapped up in thick blankets, exposed to fresh air and the year's young sun. Exactly what the *Hofrat* prescribed.

Lying there, I noticed that the sun and the air were different from what I was used to in our northern, gray latitudes. The sky was deep blue, the sort of picture-postcard blue which the people who stay at home under gray clouds have come to dislike intensely when they get the postcards. But in Meran the sky was really blue and the air had a velvety softness that neutralized the winter cold and made it pleasant to inhale. The strangest phenomenon was the mixture of warm sunshine and cool air creating a transparent blue haze that seemed to hang over the blessed landscape.

There has been some pollution lately in the larger cities of the South Tyrol but in the countryside the bluish haze has remained. I notice it the moment I cross the Brenner Pass and go south. It is a miracle that never ceases to enchant me. Nowhere else on earth have I seen that miraculous haze. On hot summer days it glistens like the air above the radiator of a car. In wintertime the haze is quite still, almost three-dimensional, a soft blanket of pure cashmere.

Lying on the terrace under the watchful eyes of my mother and later, after my mother's return to Ostrau, of "Aunt" Lamberg, I had time to think. Next to me a few children were lying on the terrace. Perhaps they too could make rasping noises in their chests, though no one asked me to demonstrate mine. There was something especially peaceful about the house, the old garden, the vineyard across the street, that appealed to me though at that time I couldn't have spelled the word "peace" and didn't know its meaning.

The Lambergs were an elderly childless couple. "Uncle" Lamberg, as we called him, was an official at the local bank. The bank is still there, now called Banco di Roma, more impressive than in the old days. Now it has indirect lighting and black marble. The foundations are not visible, which may be a good thing. Banks must look impressive even in Italy where the people make wry jokes about them. When I walk past the Banco di Roma I think of Uncle Lamberg, who was irritated when we boys came in asking for a new pencil. He was quite conscious of his duties and didn't like to be disturbed during working hours. He and his wife had always wanted and never had children, and now Aunt Lamberg took in boys and girls from families who could afford it for rest, sunshine, and plenty of food. None of the children had an infectious disease. We were probably a group of spoiled brats. Some of the children had been parked there by their parents, as one parks a car when one does not need it for a while.

Yet my feelings for Meran-Merano have evolved from that terrace, in the garden of the Lambergs, with its brilliantly colored flowers and the old, dark trees, and the scent of apples lying in the cellars of many houses. Nearby were a few palm trees, the first I had ever seen. There are not many places on earth where you can see apple blossoms and palm trees and high mountains with snow-covered peaks without turning your head. I must have sensed then that I had found a place where the noise of the outside world had only a faint echo. The end of the line.

I no longer believe in casual events. Things don't just happen. It was no coincidence when Martha, who had been so fond of my father, one day happened to drive through Merano with her husband, on their way to Sicily. They fell in love with the place at first sight. They stayed and never drove to Sicily. Instead they looked around and bought Praderhof, a large mansion in the district of Maia Alta (Obermais), with an old park, a garden, and vineyards. The mansion had been built around the turn of the century by an architect with a passion for gables and ornaments; and to make it look like a "castle," he had added a round tower. The place had that strange *fin de siècle* ugliness that is now almost beautiful. It is surrounded on all sides by friendly mountains, some of them wooded, rounded hills and others jagged peaks with snow fields and small glaciers. It is both an alpine and a southern landscape, a happy synthesis. From the vineyard one looks down on the large plain between Merano and Bolzano (Bozen), a sea of blossoms in the spring, and an ocean of deep scents in late summer, when the apples and peaches mature. There may be more beautiful places on earth but I haven't found one yet.

All year long the smell of earth is strong there, the *goût de terroir* that gives the local light red wine its characteristic taste, and there are the wooden houses of the peasants, who make their own wine. It is not only beautiful, it is real, not a resort place for transients who come and go. There is an old chapel at the corner of the road, and always fresh wild flowers in front of the Virgin. The families of the peasants and the vintners have lived there for generations. The peasants are tough and shrewd and they refuse to sell their orchards and vineyards. They know that their soil is the only safe investment in their country and they hold onto it.

All this seems paradoxical because international tourism has not by-passed the town, which was already a fancy winter resort in the final decades of the Habsburg monarchy. Empress Elisabeth, the wife of Franz Joseph, often spent the winter there, with her court. After her assassination a statue of her, made of white marble, was placed by the winter promenade. After 1918 the Italians relegated it to a somewhat hidden place; they have no pleasant memories of the Habsburg dynasty that for centuries kept a tight rein of them. But today the Italians, civilized people, try to forget. The Habsburg Empress is back where she used to be, in a prominent place, and there are always fresh flowers in her cold marble hands.

For a long time people have come to Meran for the *Traubenkur,* the mysterious "cure of the grapes," which is pleasant and innocuous. You eat the small aromatic grapes by the kilo, and drink freshly pressed grape juice, and hope for consequences. My friends think I am crazy when I identify today's Merano with peace and tranquillity. The tourists arrive in their big buses in the morning; some come in their cars. They walk under the old arcades of the medieval town and do their hectic shopping in the stores—souvenirs, pullovers, wine, and gold jewelry, said to be "inexpensive"—and if they have time they run up the Gilf Promenade and the Tappeinerweg before they leave in the afternoon, hot and exhausted. The poor people haven't seen the place, they've made it another stop on their crowded program. How should they know that the softly ascending promenades, leading up through gardens and past vineyards high above the Passer and finally forming a balcony from which one looks down upon the town, were originally built by a wise physician who prescribed a comfortable one-hour walk every day for his patients, suffering then, as they do now, from stress and circulation troubles? This is not a place for running but for walking slowly.

❖ ❖

I remember the short and happy time, prior to the Second World War, when Martha and her relatives inhabited the Praderhof. A kindly, childless woman, Martha was close to her large family and wanted to have as many of them as possible in her large house. But then the place became too expensive to run, and they began to take friends as "paying guests," to cover the high overhead. The kitchen was underneath the dining room, in the spacious cellar, and the dishes were sent up in a dumbwaiter. The feudal arrangement worked well as long as they could afford a woman cook and a couple of girls in the kitchen but it became difficult when there was no more help after World War II. Elderly members of the family had to work in the kitchen, and others had to look after the garden, the park, the vineyard. During the war Martha and her husband, a Catholic, had left the house and hidden in a monastery overlooking Lake Garda. The kindly abbot, a true Christian, often risked his life by shielding Jews. Such things did happen in Italy. Many people had no use for the German friends and occupants.

Meanwhile, in Merano, the local German S.S. *Kommandant* requisitioned the Praderhof as his official residence because it was so pleasant to live there. *He* had plenty of help; the kitchen downstairs did not bother him. He didn't take anything with him when he decided to run away from the approaching U. S. Fifth Army. Some people later said he had been "decent enough." And after a while the American liberators left and the German occupants came back, cautiously and often under false names. In the 1950s, Merano was one of the least-known hiding places of former Nazis. If they didn't go to South America they stayed in the town at the end of the line. Dr. Josef Mengele, the mad concentration camp doctor who tried to grow a new Aryan species of blue-eyed babies by ocular injections, was in Merano for a while before he went to hide in South America. His wife still lives there. The wife of Martin Bormann, Hitler's deputy, the highest Nazi war criminal not yet accounted for, is buried in Merano. Her husband is believed to have lived for some time at Castle Labers, on a hill just behind the Praderhof, surrounded by vineyards and orchards. During the war Castle Labers was the site of the ultra-secret printshop where the Nazis produced millions of counterfeit British pound notes. The operation was so successful that it disturbed the British war effort until the Allies were able to identify the counterfeiters. Merano was a logical place for the enterprise. Who would expect counterfeiters in paradise?

As long as Martha was there I went back to Merano. I went there when I had troubles and needed her understanding. It was so good to talk to her. Once, I remember, I went there in serious trouble. She listened patiently—she had the great gift of listening—and told me it was better to suffer, knowing one had really lived, than to live without suffering and without joy. She was a wise woman. Merely walking next to her under the arcades of vines, with their white and red grapes, made me feel better.

Martha died in 1949, and six months later her husband followed her. She is buried in the Jewish cemetery, and he in the Catholic cemetery. The cemeteries are side by side.

Suddenly the Praderhof was too big, too expensive, needing too many repairs. Martha's sisters rented the big house and moved to the small house below the vineyard, once the servants' house probably. After the birth of our daughter Poppy at the local hospital—it is located in a street named for Goethe—my wife and I joined them. Yet the arrangement didn't work out and the big house had to be sold. The sisters took the money and went to America to join some members of the family who had emigrated earlier. They lived in a small apartment in the Bronx and grew homesick for Merano. They couldn't forget the bluish haze, the stillness, the scent of fresh fruit, which everybody could enjoy in Merano because they were free.

❖   ❖

I've often walked past Martha's former home and regretted not having bought it. When they wanted to sell it I didn't have the money. And I now know it would have been a mistake. The problems of upkeep, costly repairs, dealing with the local petty bureaucracy would have spoiled my joy of ownership. The buyer surrounded the property with two rows of barbed wire (some people are addicted to barbed wire) and keeps three shepherd dogs near the gate.

Eventually Time, the great mover that ousted the counterfeiters and the members of ODESSA who helped Nazi war criminals to escape, will remove the dogs and perhaps the barbed wire. Unfortunately it has already moved out the lovable eccentrics and bizarre types who were at home in the town at the end of the line. Near the Praderhof there is the old wine castle of Rametz, whose vineyards produce one of the better local wines. During the last war the small apartment up in the castle tower was occupied by Fritz Herzmanovsky-Orlando, the Austrian novelist and artist, then almost unknown, now posthumously admired as social critic and ironic historian of the Habsburg monarchy. He would often come to our place jingling coins in the right pocket of his pants. He said they were gold coins, and when we looked skeptical he showed them to us. And they *were* gold coins. He said they were his savings and he carried them around wherever he went. He called this "total financial mobility." He was not being sarcastic; he was right.

In November, with the advent of cool weather, the tourists disappear. For a while Merano belongs to the Meraners, who seem totally unaware of the attractions of their home town. I know some who have never walked on the Gilf Promenade. They claim it is "for the foreigners" but they don't know how much they miss. Unlike them, Ezra Pound was aware of the beauty that surrounded him when he spent several years at Castle Tyrol, overlooking the landscape. There he brooded and wrote and tried to find peace before he went to Venice.

Personally, I would rather stay at Merano. I won't miss the smell of decay and the sense of death on the canals in Venice, picturesque and depressing. There may be little of Venetian beauty and color in Meran, but there is also none of Venetian disease and decay. No matter what others think, Merano remains a good place to live in and a good place to die. The contours of the mountains are as intimate now to me as the faces of my last few true friends. Hidden corners and small spots remind me of something that is very personal and very important. It is *the* place.

6.

I AM ONCE again ahead of myself—switches in time help me to explain my life to myself. In 1913, after I had been in Meran for two months, I seem to have been as good as new. The rasping sounds in my chest had gone; the cod-liver oil twice a day continued. My mother was notified by the Lambergs and came to take me home. She too loved Meran and often went there in later years.

Back in Ostrava I rejoined my classmates at the Jewish School. With the help of a tutor I managed to catch up with them and finished the year with a good report. My father was pleased but not surprised. He said he'd always expected this from me, and that pleased *me*. My mother, always more pessimistic, had expected I would have to repeat the class. She was overjoyed, and she and I went on our summer vacation.

When the shots of Sarajevo were fired, on June 28, 1914, my mother and I were on the Semmering, a three-thousand-foot-high hill sixty miles south of Vienna. Some wealthy Viennese had villas there. People from the provinces would spend the summer holidays in one of the comfortable hotels, to be close to their Viennese friends. Going to the Semmering had been Aunt Bertha's idea, naturally. She thought it would be nice to have us "in the vicinity." She promised frequent visits. But after Sarajevo she had no more time to come.

I don't remember much about the assassination of Archduke

Franz Ferdinand, the heir to the throne, and his wife. My mother was very upset. When my father joined us there, a day or two later, she was much calmer. She had expected he would talk about Sarajevo and the terrible danger of war. Everybody was talking about it, and no one dared think about it. The very thought of war was horrifying.

My father seemed unconcerned, though I wasn't sure. He told her not to worry. At home everything was well. My two-year-old brother Max had been left in the care of Fräulein Gertrud and Marie. To be sure, there had been minor domestic intrigues between the two women, jousting for position and power, but my father had managed, with tact and justice, not to offend either one.

"Of course," my mother said. "You are always the diplomat."

My mother called my father "the diplomat." Uncle Alfred and Uncle Eugen, who worked with him at the bank, were "the charmer" and "the militarist." She asked my father what his brothers had said about Sarajevo. He shook his head, smiling. He didn't want to discuss it. But I knew he was thinking about the future and war. I had already learned to observe my father. I was almost seven. He had often indicated that there were moments when we men—yes, he said "we men"—must form a common front. He didn't say against whom, he sometimes would leave a few things unsaid, but I had a pretty good idea whom he meant. The common silence and the common knowledge created a strong bond among "us men." I worshiped my father. In my childish heart I wanted to be like him when I grew up. I was watching him closely during those days on the Semmering. In some moments when my mother felt unobserved he would give her a thoughtful glance. Perhaps (I feel today) he sensed what was going to happen and wondered how she would be able to cope with the future.

This is not a chronicle of the outbreak of the First World

War. It is a seven-year-old boy's vague reminiscences of the last weeks preceding the war. Old people in Vienna still call it "the war." The Second World War is "the last war." Much of what I know about "the war" so far as it concerned us I learned later from my mother, who time and again went over every moment of what had happened. These were the last weeks of her life, she would say, what came later . . . She gave a meaningful shrug.

I believe she and my father tried to shut out the thought of war. They both knew it was going to happen but never mentioned it. When we walked in the countryside they enjoyed the little things that matter: the trees and the mushrooms in the woods, the wild flowers, the scent of summer over the meadows where the peasants cut the grass and put it up in bales. The peasants seemed unconcerned about the future; they followed as usual the rhythm of nature. It was peaceful and remote, and completely natural. I still remember the sound of the small bell from a nearby chapel.

It was hard to realize that Vienna's Ballhausplatz was only two hours away by fast train. (Fortunately my parents didn't know that the bureaucrats were drafting the fateful ultimatum to Serbia in their stilted, diplomatic French.) On our walks through the countryside we often watched the trains going to Vienna. The Semmeringbahn was part of the Südbahn, the Southern Railroad from Vienna to Trieste. My father had come through this region as a boy when he ran away to Trieste. The Semmeringbahn was the monarchy's first mountain railroad, built after 1848. The bewhiskered old Emperor had been a very young man then. It was hard to believe that he had ever been young. With its many tunnels and daring viaducts, the railroad had been admired as a masterpiece, another symbol of the Empire, like the Ringstrasse and the Court Opera in Vienna. The

Habsburg monarchy no longer had any solid foundations and depended mainly on symbols.

The shots of Sarajevo did not "start the First World War," as we learned in school. Not immediately. It took four long weeks of hope and despair, of diplomatic stupidity and political quid pro quo to set in motion the devilish machinery that finally turned Europe into an immense battlefield. The summer was warm and beautiful. The casual observer might not have seen anything unusual. There was no dancing-on-the-rim-of-the-volcano mood, not even in Vienna, where the people went into the parks, to the Danube, and to the *Heuriger* inns in the suburbs, drinking young wine under the chestnut and linden trees. There was much talk of politics but no one really believed that "it" might happen. "They" would straighten it out, the people at the Ballhausplatz. There was an editorial in this morning's paper but you know these newspapers. They need some sensation during the dog days. Thriving on bad news, on disaster.

My mother heard about the strange ritual in Vienna's Capuchin Vault, where the coffin of Franz Ferdinand had been surmounted with the symbols of Habsburg power: the crown, the helmet, the saber, his decorations. But the coffin of his wife stood on a lower level. No crown on it; just a fan and a pair of white gloves to remind the people that the Archduchess who would have been the Empress had been "only a former lady in waiting." Countess Sophie Chotek von Chotkova und Wognin. Lower Bohemian nobility. Definitely not in the list of families into which a Habsburg was expected to marry.

The sympathies of my mother and her women friends were on the side of Sophie. They talked about her as though she were a member of our family. They were shocked that social and feudal differences were noted even in death. Obviously no one in Vienna's court circles had wanted to remember that the heir to the throne had been happily married. He had insisted on marrying Sophie. The Kaiser had, most reluctantly, given his permission but he never forgave Franz Ferdinand for it. My mother knew all the details. She loved to read *Neues Wiener Journal*, the newspaper that printed court gossip.

❖ ❖

On the Semmering the pace of life was even more deceiving than in Vienna. The somnolent, pleasant holiday routine, morning walks to the post office to get the mail and the papers, leisurely meals at the hotel. My father would carefully read the papers, the *Neue Freie Presse* and the *Reichspost*, but he kept his thoughts to himself. "He didn't want to alarm me but he became more protective as things got worse," my mother later said. She asked him no questions, though she heard all the gossip on her errands in the village when she went to buy some chocolate for me. I had given up my exclusively cocoa-and-*Würstel* diet, but I liked milk chocolate, and I got more of it during those weeks in July 1914 than I deserved.

On fine, warm days we would go for a walk in the afternoon. In Ostrau, a coal town, people were always afraid of being "asphyxiated" by all that coal dust. On weekends they would take excursions to the nearby Beskiden (Bezkydy Mountains) that were for Ostrau what the Semmering was for Vienna—a poor man's Semmering, to be sure. In the Beskiden there were no luxurious hotels such as the Südbahnhotel Semmering or the Grand Hotel Panhans, where we stayed.

I enjoyed our afternoon rambles. My father would hold my hand and we would walk slowly behind my mother, who was two steps ahead on the narrow paths. If there was space I would walk between them, but I would hold only my father's hand; I wasn't so small any more as to be held by both hands. My favorite hike was to the Sonnwendstein, almost two hours from the Semmering Pass, up to a height of forty-five hundred feet. Up there it was cool and pleasant even when the day had been sticky farther down. Below there was a fine view of the Semmering and the viaducts of the railroad. I loved trains even then and so did my father. He carried a small schedule in his pocket and knew when we might expect a fast train coming up or going down. The train would enter a tunnel, come out on the other side, and cross one of the high viaducts. I was afraid it might fall off into the abyss but it never did. Once my father showed me the relief plaque of a dignified man near the railroad station. He was Karl von Ghega, the famous builder of this wonder of the world.

From the Sonnwendstein we would walk down toward Maria-Schutz, a celebrated pilgrimage church. I didn't know what a pilgrimage was and I wouldn't have cared. I remember the glass of cold milk though, the dark peasant bread thickly spread with sweet yellow butter and sprinkled with salt. Delicious. Small squares had been drawn in the butter with a knife. I was careful not to disturb the squares with my teeth while eating the buttered bread.

We were on the Sonnwendstein on the afternoon of July 28 when a tourist, a casual acquaintance of my parents, told them that Austria-Hungary had declared war on Serbia. He had just heard it down in the village. He spoke in a low voice but he was obviously delighted to be the bearer of bad news. My mother began to cry. My father, quiet and pensive, said, "Please don't cry." He never liked the display of emotions in public. He took my hand and we walked to the balustrade to wait for a fast train which was due any moment. And there it was, like a toy, the engine puffing as it entered the tunnel, and smoke coming out of the tunnel long after the train had disappeared. Then we walked down, straight to our hotel, with no side excursions. I wanted to collect some mushrooms, but he shook his head. At the hotel my father said we had just enough time to pack and make the evening train to the Südbahnhof in Vienna. From there we would go to the nearby Ostbahnhof, the Eastern Railroad Station, and get the night train for Lundenburg and Ostrau. My mother cried and said we might as well stay until the next morning and make the trip in daytime. My father shook his head, gently and regretfully, as though he were forced to turn down a would-be creditor at the bank. He said we must be back in Ostrau the next morning. He was a reserve officer in the army and would have to report to his regiment at once.

In Vienna both railroad stations were crowded with panicky, desperate people trying to get somewhere. At the newsstand I saw large newspaper headlines. All papers had published the Emperor's manifesto *"An meine Völker* [To My Peoples]!" I've often read it since. Signed by an eighty-four-year-old man who had kept an uneasy peace for forty-eight years. Now, under pressure of his advisers, he had endorsed the document he knew to be the death warrant of his empire. One paragraph of the manifesto stands out in my mind. "I put my faith in the Austro-Hungarian army, in its bravery and dedicated loyalty." To me that paragraph always meant my father.

❖   ❖

Since then I've read many books about the beginning of the end of the Habsburg monarchy. I wanted to know the true story of what happened, if such a story exists, and perhaps to find, mainly for myself, an excuse for my father's "bravery and dedicated loyalty." He must have known that he was fighting for a lost cause. Perhaps he had some last illusions; perhaps he thought the impossible might become possible. The newspapers wrote that the war against Serbia was "a joke" and would be over in two weeks. The "ridiculous Balkan country" would be overrun, just as the advisers had assured His Majesty in his summer residence in Ischl, Upper Austria.

The Kaiservilla, where Franz Joseph signed the fatal papers, is now a museum open to the people. During the monarchy, or-

dinary people could never get in even when the Kaiser was not
there. While we had been on the Semmering, the Old Gentleman had been in Ischl. The summer had been exceptionally dry
in Ischl, which is noted for the *Schnürlregen,* a slow, steady
rain, soft and depressing, the water coming down as in long
cords. And on a beautiful evening the news was received from
the Austrian ambassador to Serbia. The Serbian government—
this is known—had originally agreed to accept the Austrian ultimatum unconditionally. There would have been no war. But
later that day, on July 25, the Serbs changed their minds. No
one knows why. In Belgrade too, some bureaucrats and diplomats may have had their way. They may have said, "The least
we Serbs can do is to reject the Austrian demand that only *their*
officials should take part in the criminal investigation." After all,
the assassination had occurred in Sarajevo, on Serbian territory.
The Austrian ultimatum offended the Serbian constitution and
Serbian criminal law. The Austrian diplomats who had drafted
the ultimatum knew this very well.

But the unholy alliance between bureaucrats and diplomats is
worldwide. The truly powerful men—emperors, dictators, presidents—have perhaps always been at their mercy. It is easier to
win a battle against the enemy's forces than against one's own
bureaucrats.

Whatever the reason, at two minutes past six a totally new answer was handed to the Austrian ambassador in Belgrade. It was
considered "unacceptable." The Austrian ambassador immediately left his embassy in Belgrade and drove across the Sava
River to the Austrian outpost of Semlin. From there the message
was sent to Ischl in Austria. It arrived after seven-fifteen. His
Majesty was about to go to mass.

The historians report that he read the message and stood silent for a long time, "a man turned to stone," as Edward Crank-
shaw describes him. He was still hesitating. He told his advisers

that this meant breaking off diplomatic relations, certainly, but it didn't mean war yet. There was still a very remote chance of peace.

Then Foreign Minister Count Leopold Berchtold and War Minister Baron Krobatin arrived. Krobatin was a leading warmonger; war ministers are often sympathetic toward war, having trained for it.

The historian Josef Redlich, a primary source because he knew the protagonists and was there most of the time, notes an early rumor in 1913 according to which the Emperor banged on the table and exclaimed, "I don't want war. I've always been unlucky in wars. We would win but we would lose some provinces." But on the same day Redlich notes that he heard Baron Krobatin say, "Austria has to go to war because it is the only way of solving the monarchy's internal problems."

These were the men at the center of power who decided life or death, more accurately death or life, for millions of people. Perhaps they were not frivolous, only afraid of their own courage, thinking of their personal careers. It makes little difference. The Emperor signed the mobilization order for war with Serbia and Montenegro. A minor local war. It will be over in a few weeks, Your Majesty, and these people will have learned their lessons.

It was all settled. The future belonged to the generals, no longer to the diplomats. Field Marshal Conrad von Hötzendorf, whose toughness was compared to that of a terrier, figured it would take at least two weeks for the Austro-Hungarian army to finish its mobilization and be ready to move against Serbia. He had not been happy in the long weeks of July, when he wasn't sure whether war would be declared. He didn't even dare move his troops into Semlin, across from Belgrade, since the Serbs might consider this a provocation. Conrad von Hötzendorf was mainly concerned with Serbia. When Armageddon was suddenly upon him, he was just a worried field marshal.

Looking back now, one is shocked by the apparently inexorable sequence of events. On July 28, Austria declared war on Serbia, the "limited" war, according to His Majesty's advisers, that would be over in a couple of weeks. But on July 29 the Russians began a general mobilization, first in Kiev, Odessa, Moscow, and Kazan, and later everywhere. On July 30, Germany declared war on Russia. On August 2, Berlin sent its infamous ultimatum to Belgium, demanding "free passage" for the German troops. On August 3, Germany declared war on France. On August 4, the British Foreign Minister, Sir Edward Grey, telegraphed a British ultimatum to Berlin. If Germany attacked France, England would come to the aid of France. Sir Edward asked for a reply by midnight, German time. He didn't really expect an answer. None came. On the morning of August 5, Europe was at war.

❖   ❖

The journey from the Semmering to Vienna and from there to Ostrau remains a nightmare. The fast train to Ostrau that we boarded at the Ostbahnhof one hour before midnight was overcrowded. We got on only after my father had talked to an army colonel. They both went to see a high-ranking railroad official. My father explained that he had to get home quickly because it was his duty to report at once to his unit. During the weeks and months that followed I often heard the word "duty" uttered, plaintively or sarcastically, never neutrally. Either "duty" was something that had to be done though no one liked doing it; or it was almost an invective. A man doing his duty was a fool; if he was smart, he managed to get out of it. If he had tried and failed, he was also a fool. The worst meaning of the word was its literal use. It seemed almost sinister to some people that a man believed he *had* to do his duty. Either he believed in the wrong things or he had joined the small group of superfools who wanted war. There were no displays of jubilation in my home town. Elsewhere, but not in Ostrau. No shouting, no patriotic speeches, no bands playing as the men went away. Too many people there knew what it meant.

My father finally managed to get one seat in a first-class coach which a high-ranking officer gave up for my mother. I sat on her lap. My father and the officer spent much of the night standing in the corridor, talking softly. Some women were crying. My mother cried too when my father wasn't watching. The men looked grim and some, I thought, were angry. I was glad when we arrived at the Ostrau railroad station, out in the suburb of Oderfurt (Přívoz). It was past four in the morning but the station was as crowded as on a weekday afternoon. There was much confusion. Men in uniforms were throwing their weight around. For the first time I heard the word "civilian" uttered with contempt. It was already shameful to be a civilian. The population was divided into "our brave soldiers" and "civilians." I asked my father about it. He gave me a sad smile and shook his head. I understood. No sense discussing it.

I have a vague recollection of the next day. Confusion, my mother and Fräulein Gertrud and Marie crying, my father's brothers coming up to see him. Uncle Eugen already wore his well-pressed uniform of a *Rittmeister,* a captain in the cavalry, with splendidly shined boots. He said to my mother that he had shined them himself, "at least for half an hour"; he considered this his "patriotic duty." She stared at him, speechless. Uncle Alfred, of whom my father was very fond, looked perturbed, though he gave my mother an encouraging pat on the shoulder as though she were a client at the bank downstairs and something had gone wrong. My father had a long talk with him in the *Herrenzimmer.* Both were serious. Then my mother joined them and when they came out she was crying, and my father didn't even try to stop her. Even Uncle Alfred was in tears.

Thereafter everything disappears behind the sort of gauze curtain which modern stage producers use when they are not sure of what they are doing and try to conceal their lack of conviction behind merciful dimness. But the curtain goes up and I see everything clearly as my father goes away and I see him for the last time. Fräulein Gertrud, holding my brother Max on her arm. Max is two years old but seemed older that day. Marie and I standing at the right-hand window of the dining room. The slightly curved window is open; in front of it there is a sill with flowers. (The architect had tried to imitate some art nouveau masters when he created a rounded façade on the dining room, jutting out slightly.) The window sill obscures the view, so I get up on a chair. Marie insists on holding me by the suspenders because I might fall out. Silly. Why should I fall out? I won't get dizzy either, one doesn't get dizzy when one is seven years old.

I didn't cry, I had promised my father some things, and not to cry was one of them. (I later forgot the promise but one day my mother reminded me of it.) I stood there on the chair looking down. The *Fiaker* was waiting at the corner of Johannystrasse, across from our house. A fine coach drawn by two horses. Then my father and my mother crossed the street and she got into the coach. For a long moment my father stood there, turning around, looking up at us, and then he slightly raised his hand, his right hand, and waved at us, just once. I was glad it was a "civilian" gesture though he wore his beautiful uniform, which I described at the beginning of this book.

I can still see my father standing there near the coach, looking up for what remains the longest moment in my life. He turned around and got into the *Fiaker* and sat next to my mother. He didn't look back any more. And then they were gone.

❖   ❖

My father's regiment, the not so famous 34th Infantry, was one of the first to leave for the front. Afterward, "the front" always meant Polish Galicia for us, the front against the Russians, though there were several other, equally important fronts during the war. "The front" was the region from which my father's family had come, when Grandfather Wechsberg arrived in my home town "on top of a loaded haycart," according to the family legend. And now my father went back there, as an officer in the Austro-Hungarian army on whose "bravery and dedicated loyalty" the Kaiser had counted.

My father frequently wrote to my mother and always added a few words for me. I already realized that I was "the older of the two boys" and I knew that seniority meant responsibility. Sometime in September 1914, while the regiment was being alerted, he asked my mother to come to Craców. She stayed two or three days and when she came back she looked distraught but she wasn't crying, and that was much worse. She told me she had stayed with him until the regiment received marching orders for the front sector of Bochnia. Life is a number of concentric circles, and it is merely another circle within the circles that my wife's father was born in Bochnia, whence he had later migrated to Ostrau. I knew no one who migrated *to* Poland. Everybody wanted to get away from there. My father had been there during the autumn maneuvers and had often said, *"In Polen ist nichts zu holen* [There is nothing to be found in Poland]." Nothing but death.

The following weeks are hazy again. I went to school, and there was the usual routine at home, interrupted only by news from "the field," written by my father in his correct, clear handwriting on gray *Feldpost* cards that bore the stamp of the censor. Sometimes my mother tried in vain to read some of the lines over which the censor had placed his black stamp. Once in a while my two uncles who lived in our house came up for a short visit. My mother disliked these visits but didn't discourage them. Perhaps she too had made a promise to my father. Uncle Alfred had been turned down by the army on medical grounds. My mother was vague about it. Later she once said, "Alfred was as healthy as your father but he arranged himself."

Uncle Eugen, the second partner in the bank, was very busy visiting people in his splendid *Rittmeister*'s uniform. He had been assigned to a quartermaster outfit in the nearby town of Teschen, a long way from the front. Teschen was later called Czieszyn by the Poles and Těšín by the Czechs. Both wanted to have it after the end of the war, and for a while Teschen had the dubious distinction of belonging to both, or to none. The Olsa River, which went straight through the middle of town, was the border. It was said that the statesmen who wrote the peace treaties had been unable to agree on the town, so they halved it, irritating both sides. No one would make the Seine a border, separating the Left and Right Banks, but Teschen was a long way from Paris, and none of the statesmen had ever been there.

Once Uncle Eugen invited me to spend several days in Teschen, where he was stationed with Aunt Irma, my mother's sister, and their two boys, my cousins Kurt and Hans. Teschen was the residence and headquarters of His Highness Field Marshal Archduke Friedrich von Habsburg, who had a castle there. We boys thought it was a beautiful old castle, but I remember Uncle Eugen said it was "typically modest" for a member of the All-Highest Arch-House of Habsburg. He almost but not quite stood up and saluted when he mentioned the House of Habsburg. He truly liked the war. In the morning we boys would walk with him from the house that had been requisitioned for him to his office in the center of town. It was a small town and the streets were crowded with more generals than I had thought existed. All looked cheerful and well dressed as though their uniforms had been ironed by their *Burschen* (batmen) that very morning; and probably they had.

Uncle Eugen saluted the generals smartly, often exclaiming, "*Respekt, Exzellenz!*" when he happened to know one personally. *Exzellenz* would salute, a little condescendingly maybe, which proved that he really belonged; he might even stop and graciously exchange a few words with Uncle Eugen. Sometimes I was introduced as "the son of my younger brother, Oberleutenant Wechsberg, now at the front near Bochnia," but the mention of "the front" didn't seem to please *Exzellenz,* and after a while I was no longer introduced. When I returned home I told my mother that the war seemed to be quite interesting in Teschen, and I told her about Uncle Eugen and the generals in their fine uniforms, with red stripes on their immaculately pressed pants. In fact, I said, the generals seemed to enjoy the war.

My mother listened, and then she said, "They might enjoy it less if they were with your father right now in the woods near Bochnia."

❖   ❖

The story of how my father died, of his "heroism"—my mother pronounced the word as though it were obscene—was first told to me by her. Later it was confirmed, officially, by a colonel from the War Ministry in Vienna, a General Staff officer who came to visit her a few months after my father's death to hand her a high military decoration that had been posthumously awarded to my father. I never tried to find out the name of the decoration, a cross studded with small diamonds. I feel about it exactly as my mother did.

She took it from the colonel, silently. She said not a word. She closed the small box lined with blue velvet, without looking at the decoration, and placed it in the laundry closet, underneath the sheets and pillowcases. She never took it out and

never looked at it. The colonel watched her stiffly, and then he
saluted and left. I don't know what happened to the decoration.
Presumably it was taken by the Gestapo at the time they found
the other things my mother had kept—or hidden, as they may
have called it—in her laundry closet. It had some value, owing to
the small diamonds. And the Gestapo didn't like First World
War military decorations in the houses of Jews. They arrested
Jewish citizens who walked around wearing the yellow Star of
David *and* their military decorations.

But the truth was told to us one day in 1924 by an old Polish
peasant who took my mother and me to the mass grave in the
woods near Bochnia where my father and his men had been
buried. It was ten years after his death. I was seventeen, old
enough to help my mother, as I had promised him the day he
went away.

The old peasant knew what had happened. The story had become almost a heroic legend in the region. The Poles had hated
the Austrians but they hated the Russians even more. Compared
to what the Russians had done to them in the course of their
long and tragic history, the Austrians had been almost innocent.
The peasant's story differed from the Austrian colonel's story
enough to prove that the General Staff officer had tried to cover
up the "lack of judgment," as he called it, on the part of a fellow
officer from the General Staff. The club spirit. But the Polish
peasant had been there—he was among other Polish civilians ordered to help the Austrians dig out the mass grave—and he told
us the truth.

I have written about this before, emotionally. Now I simply
want to put down the facts. There is no need for emotion. My
personal experiences in two armies, the Czechoslovak army and
the American army, have helped me to understand how such
things could happen. All armies on earth operate by unwritten
laws.

Law No. 1: The man who outranks you is always right, he cannot be wrong. Law No. 2: Members of the chain of command always cover up the mistakes of their fellow commanders.

The mass grave was in a clearing in the deep, dark woods, on the spot where the men had been killed. There was no time to take away the bodies. They were buried where they died. The grave was hardly visible. Ten years had gone by, and during the summer moss and wild flowers had grown all over it, according to the peasant. We saw no flowers; there are no wild flowers in November. We were there on the tenth anniversary of the death of my father on November 22, 1914. It was a cold and rainy day but I was too excited to notice the rain.

The Polish peasant said that the people living nearby often came here to say the Lord's Prayer. He knelt down and said the prayer and crossed himself. My mother and I stood motionless, as in a trance, unable to pray. There are moments when one ought to pray but cannot.

The mass grave was marked by a primitive wooden cross that had been placed there in 1914, with the names of the dead. Now, ten years later, the names were hardly visible. My father's name was on top, followed by the names of all the men in his company, according to the peasant. Not one had survived.

The peasant showed us the approximate spot where the Austrians had had their trenches, below the hill with the clearing on top. The Russians had held the top of the hill, and they had heavy machine guns posted in the clearing, exactly where the grave was now. The Russians had dug in there and might be dislocated by field artillery. But my father's infantry company had had no artillery support when the order came over the field telephone to take the clearing "at all costs." The order had come from higher headquarters in the rear, from somebody "along the chain of command."

The Austrian position was hopeless when my father, the company commander, received the order.

"There was nothing he could do but give the command, '*Sturm* [Attack]!'" said the old peasant.

But the men were reluctant to leave the relative safety of their trenches, just because some invisible commander in the rear had issued the order over the field telephone. The men knew they would never reach the clearing on the top of the hill alive. Facing disobedience and possibly mutiny, unthinkable for a k. & k. officer of the Austro-Hungarian army of whom His Majesty expected "bravery and dedicated loyalty," my father had drawn his saber and jumped out of the trench, all by himself. And the men who only a minute ago had hesitated to follow his command automatically remembered Law No. 3, "*Befehl ist Befehl* [An order is an order]," and stormed up the hill behind their company commander.

The Russians had waited. Either they were surprised by their foolhardy enemy, or they wanted to be sure of killing them. Only when the attackers had almost reached the clearing and were within easy range of the machine gunners did the Russians begin shooting.

"They cut them down right here as we mow down grass with a scythe," the old peasant said, and spat because he was deeply moved. He uttered a Polish curse, and then he got down on his knees again and said another Lord's Prayer.

Much, much later the Austrians had brought up some field guns from the rear and shelled the Russian position. The Russians retreated, and the Austrians occupied the clearing and buried their dead. That was the way it happened, the peasant said, and I believe him, though the "official" version of the War Ministry colonel was somewhat different. But then, the colonel hadn't really been interested in the truth.

7

For some time after that day in November 1914 when we knew that my father would never come back, I resented my friends and classmates who still had their fathers. Why all of them, and not Max and I? I brooded over the question. There was no answer, none that satisfied me. I sensed vaguely that I was perhaps too young to ask myself the question but that didn't help. I was hurt.

One day, after our classroom lesson in religion at the Jewish School, I approached Dr. Spira. He sat behind his desk on the platform, underneath the picture of Emperor Franz Joseph I. Dr. Spira often meditated during the intermission while we children played in the courtyard. I was all alone in the classroom with him and asked him the question.

He wasn't surprised. He looked at me pensively, nodding a few times as though he had expected it.

"You are right to ask me the question," he said at last. "Unfortunately I cannot answer it. Some of my colleagues might tell you it was God's will but that won't satisfy a boy of eight. You are eight, aren't you?"

"Almost."

"Yes. At your age I probably would have asked the question myself. . . . I could tell you, of course, that you are a chosen one." He gave a shrug. "That too is easy and convenient. But you and your brother Max are not the only chosen ones. The casualty lists keep coming in, and the war has barely started." He mentioned a few names. "You heard about them, did you?"

"Yes, but . . ."

"I know. It's not the same thing when it happens to others. It's going to happen to many children, though, I am afraid. Try not to think of the question and perhaps that will eventually help you to find an answer."

Dr. Spira got up, indicating that the audience was ended.

"Someday you might come to the synagogue. Come there once on a Friday evening. The service doesn't last long. Your grandfather often came. He still has his seat there, in the first row, a seat of honor. Now the seat is mostly empty. Your father sometimes came but I never see his brother Alfred there."

"Uncle Alfred is running the bank now," I said.

"Not on Friday night," said Dr. Spira.

❖   ❖

Our house was located between the Old (Catholic) Church and the synagogue. I walked out of our house and turned left. At the next corner there was the small street to the left leading to the church. To the right was the synagogue. Originally, the Old Church had been *the* church, but when they built the New Church, near the *Realschule* where my father had gone and my brother later went to school, *the* church became the Old Church. No one called it by its name, St. Wenceslas Church. There was also the Evangelical Church, which was bright and styleless and had no mystique at all.

Contrarily, the Old Church was baroque and darkly mystical, with an onion-shaped cupola in Russian Orthodox style. Such churches exist in many villages in Bohemia and Moravia and in the Eastern countries, and the finest are in the Kremlin in Moscow, but I still like our Old Church the best. Marie, a very pious woman, went there to mass every morning at a quarter of six, and often she went again at night. During the month of May we always had cold things for supper because Marie would leave for *Maiandacht* (the May Prayers) before 7 P.M.

Sometimes she took me along. I liked the church because it was dark and peaceful. I liked the statues of the saints best. Marie said that the saints were dead, all of them. Apparently no one was around any more who could have been a saint. Marie was too smart to say that "they lived happily ever after." She loved funerals, especially when she hadn't known the dear deceased. She attended many anonymous funerals that took place in the Old Church. Some were rather simple, without organ music, for poor people; and some had an elaborate ceremonial, with choir singers and several priests attending; they were for rich people, Marie said. So it wasn't true, as some people said, that in death we are all equal. Another lie of the grownups. I admit that I liked the rich funerals better than the poor ones. Today I would say they were a fine show. The tall candles, their flickering lights making the stone faces of the saints wince or chuckle so that they became almost alive. The monotonous voices of the priests, the organ, the choir, and the powerful effect created by the smell of incense. The rich funeral probably gave no pleasure to the person lying there in his coffin but his mourning survivors certainly enjoyed it.

My occasional visits to the Old Church in no way distracted me from my early devotion to the strict laws of Judaism. I went to the synagogue on the high holidays, sitting in the first row, the left corner seat from the middle aisle. It was a place of honor, with a small brass plate saying ALBERT WECHSBERG. My late grandfather had been a generous contributor to local Jewish charities. When he was called up on the high holidays to read out of the Torah, the whispers among the congregation ceased and everybody watched Dr. Spira, the rabbi, who would announce Grandfather's generous donations. And when Grandfather Wechsberg came back to his seat the men around him would nod gratefully.

The widespread sense of tolerance at the time I grew up, in the 1920s—I remember it because it no longer existed ten years later—was symbolized by the proximity of the two Houses of God. On Yom Kippur, when we Jewish boys were not supposed to attend school at the Gymnasium, some Catholic and Protestant classmates would stay away too. They said they did it out of respect for their Jewish classmates. This fine show of tolerance put us Jews under obligation to them, and it was agreed that instead of going to the synagogue we would play soccer with them on the stubble field, a plot of land conveniently hidden by houses on three sides. An ideal, strategic location. A lookout would be posted on the fourth, open side to signal the arrival of a professor, and we would hide in the three house entrances until he had gone.

Unfortunately we Jewish boys were dressed for the synagogue, not for playing soccer, which created complications when we ran back half an hour before the end of the service and arrived there out of breath, covered with dirt. Once the *shammes*, the non-Jewish janitor, refused to let me in. "You cannot sit down in the first row like that," he said. "Go home first and wash up."

Our synagogue had a somewhat oriental touch, owing to much filigree work in gilt and to the vividly colored frescoes that covered its ceiling. It had been built around 1890 and combined some *belle époque* features with a style that I later saw in more impressive forms in the mosques of North Africa and Turkey. Perhaps the architect had been inspired in these places. There were old Persian rugs hanging on the walls and fake marble columns. A gold-painted gallery for the women ran around three sides. People said that "a lot of gold" had gone into our synagogue. Some laughed disrespectfully, but they liked it. They said it was very "practical." If we ever had a Moslem invasion, they said, our synagogue could be used as a mosque by the invaders. More laughter. But when the invaders came to Ostrava in 1939 they were not Moslems, and one of the first things they did was to burn down the synagogue.

The liturgical proceedings were not as mystical as at the Old Church but a strong cabalistic ambiance was conveyed by the old bearded men in the rear, praying with their *tallisim* like scarves around their necks. It was an Orthodox service, and everybody wore a hat. When I went to New York and stepped into a Reformed synagogue I was asked to take off my hat. I had never known that such a service existed.

At our synagogue the men sat downstairs, and the women were upstairs in the gallery. The women also had prayer books but my mother said they rarely prayed, they were too busy looking at one another's clothes. There was a flurry of gossip when someone came in wearing something new. Once my mother, who wanted to pray, got so exasperated that she left. Usually she stayed on Yom Kippur until somebody fainted. That was the climax of her personal ritual. People were not supposed to have taken any food since the Kol Nidre meal the evening before, and on warm days some women were so weak around noontime that they might faint. Once no one fainted. My mother thought the service had been disappointing.

At the Old Church no one ever fainted from hunger. Marie had explained to me that the Catholics' fast just meant no meat, which was not our kind of fasting. The big attraction at the Old Church was to be surrounded by the dead saints. The statues all represented people who had been alive once and were now dead. I brooded about this a lot and in the end I learned about the inevitability of death. One might postpone it for a while, perhaps with the help of a good doctor, but in the end one would have to accept it. In moments of bad behavior when I wanted to hurt Marie I told her that she was old. At that time she may have been forty-five or fifty, at the most. She didn't get angry. She said,

"If you don't want to die old you have to hang yourself while you're young." Her logic made me shut up immediately. Marie was interested in death and dying. She got on so well with my mother because my mother was interested in life and living.

❖   ❖

The Friday after my audience with Dr. Spira at our school I went to the synagogue. (Until then I'd been there only on the high holidays.) I liked the organ playing, the choir, and especially the part of the service when Dr. Spira and the cantor took a sip of the wine and said the blessing. Dr. Spira looked resplendent in his white gold-embroidered robes. I had the strange feeling that he looked down at me briefly when he held up the cup with the wine, and he almost seemed to smile. But perhaps I was imagining things.

I went back to the synagogue the next Friday. My mother seemed surprised but asked no questions. It was wintertime, and darkness came around three in the afternoon. My going to the synagogue did not interfere with any domestic routine. Still, I realized that my mother was wondering. Our family was not very religious. My mother would light the candles in the baroque candlesticks on Friday evening but she said she did it "out of piety." We had no kosher food at home. Once a classmate, an Orthodox Jew, chided me for eating *Würstel* and ham. On Kol Nidre, the eve of Yom Kippur, we always had a special dinner, prior to next day's fast, which I kept strictly. During the Pesach holidays Uncle Jacques would come up. He was my mother's favorite brother, though he shouted a lot; he was then still unmarried and would celebrate Seder as head of the family. Being the youngest male around the table—Max was only three years old—I would read from the Haggadah, "Why is this night different from all other nights?" All this was said in Hebrew, which I didn't understand. The fascinating details of the Exodus from Egypt remained unknown to me.

All things considered, we had a relaxed relationship with religious ritual. Orthodox Jews from Russia and especially from America might have taken a dim view of what our family considered "religion." Maybe they would have been contemptuous. I experienced such contempt much later, as an American soldier in Germany, when I met some people who had been in the concentration camps. They knew I was a Jew and resented me for having been in the American army while they were in the camps. "How lucky can a Jew be?" one asked me once, and almost spat in my face. I didn't exist as far as he was concerned. I certainly was not a chosen one.

My uncle Leo, the "Zionist" uncle—to keep him apart from the "musical" uncle, the "deaf mute" uncle, the uncle who often went bankrupt, and Uncle Jacques, the "shouting" uncle—became so impressed with my synagogue-going and my early knowledge of Zionism that he took me along in 1925 to the Zionist World Congress in Karlsbad. I saw the great heroes of the Zionist movement—Chaim Weitzmann, Nahum Sokolow, Sch'marjahu Levin—and was deeply impressed. But what I remembered best about Karlsbad, I regret to admit, was the enormous *Wiener Schnitzel* which Uncle Leo once ordered for me at the Grand Hotel Pupp. It was so big that its sides overhung the rim of the large plate. It was delicious, the bread crumbs the color of certain Breughels, the meat inside tender and juicy. The Pupp was then one of the Western world's great hotels. Several years ago I happened to be in Karlovy Vary, as the town is now called, and stepped into the Pupp, a state-owned enterprise now, like everything else there. I suppose I was subconsciously trying to discover a link with the past but there was no thread between the garish lights and the cold stares, and there was no *Wiener Schnitzel* on the small menu. I was angry at myself because I should have known by then that one cannot go back.

8.

AFTER THE DEATH of my father, his favorite brother, Alfred, was the sole manager of the family bank. Alfred, whom my mother called "the charmer." Uncle Eugen, "the militarist," was still walking around Teschen in his shiny riding boots, doing his best to help win the war. He didn't even consider the possibility that we might not win it.

In the beginning Uncle Alfred did well for the family, by general agreement. He patriotically invested the money of his brothers and sisters in *Kriegsanleihe,* as the war bonds were called. He came up to our apartment and explained to my mother that these bonds were an excellent investment. High interest rates and practically no risk, none whatever, since the bonds were guaranteed by the State, the government of the Habsburg monarchy.

"And if we lose the war?" my mother asked.

Uncle Alfred raised both hands in a gesture expressing sheer horror. It was high treason, he said, merely to *contemplate* such a possibility. Perhaps two years later he remembered his talk with my mother. Our side had lost the war and the bonds were not worth the beautiful paper they had been printed on. In his own affairs, however, Uncle Alfred was quite astute. He sold his bonds, while there was still time, at a small loss. Later he sold the bonds belonging to his brothers and sisters at a large loss. He invested the money in common shares of the Lombard & Escompte Bank in Vienna. "Excellent growth possibilities," he said, "and minimal risk." His brothers and sisters reluctantly agreed. They said that Alfred could do no wrong, he had a "sixth sense." Hadn't he saved *some*thing from the war bonds? Only my mother was doubtful.

"When Alfred came to see me and tried to sell his new idea, I distrusted him," she told me later. "I always sensed that Alfred's charm outshone his honesty. Your dear father didn't want to hear about it. Alfred was one of his blind spots."

My mother said no, and Uncle Alfred departed.

"He knew the value of patience, he knew how to treat women customers," my mother said bitterly. And she added, by way of a non sequitur, "He knew nothing about women, though." She loved to drop such hints without explaining their meaning. She could be as evasive as a mystery writer.

Alfred returned to tell her that everybody in the family had agreed to follow his lead, would dear Minka go along?

"What should I have done? By that time the people said our money was going to be worth less tomorrow than today, and they were right. I didn't know what to do. I didn't trust Alfred but the others did, and I thought, Maybe they know better than I."

At that time Uncle Alfred knew something that his brothers and sisters didn't know yet: the family bank was lost. The few private banks in town simply went out of business, swept away by the postwar winds of disaster. Two that had a more solid background were merged with large public banks. One of them, A. Wechsberg & Co., was merged with the Länderbank in Vienna and eventually became the local branch office of the Länderbank.

By that time Uncle Alfred and his family were no longer in town. He had used his share holdings—his own and those bought with his relatives' money—to get himself elected a member of the board of the Lombard & Escompte Bank. A little later he became the managing director. After the fait accompli he notified his relatives.

My mother showed me the letter she had recieved. I was sixteen, and I knew nothing about banking and finance. Neither did I know then that many financiers know little about the mysterious science. It was a beautiful letter, typed on expensive white paper. The envelope showed the stamped name of a prestigious Viennese stationer. Uncle Alfred's name and title were engraved at the top of the letter. He carefully explained the situation to dear Minka and asked for her patience. He understood that she might need some cash but right now it was impossible to sell the shares, "owing to the generally unstable situation." She need not worry though. He tactfully reminded her that he still treasured the letter which dear Siegfried, his favorite brother, had written to him from the front, asking him "to look after my dear wife and the boys if something should happen to me." He was aware of the trust bestowed upon him by dear Siegfried and would always, always look after our interests.

It was a cautious letter, written in the legally incontestable language of a skilled banker. Vague statements and undefined promises, soothing phrases and oodles of charm. Uncle Alfred had always been the uncommitted member of the family. Uncle Eugen, the oldest partner, would say yes or no, and my father would regretfully shake his head when he meant no, but Uncle Alfred would give the would-be customer an ambiguous smile that might mean anything, from firm acceptance to flat rejection. He would have been a successful senior diplomat. He looked exactly like an elderly actor playing a senior diplomat. Tall, graying at the temples, with relaxed movements, and always that disarming smile. Always conciliatory, at your service.

"Alfred," my mother once said, "would have charmed a statue made of sandstone."

But she herself had not been impervious to Alfred's charm. When she got his letter from Vienna she wanted to believe him. Later she said she had always been a little sorry for him—because of Aunt Anna, his wife.

Aunt Anna was the *femme fatale* in our family. Every family should have one so the other women have something to talk about. Absurd, my mother would say; Anna didn't even come from Mährisch-Ostrau. She was born in Polnisch-Ostrau, across the Ostravica River near our house, just ten minutes away, and also ten light-years. The small river, perhaps two hundred meters from our house, had once been the provincial border. In my home town you didn't think, "the wrong side of the tracks"; it was the wrong side of the river, where Polnisch-Ostrau was located, a modest suburb with low houses on a hill. The houses were covered with coal dust, but so were the houses in Mährisch-Ostrau, even our house. People said that when you put on a white shirt in the morning, it would be dirty by noon. Maybe not dirty, but not quite white anymore. I had nothing against Polnisch-Ostrau. My violin teacher, Professor Fritz Landau, lived there, and I admired him.

That was different, said my mother. It wasn't really Polnisch-Ostrau that mattered, but Aunt Anna's family. I think they had run a beer and *Schnaps* house, for the miners. Well, what was wrong? I asked my mother, and she would say that there were certain things I did not understand, and shrug. End of conversation. Or almost. After a while my mother would say that I was "too young to understand," and give another, final shrug.

That meant inquiry elsewhere. I began to watch Aunt Anna, which was easy since she and her family lived in the apartment underneath ours. She frequently wore a veil, like the women in Schnitzler's plays who always visited their lovers in the after-

noon. She was often away on mysterious trips to Venice or
Paris, without Uncle Alfred. That was no secret. Aunt Anna
liked to send postcards to her sisters-in-law and women friends,
and there was often another signature written next to hers.
When the other signature was illegible, my mother and her
friends would study it with a magnifying glass during the *Jause*,
the coffee-and-cake-and-gossip hour late in the afternoon. Sometimes one of the women would say, "I wish I knew who it is this
time," and they would all sigh wistfully.

All this was intriguing, and Aunt Anna became an object of
my adolescent speculation. Not that I admired her secretly.
She wasn't attractive, and she was "much too old," in her early
forties. But Aunt Anna had *allure*. I couldn't say exactly what
the word meant, but it did fit her. She was a character in one of
the French bedroom farces given at the local theater, with Rolf
Gradnitzer playing the part of the elegant *bon vivant*.

Gradnitzer was probably the most elegant man in town, or
rather, about town. He always wore patent leather shoes and
white spats, a topcoat with a black velvet collar, and he carried
a stick and a gray derby. An irresistible combination. He walked
with a slightly elastic gait as though he had springs built into his
shoes. I remember him in Molnár's *The Guardsman* and as the
Archduke in the last act of a silly operetta who appeared as *deus
ex machina* and straightened out the improbable complications
with a subtle movement of his hand. He was so good because he
played himself. To me he seemed more aristocratic than some
real aristocrats. Walking along Hauptstrasse (Main Street)
around six in the evening, the hour when almost everybody took
a walk there before dinner, Gradnitzer bewitched the girls and
irritated the men. Perhaps, I thought, I would become a *bon
vivant* when I grew up. Certainly not a streetcar motorman or
an elevator operator. That was childish, finished.

Imagine my excitement when I jumped down the stairway in

our house, taking two or three steps at a time, and suddenly found myself face to face with Rolf Gradnitzer. He certainly wasn't walking elastically. He breathed heavily, though this was only the third floor, as he continued slowly up to the fourth floor where Uncle Alfred and Aunt Anna lived with their children, Edith and Raoul. He stopped in the middle of the stairway, took off his gray derby, and mopped his brow with his handkerchief. It was incredible. In the evening I reported the news to my mother. She wasn't surprised at all, which surprised *me*.

"Naturally," she said. "Everybody knows it. But dear Aunt Anna might have more finesse than to have him come up just when poor Alfred is away in Vienna on business."

That was in 1922, the year poor Alfred moved to Vienna with his family to take up his new position there at the Lombard & Escompte Bank. He came to say good-by to my mother. He was as charming as ever and patronizingly patted my shoulder, predicting that my mother would have every reason to be proud of me, since I was the very effigy of his dear brother Siegfried. Then he left. For a while we knew nothing about them. Then some fascinating rumors began to drift in from Vienna.

They had bought a beautiful villa in a very chic neighborhood—"naturally," said my mother—the Cottage in Döbling. Some pronounced "Cottage" in English and some in French, but either way it sounded more distinguished than our street in Ostrava, which had been renamed Těšínská (Teschnerstrasse), after we found ourselves in the young Czechoslovak Republic. Renaming streets seemed to be a favorite public pastime. The villa in the Cottage was said to have been designed by a famous architect who had been a pupil of the great Adolf Loos.

In 1910, Adolf Loos had created a minor revolution among the bourgeois philistines of Vienna by having "the impertinence" (that was their expression) to build the first functional house near the Hofburg, the imperial palace, in Michaelerplatz.

Right there, where the Kaiser couldn't help seeing it. A scandal. Unlike the "dignified" palatial buildings in Ringstrasse, which was a merry-go-round of neo-Hellenistic style, neo-Gothic, neo-Renaissance, and other mixtures of neo- or non-styles, Adolf Loos had "dared" (that was what they said) put up a house with a pure, sober façade and not a single baroque ornament, not a scroll, nothing to make it look rich and impressive. No architraves, no window frames. A straight façade with austere lines. The grandeur of simplicity. The house is still there, looking as fine as when Loos designed it. Better. Nowadays "functional" is often a convenient excuse for lack of taste and imagination, but not with Loos. He had both.

He wasn't exactly popular with the upper-middle-class burghers who lived in neo-feudal splendor in their Ringstrasse buildings, in the most expensive location in Vienna, between the neo-Renaissance Court Opera and the neo-Hellenistic Parliament (though the other direction, leading toward the Stadtpark, wasn't bad either). Best of all was to own a "genuine" baroque palace, but that came with a dynasty and a coat of arms and a "genuine" title. You couldn't buy these things, you had to inherit them. Second best was to build an ornate *palais* if you didn't mind spending a great deal of recently made money.*

So much for the social background. My mother admitted that

* The subtle difference between an old-money palace and a nouveau-riche *palais* had existed since the eighteenth century. Hugo von Hofmannsthal had fun with it in his libretto for *Der Rosenkavalier*. The story takes place in the days of the Empress Maria Theresia. The *Feldmarschallin*, the very attractive feminine heroine, is a duchess and lives in her palace. Her young lover is a nice young man, also from a good, old family, the Rofranos. (The Rofrano dynasty existed and the duchess is pure imagination, yet today a certain palace is shown as her hereditary home, a typically baroque mix-up in the baroque city of Vienna.) Contrarily, the nouveau-riche Herr von Faninal, "recently ennobled by Her Majesty's grace," lives in his atrociously ornate town *palais*. He also owns twelve houses in the Wieden district. He is trying hard to learn good manners but remains a vulgar snob.

"dear Anna" knew her social history. "Though I have no idea where she acquired her knowledge," my mother said. "Anna never read a book in her life."

❖   ❖

And so a pupil of the great, unforgotten Adolf Loos had built Uncle Alfred's villa at the Cottage. Everybody in town talked about it though no one had seen it. The general manager of the Witkowitz Iron Works, who "knew" the Rothschilds since he worked for them, was quoted as having said that it would have been "more appropriate" if Uncle Alfred's villa had been built by a pupil of Makart. The general manager lived in an atrocious, Makartish† mansion in Witkowitz that was called *das Schloss* (the castle). It looked exactly like a setting for Franz Kafka's novel, *Das Schloss*. A few people in Ostrava defended the villa built by Loos's pupil, which they had never seen—but they were known even then for their "radical" beliefs. However, there was agreement among the members of all strata that Uncle Alfred and Aunt Anna had made a steep climb up the social ladder. Too bad, some people said, that they couldn't have a real town *palais*. Still, the villa in Vienna's Cottage was light-years away from the middle-class fourth-floor apartment in the Wechsberg house in Ostrava. There were even a few people who said it was a shame that Austria was now a republic and that Uncle Alfred had no chance of being given an aristocratic title.

The temptation or the danger—depending on how you looked at it—of being made a "Herr von," the lowest title in the Habsburg monarchy, hadn't existed in prewar Ostrau. In Vienna

† Hans Makart, a painter from Salzburg, became the grand master of *superkitsch,* the living symbol of the new Ringstrasse grandeur. Adolf Loos, the ascetic heretic, called Makart's Vienna "Potemkin's City." But Makart was commissioned to arrange the "historical" costumes for the procession celebrating the silver wedding of Franz Joseph I and Elisabeth in 1879. Makart was in, and Loos was out.

some people were ennobled for having "done" something. They had contributed generously to charities or rendered some services to members of the Habsburg house—they might have forgotten to remember that they had lent a lot of money to an archduke, or they just had friends in high places. All this wasn't possible in my home town. When somebody thought he was becoming prominent, he might move to Vienna where a man's opportunities were less limited and the rewards were higher. Vienna's attractions remained irresistible to the Germans and German-speaking Jews in Ostrau. Even a few wealthy Czechs were said to be wistful about the capital. My mother's annual visits, as long as Aunt Bertha was alive, were considered almost a status symbol at home. It was said, perhaps not jokingly, that some people stayed up late at night trying to discover a relative in Vienna whom they might visit, just as a start.

But after 1918 Vienna was "only" the capital of a new republic which was small and bankrupt. Even the titles had been abolished. The private china of the Habsburgs was used at state banquets by the elected representatives of the people. Some eternal-yesteryear people said it was worse than during the French Revolution. Aunt Anna knew she could do nothing for Uncle Alfred and herself by way of social improvement. Ergo, she decided that Edith, their beautiful daughter, must not marry a commoner "no matter how much money he's got." Money meant nothing. No, Edith was going to marry "a title," even if the title was a broken-down minor aristocrat on the lookout for a rich bourgeois wife—or her father—who would pay his debts. A simple barter but this was a time of widespread bartering.

My mother said if anyone could pull it off it would be dear Anna from Polnisch-Ostrau. "She must regret very much the demise of the monarchy," my mother said. "Anna would give a lot to see Alfred made a baron. Baronin Wechsberg!" And suddenly she added, with feeling, "Poor Edith!" Much later I understood how perceptive my mother had been.

Similarly, Aunt Anna had taken firm charge of the education of her son Raoul, who was about my age. I was rather fond of him. He was good-natured and very fat and he liked to laugh a lot. Aunt Anna mothered him and gave him whipped cream three times a day. He was always in and out of school. He had private tutors and appeared at the Gymnasium only at the end of the year to pass his examinations. He always passed them. There were rumors that Aunt Anna had "influenced" the professors but I didn't believe them. Raoul may have looked dumb but he wasn't. And he had the courage of his convictions. When I began to have violin lessons Aunt Anna forced Raoul to take lessons too. I had a factory fiddle that sounded like a cigar box and probably hadn't cost much more. Raoul had a minor master instrument. He hated it, he hated practicing scales, and he told me he would throw that damned fiddle out of the window. And one day he did just that, in my presence. From his room on the fourth floor. I still hear that awful sound in my ear as the minor master instrument hit the courtyard in the back of the house with a hollow, almost human cry.

Everybody was aghast except Aunt Anna, who hailed Raoul's decisive action as the expression of his "free, independent spirit." Some of my classmates were much impressed by Raoul's forthright courage. One of them, who had to practice the piano every day for an hour, told me he wished he could follow Raoul's splendid example—but how does one throw a Bösendorfer piano out of the window? At the Gymnasium we were then studying the history of the Thirty Years' War, which followed the Second Prague Defenestration. Throwing people out of high windows was a time-honored Czech custom. Even some Czech boys in town who had often called Raoul a fat idiot now spoke of him with respect.

In Vienna, Aunt Anna was said to have declared that her bright son wouldn't have to go to school. The school would come to him. Aunt Anna knew how to irritate people. Raoul was reported to have several tutors; he was "difficult." Remembering what had happened to the minor master instrument in Ostrava, we waited hopefully. We would not have been surprised if he had thrown one of his tutors out of the window of the villa which the pupil of the great Adolf Loos had designed.

That was the situation when, one day in 1923, the letter from Vienna came.

❖   ❖

It was addressed to me, typed on Uncle Alfred's exquisite stationery and signed by him. My mother said it had probably been dictated by Aunt Anna to her husband's secretary. She thought she recognized Aunt Anna's style. The way she said "style," she naturally meant the lack of any style. Alfred had his shortcomings, she said, but at least he wasn't tactless. *He* would have addressed the letter to *her*.

The letter was short, almost formal. Uncle Alfred—writing "Aunt Anna and I, all of us . . ."—was inviting me to come to Vienna for a week during the Easter holiday. They would show me Vienna, hoping I would enjoy it. Let us know when you plan to arrive. Be sure to give our fond regards to your dear mother.

"Show you Vienna, show Vienna to a sixteen-year-old boy," my mother said irritably. "What are they going to show you? The Wurstelprater?" She had shifted her attack against me. She knew well that the Wurstelprater was strictly for kids, with merry-go-rounds, silly fire-eaters, and third-rate magicians.

"Maybe we ought to turn down the invitation," my mother said. "If Anna wants to show off with her villa, she might invite Uncle Eugen or some of *her* relatives, over *there*." In Polnisch-Ostrau. "And why didn't they ask me to come along?"

My mother had not been to Vienna since the funeral of Uncle Storch, Aunt Bertha's husband. When he shot himself, late in 1918, Aunt Bertha had a terrible shock and died shortly afterward. Their daughters had to give up the beautiful apartment. There was no money. It was the story I knew so well by then.

❖   ❖

History was a nebulous thing that eluded me, but the astronomical inflation in Austria and Germany and the breakdown of all former values were all too real. On September 20, 1922, the Austrian National Bank issued bank notes with a face value of 500,000 crowns. I still have a few of them. Curiosities. A friend found them in a safe. They are brand new. They were probably never used. By the time they were issued they were worth only a fraction of the amount printed on them. People came from Vienna and told astonishing stories of streetcar rides "that were more expensive at the end of the ride than at the beginning." I couldn't figure it out, I was not good in mathematics. Probably Professor Einstein couldn't figure it out either. People carried bags filled with high-denomination bills, bank notes that were worth several millions, and handed them over to a small shopkeeper as payment for three eggs. Our knowledge of algebra was not sufficient to solve these mysteries. Gold coins and dollar bills were said to be "worth more by the hour," whatever that meant, but I knew no one who had gold coins or dollar bills.

There was less food than before. Many things had simply disappeared from the shelves. Strange deals were made at our Gymnasium during the ten o'clock recess. Two or three of our classmates had not merely a piece of dry bread, like the rest of us. Their fathers owned a food store, a delicatessen, and the boys had bread with something on it, a sardine, a piece of sausage, a slice of cheese. A new scale of values was immediately worked out. For a sardine, a lucky boy would get his Latin homework done. A piece of sausage bought help during the next mathematics exercise. I needed help badly but I had nothing to pay with. I thought bitterly of the sausages I had foolishly refused to chew and swallow during my silly childhood years. Now I could have bought myself security in mathematics with all the *Würstel* I had been asked to eat.

It was hard for my mother to get enough food for two boys who were always hungry. I had become quite "normal," as Dr. Himmelblau had predicted, at the worst possible time. My mother took out of the closet the rucksack she had carried on weekends in happier years when she went hiking with my father in the Bezkydy Mountains. She knew some peasants in the countryside who would let her have a few eggs, a pound of pork fat, some fruit in return for her Copenhagen china, of which she had been so proud. My father had given it to her soon after they were married. She used it only on holidays and when we had guests.

I wondered what the peasants would do with the dainty, fragile cups and saucers, delicately painted in light blue. I saw the rooms where the peasants lived when I accompanied my mother on some errands. The rooms smelled of the stable which was nearby in the house. They combined the sadness of a pawnshop with the indiscrimination of a flea market. I saw the pile of things in a corner of the room, silver candlesticks, worthless trinkets that might have had some sentimental value for their owners, assorted horrors and suddenly two or three fine pieces. Everything stacked together, mindlessly and greedily. After my mother had traded in her china and silver she was forced to part with some jewelry. A brooch, the earrings my father had bought her in Monte Carlo when he was so glad to know she would never gamble again. She pretended not to mind. I knew better.

❖   ❖

My mother tried her best to spare my brother and me the impact of the hard times. Our menu became monotonous but we were never hungry. She never sent me to the local streetcar station to queue up for a kilo of potatoes, as some of my classmates had to do. We spent two summers in Igls with my mother and Aunt Lamberg from Meran. Igls, a small village near Innsbruck, is now a famous winter sports resort. Then it was inexpensive. We stayed at the farm of a peasant, where I became acquainted with chickens, horses, bulls. We would stroll through the woods looking for fine mushrooms. These were pleasures that are unknown to city dwellers. But sooner or later we had to go back home to Ostrava.

The Wechsberg family house had been sold shortly after the bank disappeared. The new owner, an affluent dentist, moved into Uncle Alfred's apartment, just below ours. Dr. Kreml was a serious man with a small mustache, serious after looking for many years into other people's mouths. The bank's former counter room on the street floor was taken over by Süsser's Delikatessen. I thought it was a vast improvement, but some sort of vendetta was going on between our family and Herr Süsser. We were not supposed to do any shopping there. I went of course, when there was an emergency. A guest might have come in the evening, shortly before the shops closed, and I would be sent down for some cold cuts and pickles. I was fond of Süsser's pickles, which were kept in a large barrel standing next to the entrance door and were fished out by Herr Süsser with a wooden fork. He wore a white pharmacist's coat and always a hat because he was bald-headed. He didn't remove the hat even when the police director, Herr Lustig, came into his store around 6 P.M. for a snack and some gossip. "We criminologists," Lustig once told Süsser while I was in the store, "we have to listen to lots of people if we want to catch a criminal."

The affluent dentist offered my mother an apartment "in one

of the new houses" but she said she wanted to stay where we were, "at least until the boys are grown up." She was right and she made many sacrifices so we could stay there. The boarders were the worst part of it. My mother had a strong sense of privacy. She hated to have to share the hall of our apartment and the bathroom with the boarders. By then Dr. Michalitschke, the editor of the *Morgenzeitung*, had left. He had slept late in the morning, and Marie considered sleeping in the daytime a sin. She would make so much superfluous noise in the morning that the editor woke up. He was succeeded by Fräulein Stross, a noted fashion designer, a tall and forceful woman with a loud voice and tough manners. She was a sort of early women's lib woman long before the expression became popular. My mother didn't get along with her at all.

Conversely, the boarder in the *Herrenzimmer*, at the other end of the apartment, rated highly with her, though he used the bathroom, next to our bedroom, every morning for forty minutes, coughing and spitting, sounding like a serious candidate for fatal tuberculosis. In the bathroom were a much-admired bathtub and a washbasin with hot and cold water faucets. The toilet was in a special room, two doors away. Herr Harmat, the roomer, was a polite man from Hungary who often apologized for his morning cough.

"The moment I leave the bathroom I no longer cough. I do it only because I try to avoid it. Must be nerves."

Then my precocious brother Max imitated the cough and poor Herr Harmat became even more nervous. He seemed very old—everybody with graying hair looked very old to me—and he managed a small firm that made liqueurs. He had brought the "formulas" from Hungary. Occasionally he would present small sample bottles to my mother, bowing deeply from the waist. He was old-fashioned and bizarre, and my mother was pleased. Once in a while he gave me a tiny bottle with something "quite harmless," meaning low in alcohol content. I remember his *Eier-cognac,* a concoction made of egg yolks and brandy that tasted of neither one, and perhaps for this reason was popular with the women.

Herr Harmat always seemed to have a new letter from dear Georg, his grandson who played the piano and had been a child prodigy, according to his grandfather. Later he had become a conductor and a protégé of Richard Strauss. I didn't believe a word of it and couldn't stand listening to dear Georg's letters. When Herr Harmat read them to us he became excited and had another coughing spell, though it was afternoon, not morning, and he was not in the bathroom. I wondered briefly whether dear Georg existed or whether this doddering patriarch had made him up. In the years and decades that followed I met Georg several times. First in Prague where he conducted opera at the Deutsches Theater and was popular at the editorial offices of the Prager Tagblatt where he regaled us with good, mostly unprintable jokes. Later I met him again in New York where he conducted at the Metropolitan Opera; in Hollywood, where he spent a few weeks every year; and in Cleveland, Ohio, where he had built, trained, and conducted the local symphony orchestra, which was then considered the best in the United States. He rarely told jokes in the presence of his musicians, for he was very serious about his music, but he had preserved a genuine sense of humor. By that time we were friends and laughed about the former roomer, Herr Harmat, who had been absolutely right about his gifted grandson George Szell.

❖   ❖

My mother had been spoiled by her husband during their brief marriage. She often said later—and not only because of the roomers—that it wasn't nice to be suddenly poor. Our money, whatever was left of it, was still being managed by Uncle

Alfred, who took care of all the assets of the family. He wrote dilatory letters from Vienna, asking his relatives for patience and promising eventual results that would be "gratifying." Such letters alleviated for a while the fears expressed by my uncles and aunts. Alfred was "doing things" with their money in Vienna though they didn't know exactly what. Uncle Eugen, the former banker, and something of an authority in money matters (whose money was also managed by Uncle Alfred in Vienna), explained to his worried relatives that banking had become a complex business, and he lifted his arms and looked a little like the Delphic oracle. (We had just studied Delphi and the oracle at the Gymnasium.)

My mother consulted Uncle Eugen about the invitation from Vienna. Uncle Eugen seemed to be thinking it over—you could almost see him thinking—and after a while and some hesitation he suggested that I go as an "advance patrol." He was still a militarist at heart, liked to be addressed by his former rank of *Rittmeister*, and spoke a pseudo-military idiom that greatly impressed his customers, the former comrades who had become managers of local enterprises. Uncle Eugen had sold them the services of Martha's Guard-and-Lock Company. Employing retired policemen, the company guarded the premises of its clients for a monthly fee. The watchmen would patrol the offices, houses, storerooms of the clients, carrying a large bunch of keys. If someone had forgotten to lock a door they would do it. At certain points there were control clocks that forced the watchmen to make their rounds instead of sleeping it off. Everybody liked the system, especially the police, since Martha's private outfit did exactly what the police were supposed to do. This left their own men, as Police Director Lustig said, "to go after crime." Uncle Eugen was pleased because he earned some money, and the job gave him a chance to visit his former army comrades and talk about the past days of glory. It was not as dignified as bank-

ing had been, but in the early 1920s so many banks had gone
bankrupt in Central Europe that "banker" had become a dirty
word in Ostrava.

A family council, presided over by Uncle Eugen, agreed with
him and advised my mother to send me to Vienna. I was just a
teen-ager but I might "find out some things."

"He might reconnoiter the terrain and bring back some useful intelligence," Uncle Eugen said. "I'll give him a special
briefing."

I don't remember the briefing but I remember closing my suitcase with the help of my mother and Marie. We had to summon
her because the suitcase was packed too full. My mother said
that Easter might be quite cold in Vienna and put in lots of
warm things, as well as my new blue suit, especially made for
the trip by Herr Aksak. I was proud of the suit. Herr Aksak was
the former head cutter of the firm of Weiser where Uncle
Eugen, sartorially the outstanding member of the family, had
"let work" as long as he had been a banker. My father had had
his suits made in Vienna but the tailor no longer existed. My
mother couldn't afford the firm of Weiser but Herr Aksak, "the
soul of the firm," had gone into business on his own, and anyway, what is a tailor's firm without a good head cutter? I was to
wear the new blue suit with a white shirt and a stiff white collar. My mother hinted darkly, "They will look at your clothes
carefully in Vienna." She didn't say who "they" were but I had
a good idea.

A letter from Uncle Alfred's secretary notified me that I
would be met upon arrival at Vienna's Ostbahnhof. I had hoped
Raoul would be there but instead I was approached by a uniformed chauffeur who took off his cap and asked whether he
might take the suitcase of *"der junge Herr."*

"Der junge Herr," the young gentleman, was I. No one had ever called me that in my home town, where we were either boys (*Buben* or *chlapci*) when we behaved, or *Chacharen, cha-chaři,* no-goodniks, when we didn't. (The word *"Chacharen"* has a Middle Eastern, guttural sound, and you had to be born in Ostrau to pronounce it well, like "Bach," not like "Back.") No German or Czech dictionary lists the expression *"Chacharen"* or *"chachaři,"* which was strictly a local term. I never found out the etymology. We were proud to be *Chacharen;* it was a local distinction. When the dull inhabitants of the nearby towns of Troppau (Opava) or Teschen (Těšín) wanted to characterize the depravity of Ostrau (Ostrava), they would say, "No wonder, with all those *Chacharen* there." We were strictly a home-grown product, *appellation contrôlée,* as the French wine people would say. No matter how hard the young rascals tried elsewhere, they would never be *Chacharen.* Only our town had them. We belonged to it like the coal mines and ironworks, the dazzling coffeehouses, the pretty girls, for which the town was famous, the crooks and the *bon vivant* Gradnitzer.

Perhaps the *Chacharen* owed something to the fact that Ostrava was a coal town, an industrial town. From almost everywhere one could see the pit tower of a mine, with the big wheels inside. I never went down into a mine, because it was not "officially" requested when a boy joined the *Chacharen*. But we often played our mysterious games on the *haldy*, the slag dumps that were found in many places near the mines, even right behind the local theater. There the *haldy* were almost as high as the low hills. (Even German-speaking people used the Czech word *"haldy,"* because the people working there were either Czech or Polish miners.)

Linguistically, my home town was a complex place. The Czechs spoke Czech, the Poles spoke Polish, the Germans spoke German, the Jews spoke Czech at the tax collector's office or in court and German among themselves. It was a fine melting pot in which no one really melted. Some people used *Wasser-polakisch* with their servants. "Watered-down Polish" was bowdlerized German that sounded like Czech. I don't expect anyone to understand this who is not from my home town; in Prague no one understood this local dialect. It is the pure expression of linguistic tolerance. When someone at home said, *"Dienstmädchen putzovala Hausrock ve vorhausu,"* only a born-and-bred Ostrauer (*Ostravák*) knew that it meant, "The maid cleaned the coat in the hall." *Putzovala* came from the German *putzen*, to clean, but was used as a Czech word, with the Czech ending *-ala*. Whether *Wasserpolakisch* ever became a literary language I cannot tell since it was made up at the moment and often underwent subtle changes that outsiders were not supposed to know about. It was more or less a secret dialect. We *Chacharen* used it in our written messages. Sometimes the *conferenciers* and comedians used it at the two local night clubs, the Boccaccio and the White Raven Bar, when they were quite desperate and badly needed a few laughs.

The best feature about us *Chacharen* was our absolute lack of national sentiment, more exactly *ressentiment*, as it is nowadays called. Among us there were Czechs and Germans and Poles and Hungarians and Slovaks and Jews, Christians, atheists. No one cared. We had neither an organization nor rules; the whole thing was beautifully informal. Everybody automatically belonged who had demonstrated, in word or action, that he was against some kind of authority. To be a *Chachar* was a state of liberated mind. You couldn't train to become one. You had to be born in our town (the proper heritage), and you had to live in town (the right environment). At some time during the process of growing up you stopped being a *Chachar*, but there was no age limit, and some adults, it was said, behaved "like *Chacharen* though they are grown up and should know better." Basically, though, it was a distinction that came with youth and background. All *Chacharen* were at least second-generation hometown boys. There were no girls among us. (Today it might be different.)

We didn't believe in the statutes of authority, we were early protesters, but brutal violence was out. We didn't take ourselves very seriously. We just had good fun, sometimes at the expense of the grownups. We played hooky from school when we had arranged an important soccer game, but we would commit no criminal acts, as some humorless people claimed. You wouldn't call falsifying a parent's signature a criminal act, or would you? Why disturb the dear parents with a bad school report to be signed? Instead a *Chachar*, an expert in imitating the parent's signature, would sign. One promised oneself to do better next time, and one might even keep one's promise. Then the parents would be shown the *good* report and would be pleased. Or was breaking into the teachers' conference room to copy the questions for the next day's mathematics exercise a criminal act, as some silly professor might say? Nonsense. It was a healthy expression of self-reliance. In five years it wouldn't matter any more. We *Chacharen* understood that life was complicated enough, even without the mathematics exercise.

The whole operation was probably an act of Christian charity

—please-your-parents. No *Chachar* would ever have forged a check. And breaking into the teachers' conference room—it *does* seem to bother me a little now—might be explained as proof of our youthful resourcefulness. Direct action was sometimes necessary to protect ourselves against the devious ways of adult authority, such as the sinister problems of the math exercise. They were full of traps put there by the professor, who hated us, the world, and himself. The real problem after we had got hold of the questions was to convince our classmates that not everybody should hand in a perfect paper. This would inevitably create suspicion and might lead to discovery. But we *Chacharen* were conscious of our obligations to our kind of society. Suitable allotments were decided upon and many of us would put in a few carefully calculated mistakes. Only Abrahamer, the best mathematician in class, who usually finished an exercise in twenty minutes while the rest of us were still halfway through, would hand in a faultless paper. In his case anything else might have been suspicious. We were ready for all contingencies.

It was really a sort of higher ethics. Certain things were just not done, and everybody knew it. A *Chachar* respected the other person's nationality, language, religious belief or lack of it, girl friend, property (which was minimal anyway), and soccer ball. There were those who called us "dirty Jews," but they were not *Chacharen,* they were hoodlums. No real *Chachar* would have anything to do with them. We were justly resentful when Police Director Lustig, the noted criminologist, a heavy-set man with a bushy mustache and a large bald head, in moments of exasperation talked about "criminals, thugs, and this whole band of *Chacharen"* that made life difficult for his policemen. It was an unfair statement. Criminals used knives to settle their arguments. We used our fists, and often we used only our heads. Once there was a sort of protest meeting of the *Chacharen* at the Old Shooting Range to discuss what should be done about the police director. The meeting soon broke up in a mass of private arguments, but in the end a deputation of *Chacharen* went to see him. They convinced him that he had been unfair when he mentioned us *Chacharen* in the same sentence with thugs and criminals. I was a member of the delegation. Lustig was no fool and his humor had remained intact in a humorless profession. He said he retracted his statement so far as the *Chacharen* were concerned, and we shook hands with him. He was still chuckling as we left.

❖   ❖

And now I, an Ostravian *Chachar* in good standing, had arrived in Vienna, the city of my mother's dreams. Uncle Alfred's liveried chauffeur carried my suitcase, respectfully preceding me by one and a half steps. Every few steps he turned around to make sure that I, the provincial, wouldn't get lost in the big-city confusion, and all the time he addressed me as *"junge Herr,"* almost as good as "Sir." Not bad for a boy of sixteen. He put down my suitcase and opened the door of the dark gray Gräf & Stift, as exclusive in postwar Vienna as a Panhard-Levassor was in Paris or a Rolls-Royce in London. The color of the automobile was the color of the chauffeur's uniform. I wouldn't be surprised if Aunt Anna had hired the chauffeur first, afterward ordered his uniform, and finally bought the car, making sure that its shade matched that of the uniform.

With an elegant movement of his arm that seemed contrived, the chauffeur invited me to sit down in the rear of the car. My head was reeling slightly. I had to remind myself that I was a good right-inside soccer player on the class team and had once won a prize for spitting out three gas lamps in the street in less than five minutes. Still, it wasn't easy to preserve one's equanimity.

The chauffeur opened the trunk and cautiously deposited my

suitcase, handling it with exaggerated care as though it contained a priceless set of very old Meissen. He seemed less a chauffeur than an actor playing the part of a chauffeur. My mother had said, with her usual sense of clairvoyance, that she wouldn't be surprised at all if Aunt Anna had hired a temporarily unemployed actor to play the part of chauffeur. But she also said, "Maybe even somebody who once was at the Burgtheater." This illogical deduction immediately deflated her power of second sight. Why would anyone who had performed at the venerable Burgtheater play the mostly mute part of Aunt Anna's driver? Anyway, he looked handsome enough for the part. I filed the interesting problem away in a secret compartment of my mind. I might take it up later on with my cousin Raoul.

My mother had asked me to take a good look at Vienna. I was to report to her after my return on what the once Imperial City was like now that it had become the capital of a small bankrupt republic. Yet I was too busy with the trappings of luxury to look out. There was so much to see inside the car. The mahogany panels, the small mirrors, the mysterious buttons. The smell of leather and of a good cigar, and a whiff of French perfume hanging in the air.

It was not my first ride in an automobile, certainly not. A few people in Ostrava owned cars. Once in a while Herr Schramek and his wife came to take my mother, my brother, and me for a ride. But their plebeian Opel cabriolet couldn't compare with the luxurious Gräf & Stift. On these rides we had to wear white dust coats, white caps, and dark brown glasses, supplied by Herr Schramek. If I didn't have a photograph taken during one outing, I wouldn't believe that it actually happened. The dark brown glasses were the best part of the equipment. They made the grayish town more attractive, almost mysterious, dipped in a light brown hue, now the color of my Stradivari and of some of my favorite Breughels. No other event of the day matched the excitement of seeing my drab home town through these magical glasses. I wished I could wear them in school, but that was impossible. I was simply ahead of my time; my timing has often been wrong. It would be years before people wore dark glasses on all occasions, even the wrong ones.

Sitting with crossed legs in the back seat of Uncle Alfred's Gräf & Stift, I became aware that this was nothing like Herr Schramek's Opel; another class of people, one I hadn't known at home. I was becoming apprehensive. I remembered my mother's prediction that "this new life they lead in Vienna is not for you." I thought she was still angry because she hadn't been invited too. Apparently Uncle Alfred and his family had changed not merely their place of residence but also their way of life. The geographic dislocation was accompanied by social elevation.

One couldn't grow up in Ostrau without being aware of some kind of class system. The coal miners who came into town only on Saturday afternoon to do their shopping, and during the annual May Day celebration, were not in the same class as the lawyers and bankers and the managers of the mines and ironworks. The general managers were in a class by themselves. In Witkowitz the class system even separated the wives of the higher employees. The *Frau Ingenieur* was supposed to bow to the *Frau Oberingenieur* and both had to greet the *Frau Direktor*. The *Frau Direktor* didn't like it if a mere *Frau Ingenieur* sat in "her" row at the theater. It was ridiculous, we young people said, and sometimes the borderlines were vague, as in the case of Herr Schramek, ex-mechanic and now the owner of two factories. But the system existed. It still exists in today's supposedly classless society in Ostrava, though they no longer talk about "middle" or "upper" classes. Now there are workers, but there are also party officials, managers, *aparatchniks*. Only the titles have changed.

I looked out the window of the Gräf & Stift into nondescript streets as gray as those back home, though the buildings were larger and higher. The chauffeur (I later realized) had not taken the "nice" way that led straight through the center of Vienna, but the route through the drab suburbs along the Gürtel. For a moment I almost regretted having come. I was glad, though, to have my new blue suit in the suitcase. I needed something tangible to sustain my lagging self-confidence.

We turned off the Gürtel into the Cottage, a quiet district with villas surrounded by large gardens, silent streets with trees on both sides, no shops and no people walking around, everything hidden behind high walls and evergreen hedges. We had no such district in our home town, and I was impressed. Some of the villas were veritable mansions with three floors. Then the car stopped in front of a new, modern house in Lanner-Strasse. (Joseph Lanner was the erstwhile friend and later the enemy of Johann Strauss the Elder. In the end they made up and Strauss, Sr., conducted at Lanner's funeral, and played the fiddle, and everybody cried. Lanner had been a shy artist, an introvert, not at all a show-off like Strauss. His music is warm and gentle. I was glad they had named this quiet Cottage street after him. He would have liked it.)

Whether Lanner would have liked the house I cannot tell. Looking at it, I felt a little dizzy. No one was at home when the chauffeur rang the bell; I mean, no member of the family. A manservant, the first I had ever seen in a real house, not on the stage, told me that *die gnädige Frau* (the gracious lady) would be in presently. There were two chambermaids wearing black dresses, white aprons, and white things in their hair, like the ones appearing on the stage of the Ostrau theater. For a moment I had the absurd notion that the whole house and the personnel and I were on a stage, that the whole thing wasn't real, it was only a play.

It became quite real, though, when Aunt Anna arrived. She greeted me warmly and asked about my "dear mother," and my brother, and other people back home, and all the time she seemed to watch my reactions. She wanted to know how I felt about her and her family and the new house. She had a different inflection in her voice, using French words and dropping the end consonants of some German words. Aunt Bertha, whom I met only once, when my mother took me to Merano, had talked that way but her diction—which, I learned, was Viennese upper-class talk—had sounded relaxed and normal. Aunt Anna was still learning it. She was learning fast, but sometimes it was rough going and she would drop the whole thing and revert to the singsong German we used in Ostrau. People from elsewhere laughed about our "accent," which they pretended to recognize instantly. We *Chacharen* were proud of the local accent. Many of us had learned our lesson from Dr. Spira, the wise Talmudist. If you have an accent, speak it proudly. I've had and still have accents in various languages and I am totally relaxed about them. (Most Americans have some kind of regional accent.) I am now vindicated, since there are some very high-ranking American officials who are not American-born and who speak English with a foreign inflection.

Aunt Anna personally showed me the new house, like a guide in a museum full of old things. In her house it was mostly new things, some of them avant-garde and disturbingly modern. No faded Persian rugs, no upholstered furniture, no dark, heavy shelves with editions of the classics. The house in Vienna was mostly glass and very bright, and the garden behind the house was almost part of it. It was as though the architect had tried to move the garden into the house or the house into the garden. The drawing room with its large glass door led into the garden. Inside the room a few plants bridged the transition. You were still inside the house but already almost outside.

The single most stunning architectural feature, possibly put there as a challenge and conversation piece, was a free-standing spiral staircase leading from the center of the drawing room to the upper floor with the bedrooms. The stairway seemed to hang in mid-air and was gracefully curved. Its steps were covered with the bright, silvery carpet that also covered the floor of the drawing room. At parties people would sit on the steps with glasses in their hands. My cousin Edith—tall, blonde, and beautiful, and always a little remote—would sit there, surrounded by what Aunt Anna called her beaux. *Beau* means "admirer" and also "beautiful." Edith's admirers were hardly beautiful but they had titles.

Never having met a titled person in my home town, I watched the titles with what I hoped was subdued curiosity. I found their performance disappointing. Yes, they all seemed to perform, though I wasn't certain what they were performing and for whom. Perhaps for themselves. Certainly Edith was an unresponsive audience. Sometimes she gave them a speculative glance as though to say, "You poor idiots, do you really think you can fool me?" But that might be just my idea. After a moment Edith would again be friendly, nice, and still remote.

Uncle Alfred and Raoul hadn't changed. Uncle Alfred put his arm around me, smiling, the great charmer. He patted my shoulder with his right hand as he had done when he complimented people out of his private office at the family bank after refusing one of their requests. Once he explained to my father that this was his way of treating them right. "Makes them feel better and doesn't cost you anything, especially when you feel you have to say no," he explained. But my father never learned to do it. I never saw him put his arm around anybody except my mother.

Raoul was still a little strange, uttering a sentence as though spitting it out and saying nothing for a while until he spat out the next sentence. He told me he had no more violin lessons, he had fixed that for good when he threw his fiddle out the win-

dow. He was interested in chemistry and had turned the bathroom next to his bedroom into a chemical lab. There were several bathrooms in the house. His small one was wonderful, with
all the retorts, phials, acids, the *Bunsenbrenner*. It was almost as
good as the chemistry lab in our school.

"Almost blew it up twice," Raoul said, pleased with himself.
That was true. Aunt Anna was worried about his experiments
and had asked him to be careful but he paid no attention to her.
He rarely talked to his mother, but he adored his father. He was
lucky to have him. I envied him a little for the chemistry lab,
but mostly for having his father.

Uncle Alfred and Raoul and Edith had little to say around
the house. All arrangements were made by Aunt Anna. She decided where they would go at night and whom to invite and
what to serve. Uncle Alfred always agreed with her. I didn't see
much of him during the day. He spent most of his time at his
office.

One day Raoul took me to the city. Aunt Anna had said we
were to go in the car, and Raoul was to show me the Ringstrasse
and a museum there. We were not to eat anything while in
town. It was not "safe," she said, as though she was talking
about the water in some tropical country. Instead Raoul told the
chauffeur to let us off at the first streetcar stop, and we took the
No. 38 streetcar to the Schottenring. Much more fun than going
by car, Raoul said. He always did it; he had a standing agreement with Jacques. Jacques was the chauffeur. The agreement
was secret; no one else knew about it. I wanted to ask Raoul
about Jacques but was reluctant to do so. Jacques was quite
relaxed with Raoul and didn't behave like a bad actor but like a
good driver.

The streetcar ride was a great success. Raoul said the No. 38
came from Grinzing, the famous suburb with all the houses Beethoven slept in and with the *Heuriger* inns where people went in

the afternoon to drink young wine. People loved the No. 38, especially at night when they had got quite drunk and were feeling safe on the streetcar. I was surprised about Raoul's accurate knowledge and asked him whether he had ever gone to one of the *Heurigen*.

"Of course," said Raoul. "With Jacques. He knows some good ones."

We went to a nearby store that sold chemistry equipment and spent a fascinating hour looking at fascinating supplies and trying them out. Raoul bought some retorts and tubes and complex glass bowls with extensions, and told the clerk to send everything to Lanner-Strasse, with the bill. We walked through Herrengasse into a fine, old-fashioned pastry shop. We ordered *Indianer* with *Schlagobers, Sachertorte* with *Schlagobers,* and finally Raoul said what was the use pretending and bravely ordered *Schlagobers* with more *Schlagobers* on top. Everybody laughed. I knew whipped cream, which we sometimes had at home with the coffee, when we had guests, but somehow the *Schlagobers* in Vienna tasted better than ours at home. The servant girls wore black dresses and high, buttoned shoes, and even the younger ones among them had the severe appearance of abbesses. They addressed the customers, even us, in the third person plural, the old feudal style that considered it unmannerly to address a person directly. "Do the young gentlemen desire more *Schlagobers?*" one asked. The young gentlemen did. I asked Raoul whether he had any money and he looked for it. He had some but not much. Certainly not enough for all that whipped cream.

"Doesn't matter," he said and shrugged. "They'll write it down."

There were some strange people at this *Konditorei,* two overdressed elderly women who gave us boys encouraging looks, and a fat man wearing two diamond rings. Raoul paid no attention to them; he said he never did. He didn't come to see people, he came to eat *Schlagobers*. He told them to "put everything on the bill." One of the abbesses did, hoping the young gentlemen had enjoyed their degustation. It was that kind of place. I asked Raoul for the name and he said it was Demel's. He said if he died he didn't have to go to heaven, Demel's was good enough for him, and he laughed. He was strange but I became very fond of him.

We walked back and dropped in at Uncle Alfred's office. The Lombard & Escompte Bank's premises were in a palatial build-ing overlooking Ringstrasse at the Schottenring crossing. Uncle Alfred's private office, a corner room with a fine view of the Vo-tivkirche, a noble structure in neo-Gothic, was as large as the private offices of the three brothers and partners of the family bank had been at home, on the upper floor. The office fitted Uncle Alfred's stationery; or maybe it was the other way around. Wood-paneled walls, a large, dark rug, a copy of a Caravaggio in a gilt frame on the wall, photographs of Edith and Raoul on Uncle Alfred's desk. The doors were soundproof, covered with black leather upholstery. I began to understand what the people in Ostrava meant when they said Uncle Alfred was no longer a banker, he was now a financier. The office radiated monetary confidence and financial stability. This had been important re-cently when old values tumbled, people's savings were wiped out, and no one trusted money. Now, in 1923, the worst was over, some real values had been re-established, and black-market operators were going broke. It was the time of the great finan-ciers, of Bosel and Castiglione. A new generation of traders and industrialists who made their money fast and tried to spend it even faster before it could be lost again. Too bad Aunt Anna had arrived relatively late.

Uncle Alfred gave Raoul a questioning glance, saying not a word, and Raoul understood and nodded, also saying nothing.

"Was it good?" Uncle Alfred asked, having decided that I was safe and wouldn't report the conspiracy.

"Five portions," said Raoul. "What shall I say at home? I cannot possibly eat lunch. I am full of *Schlagobers*."

"You will have an excuse," Uncle Alfred said. "Usually you have one." They both smiled at each other. It was one of the really pleasant moments of my trip to Vienna.

❖   ❖

Perhaps it is ungrateful to mention some other moments, but they happened and are part of this report. On the first evening I was in my room upstairs. A beautiful room, not cozy, but very functional, everything within easy reach. There was a knock at the door, and Anton, the butler, coughed discreetly and informed me that dinner was at eight and the *Herrschaften,* as was their habit, would dress for dinner. Should he put out my things? I thanked him rather hastily and he left me with my thoughts. At home, when we had guests, we might dress for dinner; I would be told to put on a white shirt. So that was what I did now, and I also put on my blue suit. I thought I looked rather dandy in Herr Aksak's masterpiece when I went down the marvelous staircase. Aunt Anna was already there, looking distinguished in something long and transparent, with lots of pearls and silver thread. When she saw me she frowned.

"Weren't you informed to dress?"

"Yes, Tante Anna." I looked down at my fine blue suit, by way of explanation.

"We do it the English way here. The men put on their *Smocking*." It might have been the English way, but she still pronounced the word as we did back home, with a short *o*. "*Smocking*" meant smoking jacket, tuxedo.

I should have said something. But there was nothing I could say.

"Oh," she said. "You haven't got a *Smocking?*"

I managed to shake my head.

Aunt Anna was used to minor social-sartorial crises and efficiently took command of the situation.

"It doesn't matter tonight. We are alone. Tomorrow, first thing in the morning, we'll go to Humhal's."

Raoul and Edith came down. Edith was a fairy-tale princess, perhaps even a queen, in red velvet. Raoul seemed to have put on his dinner jacket in a hurry; his black tie was askew. Aunt Anna told him to go back and wash his hands, and he went. Uncle Alfred was the last to join us, looking like a man of honor and high principles, just the man to look after your investments and manage the family fortune. I looked very shabby in my blue suit, exactly what I was, the poor relation. I decided never to wear it again. Might leave it for my younger brother. Max was growing up fast.

In the morning Aunt Anna ordered the car and we went to Humhal, the famous tailor, "about the same class as Kníže," said Aunt Anna. I asked her why we didn't go to Kníže.

"Oh, everybody goes there," she said vaguely. "You know . . ."

I didn't know.

Humhal occupied the whole second floor of a large building on Ringstrasse, almost across from the Opera. Deep rugs, enormous mirrors, and the smell of fine imported textiles. Poor Aksak, he would never have a place like that. Aunt Anna seemed well known. She was almost ceremoniously welcomed by a stylish gentleman who had a faint resemblance to Rolf Gradnitzer, the *bon vivant*. He kissed her hand and asked what he could serve the gracious lady with. Aunt Anna pointed at me with her thumb and said "we" needed a "*Smocking*" tonight.

The *bon vivant* seemed slightly shaken but managed to recover his poise. "Did you say *tonight, gnädige Frau?*"

Aunt Anna smiled.

"I know you *can* do it and you *will* do it. . . . Let me see some samples."

I was never consulted. She selected the material, decided about cut and lapels and the black silk stripes on the pants, and certain buttons, and everything. Only the best.

Remarkably, my new *Smocking* was delivered to the house in Lanner-Strasse that evening, in time for dinner. They could do it then, if they had to. My present tailor in Vienna, Mr. Adalbert Šilhavý, a gentleman in his eighties who had worked for one of the great houses in Vienna before the end of the monarchy, told me they would do tail coats or morning coats on short notice within a day when somebody had to attend a funeral or appear in court to receive a decoration.

I had to go back to Humhal for a first fitting around noon and for a second fitting at four in the afternoon. By that time I felt like a habitué of the house. They were quite busy. Strange-looking characters were trying on new suits in discreet colors, but I wondered whether they would look discreet in *anything*. Vienna in 1923 was certainly an exciting place.

I remember that my hands trembled when I put on the new *Smocking* upstairs in my room and tried to knot my black tie. I couldn't do it and had to ask Raoul to help me, and he did, standing behind me in front of the mirror, as though he were doing it himself. Aunt Anna looked pleased as we came down. She nodded as though remembering something, and asked, "What happened to your father's *Smocking?*"

"I don't know. I suppose it disappeared."

"Disappeared?" She seemed surprised.

There was no point in trying to explain. She wouldn't understand. It suddenly occurred to me that I hadn't thanked her for my new outfit. I had been taught at home to thank when I received a present. Grandmother Krieger had expressed it more clearly. "If one gives you, take, and if one takes from you, scream!" But she had chuckled as she said this and I assumed it was a joke. I couldn't imagine Grandmother Krieger, the very image of dignity, screaming.

"Aunt Anna, thank you and Uncle Alfred for . . . for . . ." I stammered, and pointed at my silk lapels.

She smiled and was about to say something, but the first guests arrived, and she went to greet them. I proudly wore my *Smocking* every night in Vienna and began to feel as though I had been born in it.

Aunt Anna talked a lot about her friends in England, their strange and wonderful habits. We tried to be more English than the English; it was black tie even on Sunday night. The dinner parties in Lanner-Strasse were distinguished. After dinner the ladies would retire to Aunt Anna's "boudoir" and we "men" stayed in the drawing room. Uncle Alfred, smiling, handed out cigars from a box that reminded me of my father's Trabuccos. Cognac was served in enormous fishbowl glasses. Raoul and I were offered neither cognac nor cigars. I never liked to smoke— an aversion which bothered me greatly during my formative years, when smoking seemed almost synonymous with "being a man." A few times, in desperation, I took a cigarette and lighted it, until an early girl friend, a passionate smoker, informed me that I did not hold the cigarette between my fingers like a real smoker and looked ridiculous. Then I gave up the silly attempt.

Aunt Anna and her family led a busy social life. When we had no guests at home we would go to the theater. They liked the Burgtheater because it was a sort of cultural status symbol. Aunt Anna said it was nice to listen to the impeccable German, the Burgtheater German, spoken on the stage by the actors and actresses, and she sighed wistfully. She would never be able to learn it, she admitted to me in a candid moment. I already knew that some of the actors didn't speak that impeccable German offstage, but I didn't mention it. Aunt Anna had always been fascinated by stage people, *viz.* Rolf Gradnitzer. In her fantasies she certainly saw herself as a star of the Burgtheater, not a Greek heroine, but something like *une grande dame,* with or without camellias. The few celebrities of her "salon" were actors.

As a socially aspiring hostess she had to have a salon, but she couldn't shake off the memory of small-town life and her experiences with actors. The local passion for the stage goes back to the baroque pageants of the seventeenth century. Arthur Schnitzler said, "We all act parts, and wise is he who knows it." At that time Schnitzler lived a short walk from the house in Lanner-Strasse; Aunt Anna didn't know and wouldn't have cared if she had known. Her world was light-years away from the world of Schnitzler, Hugo von Hofmannsthal, Stefan Zweig, Arnold Schönberg, Alban Berg, Gustav Klimt, and Egon Schiele.*

I've since read the social history of Vienna before and after the turn of the century, the accounts of the celebrated hostesses. Aunt Anna was only a modest beginner but she had talent and might have gone far if circumstances had been different. She was a snob, but she believed in it, she was a snob at heart, she did what she felt she had to do; and that should grant her at least partial remission. She said she had always hated the narrowness of provincial life in Ostrau. I had never been aware of it. Back home most people seemed relaxed and didn't try to

---

* The local obsession with the stage has not changed. Famous conductors, singers, actresses are more popular in Vienna than painters or sculptors, writers or composers. During the bicentennial celebration of the Burgtheater in 1976, prominent actors and actresses, famous members of the house, made speeches. There were tributes by famous performers from other countries. Finally the Minister of Education, the Federal Chancellor, and the Federal President made their *éloges.* An impressive list of speechmakers, and not one author among them, speaking on behalf of the Burgtheater playwrights, dead or alive, who wrote the lines spoken on the stage.

speak with a phony inflection. They didn't try to be something they were not. Aunt Anna did it all instinctively. It was astonishing.

Aunt Anna had feminine intuition. She knew nothing about the families who had come half a century before from the provinces to Vienna, attracted by the Imperial City's glitter and phosphorescence, and had worked hard, with imagination and tenacity, to change themselves from outsiders into insiders. Some tactfully financed members of the imperial house were often in financial trouble, especially those who loved to gamble. All this is a matter of record. The benefactors might indicate that there were various ways of being repaid, perhaps with a title or a decoration. They didn't want to realize that if you have to go after a decoration you don't really deserve it; and if you deserve it, and know it, you don't really need it. Some did manage to acquire lesser titles. A few, like the Rothschilds, did so many good things with their money that their Jewishness became a cherished mark of honor.

Aunt Anna was no fool. She realized that her possibilities were limited. She deplored the end of the monarchy and of the various rewards. The Republic of Austria had abolished aristocratic titles and in its early years, after 1918, didn't even recognize inherited ones. Even today the truly noble Schwarzenbergs list their name, with no title, in the Vienna telephone directory. The oldest son of the last Habsburg ruler is now officially known as Dr. Otto Habsburg. Not even "von," though some of his loyal subjects still address him as *Majestät*. On the other hand, various Herren "von" and "de" are again listed with their mini-titles in the directory. It's bizarre and very Viennese. In Vienna imaginary titles have always been bestowed by coffee-house waiters, coachmen, and taxi drivers.

❖   ❖

After I had worn my *Smocking* a few times, Aunt Anna considered me almost a full-fledged member of her immediate family. She confided to me that Edith was attractive enough "to marry a count," but counts were becoming rare, or she hadn't been trying hard enough. The best she could do were two minor noblemen who came to the house when I was there, two Herren "von." Aunt Anna said that both came from "old" families, though. Raoul said that both were "decadent." Raoul demonstrated powers of observation I hadn't suspected when he lived in the apartment below ours in the family house. He now seemed to have few illusions about Aunt Anna's aspirations or Edith's admirers. He would shrug off both. He knew that Uncle Alfred went along with the whole *Klimbim* (a minor silliness) only reluctantly but was too weak to resist. This created a firm bond between the two men in the family.

I knew little about Edith. She was a few years older than I, which created an abyss in those years; she plainly considered me a silly boy. She talked to me rarely, often in a somewhat patronizing way, as though I had recently been released from a home for retarded cousins. I ignored her; she probably didn't even notice. But she looked chic in her red coat and shining riding boots, her blonde hair smartly done up in a knot, when she went riding in the Prater. Raoul had to go along because Aunt Anna demanded it. The two Herren "von" would be in the Prater and Edith must not be seen alone with them. Raoul said he would have preferred to stay in his chemical lab bathroom but there was nothing he could do.

I had wished for two things when I came to Vienna. I wanted to see a First League soccer game and a performance at the State Opera. The soccer game, my first priority, was ruled out by Aunt Anna, who declared that soccer was "vulgar." I had hoped for support from Raoul, but the sport that interested him was ice hockey. Aunt Anna remained unyielding even when I suggested a match of the First Vienna Football Club, Austria's oldest club, founded in 1893.

Impossible, she said; soccer was for "rowdies." She was "responsible" for me while I was in Vienna. What would she tell my dear mother if something should happen over there—she waved vaguely toward an invisible soccer field—and she couldn't explain it? No, no. And she called Jacques, the chauffeur, and told him to get a ticket at the Opera. That was what I liked, wasn't it? I didn't ask why *they* didn't like it. She felt she owed me an explanation and said they were busy that night. I put on my *Smocking* and Jacques drove me to the Opera. Very early, because he had to go back right away and take *die Herrschaften* to the Volkstheater. After the theater I was to meet them at the Sacher. Jacques showed me the Hotel Sacher, behind the State Opera.

❖   ❖

I had never been at a theater even faintly approaching the glory of the State Opera, and I was overwhelmed. I had only recently discovered the magic of opera. Until 1918 popular operas were occasionally performed at the City Theater (Stadttheater) in Ostrau. The performances were provincial and real connoisseurs wouldn't attend. Instead they went once a year to Vienna. That proved that they understood opera and appreciated only the best. When the monarchy collapsed and the young Czechoslovak Republic was born, the City Theater remained closed for a while and then was reopened under Czech management. The take-over of culture was symbolic. We youngsters went to the City Theater once in a while. It didn't bother us that the performances were now given in Czech. We ignored the complaints of the older people, who said it was a tragedy they had lost "their" theater, which had been built during the monarchy with "their" money, when "those people," meaning the Czechs, wouldn't know what to do in a theater. It was a nice small house, with gilded stucco and neo-Renaissance frescoes on the ceiling. The house was a replica of other theaters built in the Habsburg Empire between Craców and Trieste, with several circles of boxes, stalls, galleries. In Vienna the Volkstheater had the same design. This was no coincidence; all theaters had been designed by the same firm, Fellner & Helmer, in various sizes, according to the size of the town. One of the very first decisions an Austrian city made after reaching a population of thirty thousand was to "order" its own theater.

For a while after 1918 there was no German-speaking theater in my home town. Then the German-speaking people set up a private organization called the Theaterverein and began collecting money. It was said that a theater was more important than food: food was good for the stomach but a theater was food for the mind. Funds were solicited from enterprises, leaders of industry, and private donors. My mother, always an enthusiastic theatergoer, served two years on the board of the association. The chairman of the board was Herr Strassmann, a Jewish brewer, a great art patron. He was a fat man with a triple chin who seemed always to be on the verge of a stroke, with immense energy whether he was selling beer or the arts. Eventually enough money was collected to hire a manager who organized a small ensemble of actors and actresses and produced plays with small casts at the ballroom of Deutsches Haus.

Though my knowledge was limited, I considered myself something of an authority on the medium when I walked into the Vienna State Opera that night in the spring of 1923. I saw at once that it was a fine building dedicated to music. The staircase, the foyer, and the loggias are decorated with statuary and paintings on musical themes. The building itself seems to emit the sounds of great music. The poetically conceived paintings on the lunettes of the loggias, showing scenes from *The Magic Flute*, were executed by Moritz von Schwind, a close friend of

Franz Schubert. The auditorium is dark and at the same time intimate despite its size.

My seat was in the middle of the fifth row on the right side. I don't know why I remember such an unimportant detail, but I do. I was close to the orchestra pit and the stage, but I was uneasy sitting there among the grownups. I seemed to be the only youngster in that part of the house, and the only person wearing a dinner jacket. I had the silly feeling of being a *Pikkolo,* a waiter's apprentice at the coffeehouse, the little boy wearing a mini-tuxedo and a small black tie who brings the guest another tray with glasses of fresh water. There were young people at the *Oper* that night but they were in the rear, among the standees, or way up in the fourth gallery. I felt a sudden resentment against Aunt Anna. I didn't belong where I sat. I would have liked to stand up there with the other young people.

That night the performance was *The Marriage of Figaro,* which I had never heard at home. I paid no attention to the cast on my first night at the Opera, though in fact it was a great cast. Lotte Lehmann and Hans Duhan were the Countess and Count Almaviva, Elisabeth Schumann was Susanna, and the great Richard Mayr was Figaro. Today I would make a special journey to hear such an ensemble. The conductor was a "Herr Schalk," and I was unimpressed. My ignorance was abysmal. Franz Schalk had studied with Bruckner, worked under Mahler, and later shared direction of the State Opera with Richard Strauss. And the production had been designed by Alfred Roller, who was Mahler's stage designer when they produced their great *Tristan* together, creating a new style that has affected successive generations. The principles of space and light and color are still valid today. Yet memory is a strange thing. I remember where I sat but little about the production and much about the audience.

The audience was incredible. Fat men and vulgar women in

the boxes, overdressed and unkempt, as though they had been collected in the street by a producer with a diabolic sense of humor who ordered them to attend the performance, of which they understood nothing. They talked and coughed through the arias. During the intermission following the first act, when most people remained in their seats, I watched such an improbable couple in the parterre box next to me. They opened small pack-ages containing rolls with sausage, peeled the sausage skins off with their teeth, and threw the skins into the stalls. A man in front of me got angry and threw the skins back at them, and ev-erybody laughed. Those were the people who could afford ex-pensive seats. The real opera lovers were up in the galleries, but I didn't know it then.

❖   ❖

After the performance I walked over to the Hotel Sacher. In a corner of the dining room Aunt Anna presided over a table of what later were called beautiful people. Edith was flanked by her titled beaux. Uncle Alfred seemed to be dominated by a for-midable woman with a loud voice, the mother—he called her "Mamma"—of one of the beaux. Next to Aunt Anna sat an in-teresting man with dark locks falling onto his forehead. He had a sonorous voice and gave the German vowels a musical, Italian-ate sound. Aunt Anna didn't notice me, no one did, and I sat down next to Raoul, who was eating chocolate mousse with whipped cream. I was hungry. Nowadays I seemed always to be hungry. The sight of the people at the Opera biting into their rolls and sausage had made me swallow greedily.

My first impression of the celebrated Sacher's was disap-pointing. My mother had told me some of the famous Sacher stories, laced with hearsay, perhaps apocryphal. She went there with Aunt Bertha when Vienna was still the *Kaiserstadt* which, according to a popular song refrain of the time, existed nowhere else on earth. The song is still popular. Aunt Bertha knew all the famous stories, my mother heard them from her, and I was the thirdhand recipient. By that time the stories were more legend than truth.

The Sacher—hotel, restaurant, coffeehouse—is surrounded by legends. More books have been written about the place than about any other hotel I know. It is probably true that the young, hungry archdukes came there because the food was good. At the Emperor's table the daily fare was rather frugal except on festive occasions. Furthermore, according to protocol, His Majesty was always served first. The moment he finished no one at the table was permitted to eat. Since the young archdukes were not served until the Emperor had nearly finished, they were inevitably frustrated. The Sacher was located close to the Hofburg, and whenever they could get away they ran over and ordered a substantial meal, and to hell with court protocol. They became habitués of Sacher's and brought their girl friends there. They couldn't present the girl friends to His Majesty since many happened to be members of the Opera's corps de ballet.

Today dancers deny, often indignantly, that their predecessors might have dallied in the *chambres séparées* of the Hotel Sacher. Ballet dancing, they say, is hard physical work, often exhausting. No *danseuse* is in the mood for sexual divertissement after a long day's hard work on pirouettes, glissades, rondes de jambe. The poor woman is just tired. But the story survives, as it does in Paris and London. In Vienna a generation of playwrights capitalized on the goings-on at the Sacher and on the alleged anger of His Majesty about them. I hope one story in particular is true. They say an archduke came down into the lobby after a long night, wearing his shako, boots, saber, and absolutely nothing else. It *sounds* true. Only a born and bred archduke would walk around in this attire on a cool morning. Ordinary people would be afraid of catching cold.

The best Viennese stories have that tantalizing element of

whether it really happened and how, and there is always a grain of fact. As the song goes, Vienna, the *Kaiserstadt*, exists nowhere else on earth.

Yet sitting next to Raoul on my first visit to the famous oasis of life and love and good eating, hunger remained my first concern. Lots of waiters stood around, watching themselves instead of the customers. No one paid any attention to two teen-agers at the end of the big table. I remember a waiter who walked by, balancing on a silver tray an enormous *Wiener Schnitzel*—just what I needed.

I never got one. Raoul called another waiter—maybe the Sacher wasn't so fancy, when one had to call a waiter—and pointed at the rest of the chocolate mousse on his plate.

"Two more," said Raoul. That was all I got that night, after my first *Figaro*. I decided to tell my mother nothing about it. She might have said something about divine retribution; and she would have been right. I've been hungry on other occasions in my later life and I always accepted hunger as the just punishment for my youthful cocoa-and-*Würstel* sins.

❖   ❖

I left Vienna the next day. The week was over. My departure was as informal as my arrival had been. No member of the family was at the house when Jacques helped me close my suitcase. My mother had told me to tip the staff "because they expect it," and they certainly did. Anton, the arrogant manservant, didn't bother to say thank you. Perhaps he had expected more. Jacques said that he had taken the family into town, they all had important appointments, as though he had a sense of guilt about their going away without saying good-by to me. They were simply glad not to have me around any longer—except, perhaps, Raoul. I should have heeded one of Grandfather Wechsberg's axioms, *"Ein Gast und ein Fisch/ Sind am dritten Tag nicht mehr*

frisch [A guest and a fish are no longer fresh on the third day]."
It sounds better in German, with the rhyme.

It was a fine, sunny day, and Jacques took me through the
heart of the city, of which he was proud, as all Viennese are.
The old districts are beautiful. This time the ride was pleasant
and informal. Jacques no longer called me *"junge Herr"*; he
called me nothing, he had accepted me. I knew that Raoul was
the only member of the family Jacques approved of, and now
perhaps his approval included me. I sat next to him, not in the
rear. But he insisted on holding the door for me and closing it,
and then he went around the back of the car and sat down
behind the wheel. He threw his cap on the back seat and said,
"My goodness, if the *gnädige Frau* could see that!" We both
laughed at the absurd notion. Aunt Anna would have had a fit,
and her fits were not too pleasant. I asked Jacques whether he
had ever been an actor.

He shook his head.

"No, but I often wanted to be one. Even studied one semester
at that acting school. But then I saw that there were more
would-be actors than jobs. Besides, I wasn't good enough."

His frankness was refreshing and unusual in Vienna, where
people are often evasive. Frankness is considered clumsy.

"So I became a chauffeur. That is, I play the part of a
chauffeur, and I seem to be doing it well."

"Yes, very well."

"Someday I hope to have enough money to buy a car and to
drive my own taxi."

I said he might have more worries than he had now.

"Yes, but I'll be my own boss. And I won't have to wear that
sort of thing." He pointed at his uniform. "I believe these things
are part of the past and should be forgotten."

We rode down Nussdorferstrasse and Jacques showed me the
house where Franz Schubert was born. A small, two-story house

which most passers-by wouldn't notice. Most Viennese hadn't noticed Schubert when he lived among them. Today they are proud of him because he is one of the very few composers who was born and died in Vienna and rarely left it. He expresses the musical soul of the city, but a great many people even today do not understand his greatness.

At the corner of Währinger Strasse and Schottenring we both glanced at the palatial building where Uncle Alfred had his office, and we both laughed. No need to say anything; we understood one another. In Herrengasse, Jacques drove past the Hotel Klomser where one day in 1913 Colonel Alfred Redl of the Austrian General Staff had shot himself as befitted an officer and gentleman. Redl had betrayed the Imperial and Royal Army's mobilization plans to the Russians, and he had been found out. The "affair Redl" had shaken the confidence of many people in the system. The army had always been considered one of the last strong links that held the Habsburg monarchy together.

I was a child when the affair was discussed by my parents at home. I didn't understand what had happened, and I listened, in the half-conscious way of kids who listen though they know they shouldn't. When I grew up I read all I could find about the mysterious affair. I remember the fascinating report that Egon Erwin Kisch wrote. Redl had been a gambler and in debt. He also became a victim of blackmail, because of his homosexual private life.

The end of the affair was real melodrama. General Franz Conrad von Hötzendorf sent two of Redl's fellow officers to the Hotel Klomser. Conrad von Hötzendorf wanted war. The members of the "war party" claimed that the war would inject "vigor" into the ailing body of the Empire. Generals in Europe often—though not always—convinced themselves that war could be useful, the *ultima ratio*. The two officers left a loaded pistol in Redl's room and went back downstairs, and there they waited until they heard the shot. Conrad von Hötzendorf was pleased. One year later he had his war against the Russians.

Jacques spoke about Redl without passion, rather with detachment, but also with an inside knowledge that surprised me. I'm still wondering what became of him. He might have done well in politics, certainly better than as a taxi driver. He had no illusions about the society he worked for. As we drove past the Hotel Sacher and the Opera we were still talking about Redl and the war against the Russians and the people who had hoped to win it and thought it might settle something. It did settle only one thing: the fate of the Habsburg monarchy.

At the Ostbahnhof, Jacques carried my suitcase. It was heavy, with the new *Smocking* in it. He placed it in the rack above my seat and made sure that everything was all right. We shook hands. He politely refused to take a tip.

"No, not from *you*," he said, and smiled. Once more we shook hands. At the end of the platform he turned around and waved at me, and I waved back. We were friends now. Jacques was one of the best experiences I'd had during that week in Vienna. Then he was gone, and a minute later the train started moving.

❖   ❖

My mother was waiting for me in Přívoz, at the Ostrava railroad station. I carried the heavy suitcase. We rode home on the streetcar, but the ride was not fun, as it had been in Vienna. Perhaps it was fun only when you knew you could always take your Gräf & Stift, but not if you had to depend on the streetcar for transportation. My mother asked about "the house." I told her about the villa in Lanner-Strasse but she shook her head, impatiently. No, she meant the house in Neubaugasse where Aunt Bertha had lived. I had promised to look it up, but I had forgotten to go there. My mother shrugged; she was disappointed.

I carried the heavy suitcase all the way up to the fifth floor. There was no Jacques to give me a hand. I opened the suitcase and took out the dinner jacket with the label of Humhal, the famous Viennese tailor, inside. My mother looked at the jacket for a long time. She said nothing—always a bad sign.

I asked whether I should put it on for her. She shook her head.

"No. What for?" And then, "What did you need it for?"

I told her how it had happened, that Aunt Anna had ordered it for me at Humhal's, that I had worn it every night in Vienna.

"They gave it to me," I said hopefully. "Really, they did."

My mother looked at me sadly. "That is the first time they ever gave something to anybody."

But they had given me nothing. A few weeks later a letter addressed to me arrived from the firm of Humhal in Vienna. It contained a beautifully engraved bill for "One smoking, with silk lapels." I don't remember the amount, but I saw my mother's face and knew that it was a lot of money. Underneath the amount there was a "Special fee for express work, garment delivered same day." It was also high.

My mother took the bill and paid it the same day. She had the habit (which I inherited), considered ridiculous in some circles, of paying a bill as soon as she received it. Later, as a young lawyer, I met many people who wouldn't pay their bills unless they were admonished or sued. In the end they had to pay the bill plus the bill from the lawyer.

❖   ❖

During my oral graduation examination I proudly wore my fine blue suit. I passed with honors and wondered whether the discreet elegance of the suit might have had something to do with it. Probably not. Most of my classmates wore blue suits. We also wore them for the party that followed the examinations, the good-by party. No one wore a *Smocking*, not even Egon Goliat, the class Casanova and *arbiter elegantiarum*. Egon's parents were separated but lived in separate apartments on the same floor. Egon spent half a year with his mother and the other with his father. We were envious of the glamorous arrangement but Egon didn't like to talk about it. Sometimes he and his father, a noted lawyer, shared a *séparée* and two ladies at the Boccaccio Bar, the leading night club in town. The citizens were scandalized but Egon said they were idiots, it was less expensive to share the *séparée* with his father.

I told him about the *Smocking* from Humhal's. He laughed. "Sounds pretty silly," he said. "My father ordered one for me and he had the good sense never to ask me to wear it."

"I suppose we are just hopeless provincials," I said.

"I certainly hope so. Remember Dr. Spira. If you are a provincial, be proud to be one."

Years later, when I returned home from a trip around the world, I put on my elegant dinner jacket from Humhal, just for fun. The sleeves were too short, and I couldn't button my pants. I seemed to have grown in all directions. Some people said that I had become a man. I never put on the elegant tuxedo from Vienna again. I didn't take it with me to America. I have no idea what happened to it.

10

I NEVER SAW Aunt Anna again after that visit. Uncle Alfred would occasionally come to Ostrava to appease his relatives when they threatened to sue him. He implored them to be "patient." They must not start any action simply because the investments in Vienna "had not gone as well as expected." True, the astronomical inflation and the economic collapse had been halted with the help of League of Nations loans, and the bust had been followed by a boom. But, Uncle Alfred said, it might be an unhealthy boom. Many old coffeehouses had disappeared and their premises been taken over by brand-new banks and financial institutions of ephemeral status. Uncle Eugen, the ex-banker, claimed that Uncle Alfred personally was doing quite well. Uncle Eugen couldn't explain why the assets of Alfred's relatives were not doing equally well. There was new talk of starting legal action against Alfred. It was postponed, though, when Edith's wedding was announced. She would marry one of the Herren "von" I had met in Vienna.

The wedding took place at the Votivkirche across from the palatial bank building where Uncle Alfred had his office. In 1853 the Hungarian tailor János Libényi had tried to assassinate the twenty-three-year-old Emperor Franz Joseph I with a knife. He failed and was later hanged, after which he became popular and the hero of a caustic folk song. Archduke Ferdinand Max, the

Emperor's brother, decided to build the Votive Church at the very spot where the Emperor's life had been saved by the grace of God.

And in that popular, distinguished church Edith was to be married to her "Herr von." Aunt Anna had brought off her coup. *She* couldn't have a title but at least she was going to have a titled daughter. Uncle Eugen was invited and went to Vienna. He was then Uncle Alfred's only living brother. My mother didn't expect to be invited—that is, she *said* she didn't expect to be—and wasn't. Later she said she was "only" the widow of Siegfried, who had often called Alfred his "favorite" brother. She said it without bitterness but I wasn't sure. Perhaps she was secretly relieved she didn't have to go there. It would have been a strain, and there was also the question of "what to wear."

"If Aunt Bertha were still alive, I would go," my mother said. Aunt Bertha would have known exactly what to wear, though even she might have been surprised by the magnitude of the event. When Uncle Eugen returned from Vienna he regaled the family with many fascinating details, though he disappointed the women. He was unable to describe exactly Edith's bridal gown. Photographs had been taken but they had not yet arrived. Uncle Eugen said that Edith had looked "very lovely," which was certainly right. Edith always looked lovely.

Uncle Alfred had been the best man. Uncle Eugen said that Alfred "looked more aristocratic than the bridegroom and his family," and again he was probably right. The finest moment came as Uncle Alfred led his daughter down the aisle and the powerful organ sounded in the large church, which had been decked out completely with white carnations.

"White carnations!" my mother exclaimed.

"Thousands of them. From the Italian Riviera. Must have cost a fortune." Uncle Eugen shook his head as though he found it hard to believe though he had seen it. He added, "Even at wholesale prices."

"Did you hear Edith say a loud 'yes' as she stood next to the bridegroom?" my mother wanted to know.

Uncle Eugen shook his head, irritated by the question. He hadn't paid attention to such trivial detail. Perhaps he had been trying to figure out in his mind the wholesale cost of the white carnations from the Italian Riviera.

"Edith must have been baptized," said my mother.

"Certainly. I heard that Anna had tried to have the wedding in one of the older churches, such as the Augustinerkirche or in St. Stephen's. The church authorities wouldn't permit it, though. Edith had been baptized only a short time before the wedding. Good thing the wedding didn't take place in St. Stephen's. Imagine filling St. Stephen's with white carnations, at our expense. Even as things were, it cost us a fortune."

My mother looked at him questioningly.

"Alfred had to make a large donation for a church charity," said Uncle Eugen. "That's the way things are done there. And the wedding party afterward at the house in Lanner-Strasse! Anna told everybody it was a very expensive reception. In case anyone didn't know."

Uncle Eugen launched into a picturesque description of the wedding reception. I thought the whole thing was a bore but my mother wanted to know what had been served.

"Champagne, of course. Only the best, brut." Uncle Eugen sounded indignant. He didn't say, "at our expense," but I am sure he was thinking it.

"Of course," said my mother. *"Nobel geht die Welt zugrunde."*

The world goes to pieces, but nobly. Another of Grandfather Wechsberg's wise sayings conveying the essence of a situation.

❖   ❖

One day in the late 1920s, when I came back from a journey around the world—as a ship's musician, though I was "officially" studying at Prague University—my mother told me that Edith was dead.

I stared at her. It had never occurred to me that Edith, the symbol of being alive, might die. I could see her, wearing her riding costume and the shining black boots, tall and blonde and beautiful, and always a little remote.

"Her marriage was plain martyrdom," my mother said, speaking like the actresses of the Burgtheater whom she admired. "Edith was never in love with *that* man, and he didn't care about her. She married him because her mother wanted it. Anna did it all in cold blood. The man married Edith for her money, and Anna had a titled daughter. Nice deal."

I said something about *De mortuis nil nisi bonum*. Aunt Anna had died a year earlier after a painful sickness and much suffering.

"Edith had for many years been in love with a man here in town. Her mother knew it. Everybody knew it."

"I didn't know it."

"You were too small to understand." My mother mentioned the name of a well-known hotel proprietor.

"But he is married."

"He was; he is dead too. They died together. Edith came here and—they did it. Sleeping pills. Everybody tried to keep it a secret but there are no secrets in this town. Then, after it happened, everybody talked about the 'suicide pact.' Eugen came to ask me to implore Dr. Fischel to keep it out of the paper."

Dr. Fischel, who owned the local newspaper, the *Morgenzeitung*, was a friend of my mother.

"How could he? 'Suicide pact.' You can imagine what it meant for the newspapers. The whole thing, Edith's so-called marriage, had been a mess from its very beginning. Her husband didn't try to pretend to be nice to her. He got hold of her money and spent it. You know those people."

"It's all in Schnitzler," I said.

"It's always been like that, long before Schnitzler. But it didn't have to happen to Edith. She told her mother that she was much in love with the other man. He could have gotten a divorce, and they would have been happy. But Anna insisted. She didn't care about Edith's feelings. Anna insisted upon the marriage, and the title."

The death of his daughter was a terrible blow to Uncle Alfred. How much *he* had known about Edith's affair with that married man and about her unhappy marriage was a source of much speculation among the women in our family. Late in 1930, Alfred was no longer a financier; he wasn't even a banker. The Lombard & Escompte Bank was wiped out after the Bodenkreditanstalt, Austria's leading agricultural-credit institution, came close to failure. It was the spark that triggered a chain reaction and eventually became the worldwide Great Depression. It had all started in Vienna.

❖ ❖

In 1930 *the* financial power in the Austrian Republic was the Vienna branch of the Rothschild family. S. M. Rothschild und Söhne had been the financiers of the Habsburg monarchy. Back in 1881 they had launched the famous six per cent Gold Loan all over the great empire, extending their power into Hungary. Vienna's Creditanstalt, created to stop the growing influence of the French Crédit Mobilier in southeastern Europe, was almost a subsidiary of the Rothschilds. Today the Creditanstalt is Austria's largest bank.

The financiers of the Habsburg Empire remained the financial power of the young republic after 1918 though both, Austria and the Rothschilds, lost much of their influence. Austria was suddenly a mere fraction of the former monarchy. The

Austrian Rothschild firm did somewhat better. The firm remained loyal to the Republic of Austria during the astronomical inflation of the 1920s. It was managed by Baron Louis de Rothschild, the last of the "Austrian" Rothschilds, to differentiate them from the "English" and the "French" Rothschilds. Baron Louis was blond, cool, and composed, and he was pleased when people said he looked like an English aristocrat. He was a good polo player, and also a student of botany and the graphic arts. His credentials were impeccable. And being a properly brought up Rothschild, he regularly worshiped at the synagogue.

Around 1925 two upstart bankers named Castiglione and Bosel, who had no credentials at all, arrived on Vienna's financial scene and began speculating on the continuing fall of the local currency, the Austrian *Krone* (crown). Then they became power-crazy and speculated on the fall of the French franc. The crown and the franc went down, the pound and the dollar went up. Castiglione, a lone operator who was said to have a first-rate intelligence network, didn't know that the Rothschild banks in England, France, and Austria had secretly, efficiently set up an international syndicate that reached all the way from J. P. Morgan in New York to the Rothschild-controlled Creditanstalt in Vienna. The syndicate began buying up the franc. Bosel and Castiglione, the upstarts, were finished. Louis de Rothschild was completely in charge, keeping control of the Creditanstalt.

Not for long, however. In 1930, Vienna's Bodenkreditanstalt was in bad trouble. Some people lost their heads and many lost their savings. Baron Louis didn't seem to care; he was then hunting on one of his estates and was said to be "cool and composed." Austria's Federal Chancellor personally went to see him there and asked Louis to bail out the Bodenkreditanstalt. Louis's answer is a bit of Austrian lore.

"I'll do it," he said to the Chancellor. "But you are going to regret it."

Louis de Rothschild was no fool, he was a realist. His Creditanstalt took over the liabilities of the agricultural credit institution, the Bodenkreditanstalt. But it was too late, and as a result
the Creditanstalt, by that time already the country's largest
bank, had to suspend payments in 1931. It was broke; so was the
Republic of Austria. The government had to pledge to rescue
the bank by using its own treasury funds. S. M. Rothschild und
Söhne, with the help of the French cousins, contributed thirty
million gold schillings. (The new Austrian *Schilling* had replaced the earlier *Krone,* which had been wiped out by inflation.)

Only a super-financier was able to withstand such losses.
Baron Louis de Rothschild was still the richest man in Austria,
but he did sell some of his estates. Uncle Alfred was no
Rothschild, though his father, Grandfather Wechsberg, had
been called "our own Rothschild" by the people in my home
town. "Uncle Alfred's bank," as we had called the Lombard &
Escompte Bank, simply vanished. Its assets were gone, including
the life savings of our family. Everything "dissolved into thin
air," as my mother aptly though somewhat dramatically described it. She never talked about it with other people but she
reminded my brother Max and me that our father had asked
Alfred to take care of her and the boys if something should happen to him in the war.

It was little consolation to the family that Uncle Alfred had
also lost his own investments and his job and everything that
went with it: the large private office conveying the atmosphere
of solid wealth, the fine stationery, the Gräf & Stift, and the
liveried chauffeur. I wondered what might have happened to
Jacques, and I hoped he hadn't lost his savings too. Perhaps he
had bought a car and was now a taxi driver wearing civilian
clothes.

Uncle Alfred must have been very lonely. He had lost his

wife, and now Edith was dead. Raoul had left Vienna and was working as an analytical chemist in Amsterdam. He was said to be brilliant, and people said he might carry on the heritage of Uncle Hugo, the famous chemist in Hamburg who had lived in happy sin with Aunt Alma, my favorite Protestant.

Uncle Eugen told my mother that Alfred had been trying to sell the house in Lanner-Strasse. There had been no offers.

"Who could afford to buy such a house now?" Uncle Eugen asked rhetorically.

After 1930, when he had lost everything, Uncle Alfred had no reason to stay in Vienna. The people he and Aunt Anna had invited to their parties didn't know him any more. *"Wie gewonnen, so zerronnen,"* said my mother, possibly quoting Grandfather Wechsberg. Easy come, easy go. When people asked her why she hadn't sued Uncle Alfred, who had manipulated her savings into bankruptcy, she quoted another of Grandfather's sayings: *"Wo nichts ist, hat der Teufel sein Recht verloren* [Where there's nothing even the Devil cannot claim anything]."

And so Uncle Alfred, broke and ailing, returned to our home town which he had left to conquer Vienna and become a challenger to the Rothschilds. By that time Baron Louis de Rothschild had moved from his sumptuous mansion in Prinz Eugen Strasse in Vienna to a somewhat smaller place nearby—small for a Rothschild.

The mansion didn't last much longer than the Austrian Rothschild. In the early 1940s it became the headquarters of Adolf Eichmann, the architect of the Nazis' "final solution." The American air force bombed it in March 1945, the day they also bombed, by mistake, the Vienna State Opera. The ruins of the mansion were removed years later, and the Socialist Trade Unions of Austria put up their *Arbeiterkammer* (Workers' Chamber) there. It is a tall, square, functional structure, different from the red silk splendor of the original captialist-owned mansion. The present possessors, more powerful than the Rothschilds ever were in Austria, seem safely entrenched there for the immediate future. I happen to live almost next door, in Prinz Eugen Strasse, and I walk past the imposing building nearly every day. I cannot help wondering, though. The Rothschilds. The Nazis. The Austrian Socialists. Who is going to be next?

❖   ❖

In Ostrava, Uncle Alfred didn't live in the high style of his Viennese adventure. He rented a small apartment in one of the early local housing developments, a short walk from the former family bank and the former family house, where my mother still lived on the top floor. Soon after the houses were finished they looked like the slums of the future, walls cracking and paint peeling off. It was said that Uncle Alfred would try a comeback in Ostrava but perhaps that was merely gossip or a figure of speech. His health had suffered, and he was said to be tired and discouraged. All this we knew from Uncle Eugen, who went to see him once in a while.

Uncle Eugen still felt bitter toward Alfred—his life savings had also gone down the drain in Vienna—but he considered it his duty to visit his sick brother. To him the family meant everything. Uncle Eugen would at the beginning of the year note in his diary the birthdays of all relatives, down to nephews and nieces and second cousins twice removed. He never failed to come and wish me happy birthday on the day. It was a ritual with him, and then he checked my name off the list. He did it for himself, not for the others. He even kept in touch with the remote family branch in the nearby town of Friedland. I never met any of the "Friedland Wechsbergs," I just knew they existed. Uncle Eugen knew their exact genealogy, though. Once

he told me that no matter how he felt about his brother he considered it his "sacred duty" to pay him an occasional visit.

I admired Uncle Eugen's nobility of spirit but was unable to
act accordingly. I was no longer "too small to know." Perhaps I
knew too much. When I happened to see Uncle Alfred in the
street where he walked stooped, looking tired, I would cross over
to the other side, pretending not to see him. I didn't want to be
patted on the shoulder, to see the charming smile. Uncle Alfred
was still elegant—I noticed this by glancing out of the corner of
my eye without turning my head—but I felt I owed my "pride"
and "intransigence" to the memory of my father. I hoped he
would agree with me, wherever he was. I am not so sure now.

Uncle Alfred was in Ostrava in March 1938 when the Nazis
marched into Vienna. He told Uncle Eugen he thanked his
"lucky stars" not to be there. He would have been summoned to
the Rothschild *palais* by the henchmen of Eichmann, and that
would have been just the beginning. Louis de Rothschild had
been arrested, was released after complex ransom negotiations,
went to Switzerland and later to the United States, and eventually died in Vermont, where he owned a luxurious estate, in true
Rothschild style.

❖   ❖

I was briefly in Vienna in 1936, mainly to attend some performance at the State Opera. I was crazy about opera and people
said one should go to Vienna "while there was still time." Time
was running out fast. One day I took the No. 40 streetcar to the
Cottage and walked up Lanner-Strasse. I hardly recognized the
house. It looked run down, almost shabby. The once lovely garden was a wilderness. It would have been better if Uncle Alfred
had owned an older house, perhaps one built around 1900, or a
Swiss-style chalet with timberwork. Age and dereliction would
have mattered less; there are still beautiful houses in Vienna
that were built around the turn of the century. But functional

houses, made of concrete, must be kept up to maintain their function, to demonstrate the prestige of their owners. Much later I heard that the house had been sold. It went through several hands and is now the embassy of a "poor" Middle Eastern kingdom. One that has no oil.

In 1938, I went to America. Time had finally run out for us in Europe. There I had a letter from my mother telling me about "the last act of the Greek tragedy." Occasionally she surprised me with her allusions.

Uncle Alfred became very sick and died in Ostrava. Raoul was working in Amsterdam when he got the news. He tried to travel to Ostrava to see his father alive once more, but there had been passport and visa difficulties. Raoul was not tough. Aunt Anna had not brought up her children to be tough. My mother wrote, with her innate sense of drama, that that might have been the "curse" hovering about Uncle Alfred and his family. When Raoul was told that his father had died he jumped out the window.

11

WHEN MY PARENTS were together in Vienna they stayed at the Hotel Bristol. My mother would have preferred to stay with Aunt Bertha, but my father disliked being a house guest. He valued the luxury of personal freedom and was willing to pay for it. He wanted to come and go as he pleased, to order when and what he liked to eat, and he hated to sit up at night making conversation.

He wouldn't stay at the Hotel Sacher, the hangout of tired members of the aristocracy and of high-ranking officers. They spoke with the nasal upper-class inflection practiced by some characters in *Die letzten Tage der Menschheit (The Last Days of Mankind)*, the epic and often true drama which Karl Kraus wrote about the dissolution of the Habsburg monarchy.

Another good hotel was the Imperial, on the other side of Ringstrasse, where the Emperor put up official guests he didn't like having at his palace in Schönbrunn. (His Majesty also disliked house guests—another trait that made him sympathetic to my father.) "Who wants to stay at a guesthouse?" my father said. Perhaps he *had* been difficult, as my mother later implied.

The Bristol was not a guesthouse, nor was it a frivolous hangout. It was a luxurious hotel with unassuming dignity. Many years later my mother was still dreamy-eyed at the mention of the Bristol—the beautiful rooms, the unobtrusive service, the crisp *Kaisersemmeln* at breakfast, the liveried doorman, the wood-paneled dining room. She knew of the celebrities who had stayed there. Kings and queens and princes. Many maharajahs. The Duchess of Talleyrand (née Gould) and the Duchess of Marlborough (née Vanderbilt). My mother always surprised me with her knowledge of detail. In fact she told me so much that I had to visit the hotel when I first went to Vienna as a house guest at Uncle Alfred's.

I entered the small lobby and stopped, afraid they would ask me what I wanted. They wouldn't have asked. At a place like the Bristol they know exactly whom to stop and whom to leave alone. They don't look at your clothes; they know more about you than shows on the surface. All this I didn't realize when I was young.

The Bristol is still there, at the intersection of Ringstrasse and Kärntnerstrasse, which was once the fashionable shopping street and is now a pedestrian zone with supermarkets and souvenir shops. In its heyday the Bristol was a sort of palace, standing at the "best" street corner in Vienna, across from the Court Opera. Today it cannot compete with the tall, anonymous "modern" hotels that many travelers prefer. But at the Bristol you don't have to look at the bathroom towel to know where you are. You are at the Bristol in Vienna. Unmistakably.

❖   ❖

The Bristol was opened in 1894, a quarter of a century after the Court Opera had been opened. In its own way, the hotel became the inimitable mixture of chic and *Gemütlichkeit* that has often been imitated elsewhere, never successfully. The mixture remains one of Austria's great assets, though it doesn't show up in the trade balance. People from all over the world pay hard currency to enjoy it. It is this local quality that makes Vienna different from Paris, Rome, and London. The Bristol never had such superstars as César Ritz and Auguste Escoffier, but it had its bizarre personality, that light touch of decadence that made it different from great hotels elsewhere. It was the last luxurious Western outpost on the rocky road to the Balkans.

The original Bristol was built by Karl Wolff, a wealthy brewer who had come from Saaz in Bohemia and had become a "learned" Viennese, like so many others. In Vienna it is often claimed that it is better to be a "learned" than a "born" Viennese. The "learned" ones have to work hard to blend in; the "born" ones take everything for granted. Karl Wolff, long forgotten, shared with Sigmund Freud and Gustav Mahler, two other "learned" Viennese, the distinction of having arrived from the "Crown Lands" of Moravia and Bohemia. Wolff hoped that his hotel would sell a lot of his beer. He was quite wrong. Vienna's beer drinkers thought the place was too fancy and wouldn't go near it. And the people who went to the Bristol wouldn't order beer, too lowly a drink. Having realized his error, Wolff acted swiftly, putting more money into the house and importing some first-rate talent. After his death in 1904 his son decided to raise the tone of the place still higher. He brought in a brigade of twelve French chefs and sous-chefs, and a Vienna-born head-waiter who had been with Shepheard's Hotel in Cairo and had both Viennese charm and international poise, an unbeatable combination. Prices were doubled. Business was better than ever.

By the beginning of the First World War the Bristol was getting too small. Wolff, Jr., and his partner, an architect, decided to enlarge it. When the addition was finished the two buildings occupied the best part of an entire city blockfront. There was a slight flaw in the arrangement, though. Between the old and new Bristols was a narrow private house that belonged to a Frau von Gompertz, a resolute lady who refused all inducements to sell because she wanted "to die under her own roof." This would have been the end elsewhere, but not in Vienna, natural home of the compromise. After much discussion Frau von Gompertz permitted the Bristol management to put a connecting corridor through her second floor.

The old Bristol had 240 rooms, the new one 114, and there were separate guest lists and separate staffs with separate loyalties competing with each other, which pleased the owners. The guests at the two hotels were completely different. Old-fashioned people would rather have died than be seen at the "flashy" new place. People who considered themselves smart and chic laughed at the palm trees and pink marble columns in the "old" hotel.

After the death of my father, my mother never went near the place when she was in Vienna. But she knew all about the old and the new Bristol and said, "If Siegfried were still alive, we would of course go back to the *old* Bristol. There is, after all, such a thing as loyalty."

The time between 1894 and the First World War—which I still associate with my father's best years—was the golden era of the Bristol. After 1918, when Vienna almost overnight became the elephantine capital of shriveled Austria, a city of two million for a country of seven million, the white façades of the hotel gave the cold, hungry, broke Viennese the reassuring feeling that they had not been totally excommunicated from the Western world. Its brightly lit windows at night and the roster of prominent guests published daily in the local papers were an effective tonic against a latent nationwide inferiority complex.

I came to the Bristol after the Second World War. The place had gone through several metamorphoses that might seem incredible anywhere but in Vienna, where incredible events had become routine in the past fifty years. I knew so much about the Bristol from my mother that I almost thought I had lived there before. It was a sort of homecoming. I do not have many such places on earth but the Bristol was one of them, much more to me than a hotel. A place where my parents had been happy. They hadn't been there for a long time, but happiness is elusive

and cannot be measured by days or weeks. I walked through the
corridors where they had walked, and I was with them, and inevitably I wanted to know more about the time when they had
been there. I looked at the old guest books, and I talked to the
few survivors of the golden era.

The ministers of the Emperor have gone, but the members of
the Socialist government of the Republic of Austria often come
for lunch in the redecorated dining room, even the Finance
Minister who tried to do away with the time-honored privilege
of the expense account. No maharajah has been to the Bristol
for a while, but beer is still considered a lowly drink there, as it
was eighty years ago. Unchangeable despite enormous historical changes, the Bristol truly remains a symbol of Vienna. If my
parents were still around, they would be pleased.

❖   ❖

My mother often talked about her last visit to the Bristol, the
last time she was there with my father, in the spring of 1912.
She had spent *the* week in Vienna with Aunt Bertha, and then
my father had joined her. She had waited for him at the Ostbahnhof and they had gone straight to the hotel.

For a while my mother said nothing. She was looking into
space, smiling; she seemed much younger than her age. Then
she sighed and said they had still been worried about me. I had
been left in Ostrau with Fräulein Gertrud and Marie. I was five
then, on my silly cocoa-and-sausages diet. No wonder they
worried.

There had been an incident at the Bristol that still seemed to
puzzle my mother when she told me about it, many years later.
Late one afternoon they had met a high-ranking Austrian officer
in the lobby. They had come from their usual walk and he was
about to leave. He jovially greeted my father and was introduced
to her as Colonel von So-and-so, an aristocrat who had been with

my father in their early army days. It appeared that the colonel had made a brilliant career and was now at the War Ministry, "in a sensitive position," my father explained.

The colonel laughed and asked my father whether he didn't regret having turned down the invitation to stay in the army and become a professional officer. God knew, he too might now be at the Ministry. My father had said no, he did not regret it. He was content to be an innocent civilian, just an anonymous banker in a provincial town.

"He wasn't anonymous at all, just modest," my mother said, with feeling. "But that isn't the reason why I remember the incident. The colonel nodded and laughed again and said, 'I understand, Wechsberg. But we *did* have fun, didn't we?' Well, your father managed to smile and he nodded, but he seemed—almost embarrassed," my mother said.

"Why should he have been embarrassed?" I asked.

"That's *exactly* what I've asked myself since, many times. Now could it be a woman? Several women? Or this gambling business? The so-called secret I wasn't supposed to ask? . . . Well, I didn't," my mother said, with evident regret.

"You really didn't ask him, Mama?" I asked.

"Well, not directly. I tried to find out more about the colonel. A handsome man, really." My father explained to her that they had been classmates at the military academy.

"That was all he said but the way he said it . . ." My mother didn't finish the sentence.

I looked at her. I was very pleased with my late father.

She shrugged. "I discussed it with Aunt Bertha. She said, 'Minka, forget it. Don't you dare play Elsa to your Lohengrin.' Aunt Bertha sometimes quoted Wagner though she didn't really like *Lohengrin*. She said Elsa had been a silly goose to ask Lohengrin that question. On the wedding night, too."

"And you never asked him?"

"I didn't want to be called a silly goose by Aunt Bertha," my mother said, piqued. "Besides, I sensed she was right. Today I know she was. One must not know everything about a person one loves."

"Yes, Mama," I said. "There should be a law permitting everybody to have a few secrets."

"Go and finish your schoolwork," my mother said.

"It's all done, and I'm going to play soccer."

"Don't come home all dirty again," she said.

I went. I am glad I still don't know the secret.

12.

MOST YOUNG PEOPLE don't like schools. I was no exception. I remember the first names of the girls I was in love with (or thought I was) when I was a student at the Gymnasium, but I have forgotten the names of many of our professors. The Gymnasium was a severe school, strict and old-fashioned. The teachers expected to be treated with respect. Enthroned above us on a raised platform (they would never sit *among* us), they acted as though they were generals or executives. They didn't understand that genuine respect cannot be dictated from above, it must be generated from below. Most of my classmates were no fools. We respected some of our teachers and had contempt for many.

I spent eight years at the Gymnasium—a long time in the life of an adolescent. When I was enrolled there in 1917 the Habsburg monarchy still existed, though barely. Our home town was still known by its German name Mährisch-Ostrau. The picture of the last Habsburg Emperor, Charles I, hung in the classroom. He had ascended the throne the previous year, after the death of *the* Emperor, Franz Joseph I.

The end of the war was the end of the world as most people had known it. I was eleven years old. For my mother, my brother and myself, the end had come earlier. When we boys heard that the Habsburg monarchy had collapsed we didn't understand the meaning of the word. It seemed inconceivable that an almost eight-hundred-year-old monarchy could "collapse." Some said "like a house of cards," but that was nonsense. I had built houses of cards with my father's *Tarock* cards, and their collapse created no consequences. Uncle Alfred who ran the bank said gravely that the monarchy's powerful structure "had been systematically holed out from the inside." I repeated the sentence to myself, twice and three times, but it made no sense to me. Neither did I understand what the grownups meant by the "powerful centrifugal forces of nationalism." Only much later did I know the meaning. The Habsburg monarchy had not been destroyed by enemies from outside but by its own nationals, enemies from within. After the Empire had been broken up by its own people it was too weak to resist outside pressure.

I remember demonstrations and parades, speeches and flags, always flags. The whole town seemed to have gone flag-crazy. In the beginning, most of the flags were red. After a while one saw new flags, a white stripe on top, a red stripe underneath, and a blue triangle inside. It was beautiful. The old black and yellow flags of the Habsburg monarchy had disappeared. Weird stories were told about people who had "demonstratively" hoisted a black and yellow flag to show an attitude that *they* called "defiant" and others called "hopeless" or "stupid." The black-yellow people were said to be either "patriots" or "traitors."

I began to wonder about the meaning of words. How could the same person be either a traitor or a patriot? Words were dangerous, and definitions were treacherous. Gradually the last black and yellow flags disappeared. Once I asked my mother what happened to all the flags that were no longer used. She stared at me as though she had never thought of the question, but she had no answer for me. You cannot turn black-yellow into blue-white-red. At the Gymnasium the history teacher explained that the colors of the new flag of Czechoslovakia—red, white, and blue—were the colors of France and the United States, which had helped our "young" country to win its independence. There you were. The countryside around our town hadn't changed. But the town was no longer Ostrau. It was now Ostrava. The fields and forests were there, the ponds and the brooks. But the old monarchy had almost overnight become a young republic. The ways of grownups were certainly mysterious.

I was a student of Class 2B at the Gymnasium, late in 1918, when the classroom picture of Emperor Charles I was removed. One morning we came to school and there was a whitish spot on the wall above the blackboard. After a while the picture of a bearded man wearing a pince-nez appeared on the wall. It was in black and white; the color pictures, it was said, were not ready yet. Underneath it said, "Tomáš G. Masaryk, President of the Czechoslovak Republic."

The bearded man looked at us with definitive authority but not, it was agreed, without a certain warmth. The consensus was that the picture of the new President was an improvement over the glossy print of the last Emperor, with the Habsburg lip and the frightened eyes. (He had had good reason to be frightened.) And that was, so far as we students of Class 2B were concerned, the comment on the beginning of a new era. It was going to be very short—nothing like the preceding Habsburg era. Ever since, I've taken a detached view of historical events. Some seem important at the time they happen but may not matter in fifty years.

The demise of the Habsburg monarchy caused less excitement in Class 2B than a soccer game against the team of 2A. That seems strange now when I consider the number of my classmates who came from *kaisertreu* (loyal-to-the-Emperor) families. The boys from German (meaning non-Jewish) families had been brought up in monarchist traditions. And many Jewish boys—the majority of the students at the German Gymnasium were Jews—came from middle-class families such as ours. We had always considered Vienna, not Prague, our spiritual capital. Yet at the Czech Gymnasium, only two blocks away, the students had called Emperor Franz Joseph "a senile idiot." They knew all about the bearded man with the pince-nez. My personal metamorphosis occurred several years later, in Prague, where I eventually felt more at home than in Vienna.

We may have been silly teen-agers but we were no snobs. Family background and social standing were never discussed when I grew up. No one resented me for being the son of a banker and the grandson of a "financier." Some of my classmates had only a piece of dark bread during the ten o'clock intermission, and some had a slice of goose liver on it. Some rich boys didn't bring their bread from home but bought a pair of hot *Würstel* at the tiny office of Herr Kneisl, the janitor. Herr Kneisl enrolled his oldest son at the Gymnasium and said he hoped the boy would one day be something better than a janitor. We nodded, without giving it much thought. One boy's father was a shopkeeper and another's was a general manager. The war was over. I thought both were lucky to still *have* their fathers.

Inevitably we were told a great deal about the bearded man in the picture, our new President. We were surprised that he had been a professor of philosophy, a man of abstract science. Maybe there was no "money" in it but there was more—greatness, statesmanship, even a touch of history.

We in class 2B learned a great deal about Masaryk the man, not the statesman. We had a personal witness, Professor Rapp, who taught mathematics, one of the few teachers who was generally respected. He came from the village of Polná, near Pardubice, in Bohemia. In Polná, one Leopold Hilsner, an impoverished Jew, had been accused of the ritual murder of a Czech girl. "That was, of course, before you were born," Professor Rapp said, perhaps to mitigate the shock.

We didn't know the meaning of "ritual murder." Some boys asked their parents, who were embarrassed and evasive. The Czech servants were less evasive. According to them, "an old Jewish ritual" demanded "the blood of a Christian virgin" for the making of matzoh at the time of what they called "Jewish Easter." Matzoh was popular among my classmates, especially the Christian ones, who often traded for it at the time of Passover. One boy once offered his roll with a thick slice of sausage for a piece of "unleavened bread." (None of the boys noticed the taste of blood in the matzoh they had eaten.)

Higher authority was needed. A Christian classmate and I went to see Dr. Spira, our revered rabbi. Dr. Spira smiled sadly, nodding his head several times as though he had known the question was bound to come up eventually. He told us that such a ritual had never existed and that the rumor was as old as the hatred of Jews.

"It is a clever lie," he said. "Like the so-called Protocols of the Wise Men of Zion."

We knew nothing about the Protocols but were afraid to ask. Anyway we knew now that the alleged ritual was a lie. Class 2B accepted the verdict of Dr. Spira unhesitatingly. Yet, many years ago, in the Bohemian village of Polná, Hilsner had been arrested and faced the death penalty. He couldn't afford a lawyer and would have been executed if Professor Masaryk had not come to his aid. Masaryk's position was far more perilous than that of Emile Zola when he spoke up in favor of Captain Alfred Dreyfus in Paris. No one backed him up. He was already highly unpopular among Czech nationalists, having offended them badly in 1886 by writing a famous critical review in his magazine *Athenaeum*, claiming that the so-called Králový Dvůr and Zelená Hora manuscripts had been forged. These manuscripts,

pieces of parchment found underneath the church tower of
Královy Dvůr in northeastern Bohemia, had contained frag-
ments of Czech epics and lyric poems apparently going back to
the late thirteenth century. In the 1880s the Czech nationalistic
movement had been gaining momentum under the Habsburg
monarchy. Naturally the manuscripts created enormous excitement. Here was proof, the Czechs said, of the medieval exist-
ence of a Czech language and literature; proof of their national
identity.

Then Masaryk, and later Jan Gebauer, a noted scholar,
proved beyond doubt that the manuscripts had been forged by a
certain Václav Hanka, who had long ago died a national hero
and been given a state funeral. And a few years later Masaryk
again stood up against public opinion and convincingly proved
Hilsner's innocence.

All this we knew from Professor Rapp, who in turn knew it
from the Hilsner family back home in Polná. At the age of
eleven one is impressed to hear history from somebody "who was
there." We understood why President Masaryk in 1918 adopted
as his motto the old slogan of Jan Hus and King George of
Poděbrady, *Pravda Vítězí* [Truth Prevails].

Thereafter Class 2B unanimously accepted President Masaryk. Later, in Vienna, I often heard it said that Masaryk had
been a "traitor," the "gravedigger of the Habsburg Empire."
Vienna was only a six-hour train ride from Prague, where Masaryk was then venerated as a great man. My own home town
was almost equidistant from Prague and Vienna, five hours
away. Apparently a man was either a "traitor" or a "hero" depending on whom you listened to. Franz Joseph I had been
called "a senile idiot" in Prague and a sort of demigod in
Vienna.

Learning about history by being a witness, not merely by
studying it, has certain advantages. One pays little attention to

silly labels. The "gravedigger" legend of Masaryk is still wide-spread in Vienna today. In Prague he has been declared an un-person by the present regime, for different reasons. Does it matter? Eventually history will prove that he did exist. He cannot be discussed away. And someday Franz Joseph I will no longer be "a senile idiot." In Vienna he is a presence, which is more important than being immortal. He may have stepped out for a while but he is around somewhere.

❖   ❖

Much later, when I began to understand the meaning of the *Umbruch,* the great breakup in 1918, I remembered some symptoms that I had ignored when they happened. Two classmates suddenly left with their families. Their fathers had been civil servants during the monarchy. There was little coal that winter though we in Ostrava were said to be "sitting on coal." The adults carried on long discussions about "the breakdown of the old values." We young people didn't care; our values were different. Soccer games, the next mathematics exercise, later on dates with girls. Our values were not touched by the *Umbruch.* Some classmates dropped out, new boys came in. In the early 1920s we had four girls in our class. Two of them were pretty, which created minor intrigues. But on the whole we stuck together, and there were thirty-nine of us hoping to pass the *Matura,* the crucial graduation exercises, after eight years at the Gymnasium. Without *Matura* one couldn't go on to a university. The *Matura,* in fact, was the main purpose of spending those long years at the Gymnasium.

On the night after the last day of the exercises—having a name beginning with *W,* I had to sweat it out for four terrible days while the best, the easy questions all came up—we met for the graduation party. An elected committee had rented the back room of a coffeehouse of doubtful reputation, and some stuffy professors had refused to attend, which suited us well. The gen-

eral mood of relief that it was all over was overshadowed by
sadness. Two boys had not passed and were not there. Perhaps
there was also a sense of lingering regret underlying the moments of exuberance. We knew we were at a juncture. What
had been was part of the past. Life would never be the same
again, and because we knew it and didn't want to accept it, we
planned to meet again. Not just once but every ten years.

The strange graduation party broke up in the early morning
hours. We walked out into the silent, sleepy street. We walked
side by side, our arms interlocked, in a line as wide as the street.
Once, I remember, a taxi came toward us, and once a policeman
making his rounds. We let the taxi pass but we stopped the policeman. He was a good-natured man and slipped through beneath the locked arms of a boy and a girl. It must have been
four o'clock. We were a little too loud after the wine, and perhaps a little sad at the thought of parting. The year was 1925.

Ten years later my classmates were spread all over the globe.
And another ten years later, in 1945, when I, then an American
soldier, went back to my native land, I found only four of my
former classmates in the country. Four out of thirty-nine. I
talked to them and we decided to get in touch with the rest of
the class and arrange a reunion in Prague on some future anniversary of our graduation party.

During the following five years we kept up a busy and worldwide correspondence. When I came back to Prague in 1950 we
added up the score. Of the thirty-nine members of our class, five,
we found, were now living in Czechoslovakia, three in England,
two in the United States, two in Germany, and one each in Pal-
estine, China, Australia, and Russia. We could account for a
total of only sixteen in all. It would have been a sad percentage
for an American class of '25. But it was not a surprising one for
our class of '25, in that part of the world.

13

No OTHER PLACE in my home town reflected its iridescent palette as accurately as the Café Palace. The coffeehouse was, of course, not a local invention; even the most chauvinistic citizens would not make such a claim. For a long time I had believed the Viennese legend that the world's first coffeehouse had been established in Vienna, near St. Stephen's Cathedral, in 1684, the year after the Second Turkish Siege, by a certain Franz Kolschitzki, also known as Franz George Kulczycki. He was a brilliant double agent who worked for both the Allies of the time and the Turks. He did the almost impossible by surviving, and at the end of the glorious siege, Vienna's finest moment, Kolschitzki received a house, tax free, from the grateful city fathers. Earlier he had received a few bags of raw coffee beans from the equally grateful Turks. He roasted the beans—this he had learned from his Turkish friends—and served the new beverage to his Viennese friends at his home, which became Vienna's first coffeehouse.

A nice story, but today we know that the world's first coffeehouse was opened in Constantinople around 1540. From there the pleasant institution came to Europe, spreading to Oxford, London, Paris, Venice.

Vienna's coffeehouses became the most famous of all, though. Sixteen years after Kolschitzki had started the trend, there were already thirty such establishments in the city. The owners were supposed to obtain an imperial privilege, but quite a few people served Turkish coffee without privilege, illegally. In 1704 a chronicler wrote, "Vienna is full of coffeehouses where the novelists . . . get together, read the news in the papers and talk about it."

We had many coffeehouses in Ostrau, where the inhabitants had for a long time imitated Vienna's fashionable living habits. If they couldn't live in the Imperial City, at least they could try to live like the Viennese. They often exaggerated it, trying to be more Viennese than the real thing. Most Viennese had *their* coffeehouse; they didn't frequent just *any* place. It was said that some men had more than one woman but only one coffeehouse.

The custom was faithfully observed by some people in our town. My parents frequented the Café de l'Europe, an oasis of conservative elegance, as the very name implies. In our latitudes "French" was synonymous with "elegant." My mother preferred a certain French perfume. Long before I heard its name—it was Lanvin's *Rumeur*—I knew automatically when she was going out in the evening because the scent permeated the apartment. Also, it was common knowledge that French red wines were "the best." On special occasions my father would bring a dusty bottle up from the cellar. Judging by its shape, the bottle must have been a bordeaux. I was permitted to have a thimbleful. A fine, velvety red bordeaux from St. Emilion is still my favorite wine. That's something Professor Freud never wrote about.

The Europe was located in the center of town. Prior to the First World War, during the era that my mother later called "the good days," the Europe was an island of respectability, good manners, old-fashioned distinction. No one raised his voice. The tables were spaced so that it was impossible to overhear conversations. A superfluous touch, perhaps. People who listened to other people's conversations wouldn't come to the Europe. Grandfather Wechsberg went to the Europe after he became a "financier," a man of distinction. His friend Dr. Fajfrlik, the eminent Czech lawyer (later my boss), went there, as did Dr. Karl Kraus, president of several German societies. Nationality didn't matter but eminence did. My father, always something of a rebel, said the Europe was a terrible bore. "They have to have a place where they are among themselves," he said. I didn't know who "they" were—today one would call them the establishment—but I later found out, and didn't like it.

A far less distinguished coffeehouse was the Café Royal, which belonged to the father of Aschus, a schoolmate at the Gymnasium. His father was a short, sullen man who refused to believe in progress. My mother said the Royal smelled "exactly as it had smelled before you were born." She didn't like the Royal because it seemed to be the paradise of independent husbands, though she *said* she didn't like it because of the smell of the old leather benches, a smell of stale cigar smoke and fresh coffee. Aschus, who would one day inherit this monstrosity, said they had tried to get the stale smoke out of the place but failed. The smoke hung in the curtains and "had already seeped through the wooden panels." When I went there I stared at the panels, trying to see the residue of smoke there, but they were just panels.

"We tried to tear out one or two panels but gave up," said Aschus. "Too expensive. Also, the guests love it."

That was self-delusion. I went to the Royal once in a while. The guests didn't love it. They were used to the smell and didn't notice it any more. The Royal looked anything but royal. Compared to the Europe, it was downright shabby. The customers belonged to the Jewish middle classes: doctors, lawyers, merchants, civil servants, a few assistant managers of the local banks. Not the top managers, who patronized the Europe.

What surprised me about the Royal was that the customers were almost always there. I wondered how they managed to get *any* work done. Some came for breakfast, claiming that the coffee was better than at home. At the coffeehouse they could read the local *Morgenzeitung* and the *Neue Freie Presse* from Vienna, which had arrived by the night train, without being bothered by their wives and children. Some would sit there for hours before they got up, reluctantly, and went to their offices or shops. They were back at the coffeehouse before noon, "just for a jump," as they called it. A small "cup of gold" would fortify them for the impending ordeal of facing their families. The American business lunch was not known in my home town, which proudly called itself "American." People went home for lunch and, so far as I know, no one needed relief from the stress and a couple of drinks, because there was no stress.

The habitués were back at the Royal right after lunch, for their regular card game or to meet their old friends. Everybody had his *Stammtisch,* always the same few people around the same table. It was more difficult to join a *Stammtisch* than to join one of London's exclusive clubs. No one was blackballed; would-be joiners were just told they were not welcome. *Stammtisch* members had been meeting there for twenty or more years but still formally addressed one another as Herr Doktor, Herr Direktor, Herr Prokurist. Sometimes they didn't even know one another's first names. That may seem absurd but in Vienna I've played chamber music during the past twenty years with fellow amateur players whose first names I don't know. It took me several years to learn the first names of the members of my own string quartet and to find out about their professions, and I still don't know their homes and in some cases their wives. (In Vienna it is the custom that the first violinist acts as host to his fellow players. I play first violin.) And in France a man meets his *copains* in the bistro around the corner. He doesn't even know where they live and I don't think he cares.

At the Royal the habitués might leave their *Stammtisch* at

half past three. Two hours later they were back from the burdens of work to listen to the evening gossip, quite distinct from the noon gossip. Many of them certainly worked no more than four hours a day. Those who constantly complained of being overworked probably hadn't done this much, even. I am not sure now whether they were wise or just lazy.

❖   ❖

During the 1920s and the early 1930s a new coffeehouse, the Café Palace, introduced a modern style to my home town. The Palace was indeed palatial. It was built, as part of the new Hotel Palace, after the First World War, when people didn't trust the value of money. It was said that the best way to protect oneself was to invest in "things one can see." The Palace could certainly be seen. It was built by the brothers Gronner, who were "newcomers," meaning they hadn't lived in town around the turn of the century like some of the local patricians, who ignored the Palace and continued to frequent the Europe, where it was very quiet and some lights were turned off when the corner tables were empty.

The Gronners were smart, aggressive Jews who had arrived "from the East," as had so many others. They understood the spiritual climate of our town, though, better than most people born there. They looked like, but were not, twins. I don't remember their first names but people kept them apart easily. One had his right eye permanently closed, and the other the left one. When someone said that Gronner had gone through the coffeehouse, bowing to the customers and mumblingly inquiring whether everything was all right, people might ask, "Which one?" You would say, "The one with the right eye." The *good* right eye.

The Gronners were said to have surveyed the local coffeehouse scene and come to the conclusion, "What this town needs is an American coffeehouse." Naturally. The "Moravian Pitts-

burgh" needed no French- or Vienna-style coffeehouse but one
that fitted its "American" atmosphere. The conclusion was generally accepted. No one bothered to reply that there were no
coffeehouses in America. Few people had been there.

I went to the United States in 1928, at the age of twenty-one.
This made me suspect in conservative circles because I went as a
ship's musician. "Once a bohemian, always a bohemian," a man
told my mother. He wasn't referring to Bohemia, which would
not have been so bad, though not very good for a proud Moravian; he meant the Paris *Bohème,* artists living in garrets and
sleeping in the daytime. On the other hand, I earned the respect
of some of the younger people, who were glad that I had
"shown it" to these Neanderthalers. After my return I told the
people at the Palace that there were no coffeehouses in New
York, only drugstores. They laughed. It seemed absurd to them
that a big city could survive without adrenalin pumped into its
arteries by its cafés.

"What can you expect from a ship's musician?" somebody
said. Afterward I kept quiet.

Actually the Palace might just as well have been in New
York. It did have an "American" ambiance. The Gronners had
promised it would reflect the "American" spirit of our town and
they kept their promise. It was spacious, shiny, functional, full
of corners and stairways and garish lights. At the Palace everybody could see everybody else, thanks to the arrangement of various levels and large mirrors. People who had never been to
America agreed that it was "very American." Hectic, noisy,
confusing. The Palace compared to the Royal as the new Metropolitan Opera compares to the old Met. People who love the
new Met would have liked the Palace, everything bright and
glossy, chromium fixtures and glass walls. It looked like a giant
dining car.

The architects had created small islands under the same roof.

The customers had some privacy but they were all together. The tables were close to each other, to create a sense of intimacy, and because floor space was already getting expensive. At the Palace everybody knew what the people at the next table were saying. Some people went there expressly to eavesdrop. Some were masters at listening with both their right and left ears, and carrying on a conversation of their own in between.

There was no "distinguished silence" as at the Europe. The Palace people hated silence. They said, "At the Europe a man could sit motionless for hours because he was dead, and no one would notice it." There was no smell of old leather as at the Royal. At the Palace the banquettes were covered with dark green plush and frequently redone. Everything always had that "new" look. The cigar smoke hadn't seeped into the wood panels because there were none. It was widely assumed that the Gronners had once visited Versailles. In no other place except the Gallery of Mirrors have I seen a similar profusion of large mirrors. The walls of the Palace seemed to be completely covered with glass. At night the illusion of brilliant light was even more striking because of the bright chandeliers. The Gronners' idea of a "comfortable" place was one that was filled with mirrors, lights, noises, shiny metals, and confusing reflections. Many people agreed with this concept. The Palace quickly became *the* place to be; it was often crowded.

Such a place would not appeal to people who went to the coffeehouse to read or write, meditate and talk. Not too much of what is known as the coffeehouse literature in Vienna, Berlin, and Prague has survived, except in reminiscences. Ferenc Molnár's *Liliom,* written entirely at the Café New York in Budapest, often while a brass band was playing, is an exception, not the rule. Coffeehouse writing, similar to some Hollywood writing, is often better when told to others than when written down on paper. However, the Palace had no literary ambitions. The

Gronners would hardly have known how to spell "literature." It was said that they were hardly able to write their own names. But that may have been just another detail to show how smart they were. Perhaps they themselves had launched the rumor. The Gronners well knew that it is often dangerous to sign one's name.

The Palace was not a place to come to but a place to come through. The traditional tray with several glasses of freshly poured water had been accepted from the Viennese coffeehouse, where some guests were greeted by the headwaiter with "Herr Doktor, nothing at all, as usual?"—whereupon the waiter helped the guest out of his overcoat. Nevertheless, the Gronners didn't believe in traditional nonsense, but in turnover, both of goods and of people. The customers who came in to see and be seen, in the mirrors, were expected to order, pay, and go. No lingering on the plush banquettes. Time is money. Pay now, don't stay. Very American, they thought.

The waiters were smooh and sleek and often impertinent. The most impertinent was the headwaiter who would approach a couple sitting in a corner and ask, *"Der Herr die Dame schon gehabt?"* It is hard to translate adequately this lewd innuendo. It is a pun. *Gehabt* may mean both "have had" and, by extension, "have ordered." The headwaiter may have asked "The gentleman and the lady have already ordered?" or, by implication, "The gentleman has already had the lady?" Great fun. Puns were accepted means of communication. One girl I knew got so angry that she took a glass of fresh water and threw it into the headwaiter's face. She told me later that she had indeed been "had" by the gentleman, it was no secret in town, but it was none of the damn headwaiter's business.

Much of the amusement at the Palace was based on semantics and innuendo. The brothers Gronner, who occasionally walked through their coffeehouse, assuring the customers of good service and maybe even good will, were known as the *Zynicker* (cynics) because a supposedly Yiddish word, *zünicken,* means "to nod," and the Gronners nodded to everybody. Everyone knew that the Gronners were real cynics, which was the joke within the joke.

❖   ❖

The Palace became the hunting preserve of a class of people who might have formed an early café society if the expression had been known in my home town in the 1920s. When you asked, "Who goes to the Palace?" you were told, "No one and everyone." No one went to the Café Palace in search of conversation, self-education, conditions of the psyche, or interpretation of life, all of which were found in the famous coffeehouses of Vienna. Everybody went to the Palace in need of company, though not necessarily of companionship. A man who had "nothing to do" for an hour might meet a pretty woman there. And a woman who had "nothing better to do" in the early afternoon might become acquainted there with a generous cavalier. At the Café Palace a man was not actually introduced to a woman by the impertinent headwaiter, as some critics claimed. The Palace was no brothel. But the headwaiter might find "a mutual acquaintance" who might—*might,* that was the point— introduce you to the lady. The rest was up to you since the Palace was a respectable coffeehouse. Some people from elsewhere said that the Palace gave our town a bad name, but they admitted that there was rarely a dull moment there.

The only classic coffeehouse feature which the Gronners couldn't change, much as they disliked it, was the gallery. You walked up the stairway and found yourself on a gallery that ran along the walls on three sides. Not on the side facing the street, where very large windows had been installed. The Gronners didn't like the "Mediterranean" institution of the sidewalk café, which wasn't considered elegant. But they considered the street an extension of their coffeehouse, from which the customers could look out, protected by many square meters of window panes.

The best gallery tables were near the railing; from there one had a strategic view of the downstairs area. They were often occupied by attractive housewives who were honorably married but didn't mind meeting a cavalier and making a little pocket money as long as they were safely back home around 7 P.M. to prepare dinner for their husbands. The husbands were said to be blissfully unaware of their wives' extracurricular activities. As the impertinent headwaiter said, "No one gets hurt at the Palace."

Behind the tables of attractive housewives were tables along the walls which were occupied by the *Galeristen*, the "gallerists." (People who owned art galleries were also called *Galeristen*.) The Palace gallerists were involved in endless card games, as players or mere kibitzers. They had sallow faces and sat hunched, enveloped in blue cigarette smoke, living in a world of aces and kings, quite oblivious to the outside world. They seemed always to be there, like the furniture and the fixtures. Perhaps they left for a few hours to eat or sleep—the Palace practically never closed, like a well-run home away from home—but when the gallerists were not present you were told, "They'll be right back."

They were a close-knit society. None of my classmates was able to join the *Galeristen*, though some of our boys were excellent card players. The gallerists played "God's blessing at Kohn's house," the local version of poker. Some physicians sitting downstairs claimed that the respiratory tracts of the gallerists thrived on the mixture of foul air and cigarette smoke that always surrounded them. When one of them had to leave the gallery and the coffeehouse on an unavoidable errand, he pressed his handkerchief against his mouth. Breathing in the fresh, cool air outside might make him sick, it was said, might even kill him. I watched the *Galeristen* with awe. They made me think of early cave dwellers or of the silent men at the cemetery whose job it was to dig the graves and bury the dead, or of certain surgeons who were said to "deliver" the dead. Quite a few stories were told about some surgeons who often came to the coffeehouse.

The Palace was bright and young—a "typical parvenu," as the critics from the Café de l'Europe called it—but it had its strictly established and generally respected social topography. On the street-floor level the tables along the walls, the most desirable, were always considered "occupied" even when they were vacant. This was a favorite trick of the greedy (impertinent) headwaiter. A stranger might show his abysmal ignorance of local manners by sitting down at one of the apparently vacant tables. Soon he would be asked to move "over there," toward the anonymous middle of the room. When he protested that there was no RE-SERVED sign on the table, he was told that the table was *always* reserved. Yes, the next one too, and the empty table on the other side as well. All reserved. Eventually the stranger got the hint, became annoyed, and left. Everybody was pleased.

"He should never have come here," one of the Gronners once said. "Here at the Palace we like to have people who *belong*."

How to belong, and how to be promoted from an outsider to an insider, was something no one could explain. My cousin Fritz, Martha's brother, was a natural insider. He said it was a matter that could be only guessed, not analyzed. It should remain somewhat mysterious. There were people who came to the Palace day after day but didn't belong. Everybody knew it. Even *they* knew it, that was the sad part of it, but they came back always hoping that one day they might belong. They should have known better. "He wouldn't fit in," said one of the Gronners, the one with the right eye. (He was said to be the "senior chef.") After a while the outsiders would no longer come. Some said they had probably left town.

And others came rarely yet were deferentially greeted by the headwaiter, the ordinary waiters, and the *Pikkolo,* the seven-year-old waiter's apprentice. The newspapers they liked were brought—no one ever made a mistake—and often a waiter appeared with their special order, though they hadn't ordered at all: a cup of coffee of a certain hue, from black to dark brown to light brown to gold to upside down, which meant more milk than coffee. Fritz was a natural insider though he was not a regular. Sometimes he didn't appear for a week. No matter. When Fritz stepped into the Palace around six in the afternoon—at that time the place was full of people—he would get a "good" table, underneath the gallery, with his back to a large mirror. Just as an able hotel manager always keeps one last room for himself, the impertinent headwaiter always had an unreserved RESERVED table for my cousin. He expected no tip; that shows you how much Fritz was respected. They didn't care whether he ordered an inexpensive small black coffee or a very old cognac. He would sit there, relaxed and smiling, and after a while people would come to his table to present themselves. He would never get up to see *them;* that was an important difference, well understood by participants and onlookers.

Fritz was popular because he was independent, a bachelor, handsome but not *too* handsome, a definite advantage in the eyes of wise women who knew that handsome men cannot be trusted. He was the managing director of Martha's Guard-and-Lock Company, and as such was respected by his clients, often aided by the police director whose job he made easier, surrounded by lawyers who might get some business from him, and esteemed by his employees. Above all, Fritz had the locally most desirable title.

In the peculiar scale of social values in my home town, a great many men aspired to beome a *Direktor.* (The word was used in the sense of "manager" or "managing director.") Elsewhere people wanted to make a million crowns or dollars, to become presidents or full-fledged professors at a university, or members of the Academy of Sciences, or ambassadors. Not in Ostrava. To be generally respected a man had to be a *Direktor.* It was of secondary importance what kind of *Direktor* he was. It was, of course, better to be police director or director of the ironworks than to be director of a perfume factory or an even more doubtful enterprise. But the most important thing was to become a *Direktor.* It was said that certain directors had taken a cut in salary to gain the title. My aunt Anna in Vienna would never have tried so hard to have her daughter marry "a title" if her husband, Uncle Alfred, hadn't already been a *Direktor* in his home town; a *Bankdirektor.* Grandfather Wechsberg had wisely named his three sons directors when he made them his junior partners at the family bank. "That won't cost me anything and might help them," he had said. He himself wouldn't accept the title; he was, after all, a "financier," high above them in the stratosphere of success. After the death of my father, also a *Direktor,* my mother refused to be called *Frau Direktor,* which was the custom. (Wives would inherit the title.) She said she wanted to be known as plain Frau Wechsberg. People shook their heads and said she must still be suffering from shock, poor woman.

My mother was the exception. She knew that in our town the title of *Direktor* was irrevocable, a lifetime distinction. A man might commit a crime, but if he was a *Direktor* he remained a *Direktor.* It didn't matter that he was no longer director of anything. The title remained. I remember Direktor Z. who had gone to South America, taking along a couple of million crowns, not his own. He was eventually apprehended and brought back, "the biggest defrauder in local history." He was a celebrity. When he appeared in court everybody called him *Direktor,* and

the director of the prison where Z. spent several years gluing
paper bags also called him *Direktor* or *ředitel,* the Czech expression. Z. was locally remembered as the *Direktor* who never
tipped the peroxide-blonde manicurist at the Salon Proske less
than fifty crowns. More than a gentleman of generous habits: a
Direktor.

And my cousin Fritz was a director of the Guard-and-Lock
Company. The powerful police director was among his close
friends. For quite some time Fritz had come alone to the Palace,
in order to relax after a hard day at his office. He was among the
few people in town who worked long hours. And then one evening he appeared with Manja, an attractive Czech woman with
prominent cheekbones and what was known as "a good figure."
Manja was *Directrice*—the feminine equivalent of *Direktor*—of
an expensive boutique. She was not just anybody, she was *somebody* in Ostrava. She was among the local women who gave the
Palace a certain aura of voluptuousness; but she would never sit
alone upstairs on the gallery. Never. She was not that kind of
woman. Well, they came together, and came again, and Manja
remained with Fritz, much later, when he too had to run for his
life, like so many others. Manja followed him to Israel, and
there they were married. It was not easy. Manja was a Czech
Catholic and had to convert to the Jewish faith, but she did it
for the sake of her husband.

Much later I understood that it was no accident that they had
often come to the Café Palace and liked being there. The Palace
was a powerful erotic catalyst, and also a citadel of national and
religious tolerance. It was the only coffeehouse in town that was
frequented by Czechs and Germans and Jews. Each of these
groups also had its own coffeehouse where the guests were among
themselves—such as the Royal, patronized almost exclusively by
Jews. And there were "people of yesterday," as we called them,
who would never go to any place except their own. The Europe

still catered to the establishment. Then its members died or disappeared. One day the Europe quietly went out of business. The last lights were turned off. No one noticed.

In the late 1920s the Palace was more than a coffeehouse; it was a state of mind. The pragmatists and liberals frequented the Palace, showing their tolerance and independence. The first, I believe, were the actors and singers from both the Czech and the German theaters, who discovered that they had more in common than what separated them. Goethe and Schiller, Smetana and Janáček sounded good in Czech *and* in German. Shakespeare and Mozart, Verdi and Puccini, Kleist and Molière sounded good in *anything*. There followed a slow, steady rapprochement of the editors and journalists from Czech- and German-language papers. They often met on their errands, were professionally involved, and shared an antipathy toward the philistine conservatives of *any* nationality or language. To be sure, both groups had their unforgiving nationalists. But when they felt they had to discuss some matters of common interest they would meet at the Palace. President Masaryk, the country's great statesman and wise philosopher, had said, "Democracy is discussion." He might have added, "at the Café Palace," if he had ever been in my home town. Characteristically, local politicians and officials never met there though they might surely have needed a few discussions.

As the dissonances of the First World War wore off, other groups came to the Palace. Businessmen, lawyers, managers, doctors. All of them discovered that it wasn't true, what they had always heard about "the other people," who didn't share their language or religion. Members of the various soccer clubs—Czech, German, Jewish—came on Mondays, to rehash the games they had played against each other on Sundays. Even the tennis players came, though they belonged to a somewhat higher social class. Everything considered, the Palace was a pleasant anomaly in a young republic still suffering from violent childhood diseases caused by nationalism and dogmatism.

Business deals of a very special sort were also made at the coffeehouse. Such deals were considered less "serious" than those made at the office of a lawyer or a notary. They had certain advantages, though. Meeting at the coffeehouse, both parties, by silent admission, automatically waived some objections. They demonstrated that they would prefer the gentlemen's agreement at the coffeehouse table to a formal legal contract signed at a lawyer's office. They had confidence in each other. True, some coffeehouse deals were said to be borderline cases, not strictly legal, but they were the exceptions, not the rule.

Certain lawyers specialized in such "Palace deals." The local Lawyers' Chamber took a dim view of these colleagues who had no office, only a good table at the Palace. But the coffeehouse lawyers had a good case. They claimed that no agreement would be reached in some matters without their mediation. Their clients sensed that it was more convenient to come to an understanding in the relaxed coffeehouse atmosphere. Afterward the "Palace lawyers" would send their clients a bill "for services rendered at the coffeehouse." No one had ever refused to pay such a bill, and why would he refuse? The case had been settled out of court and out of office, at the coffeehouse. To be sure, some people wouldn't pay their bills regardless of where and how the services had been rendered, but that was another story.

Even physicians carried on professional activities at the Palace. It was considered bad manners to stop a doctor in the street or at a party and ask him, "Would you mind looking quickly into my throat?" or "I need sleeping pills, could you please write me a prescription?" But it was perfectly all right to approach the doctor at his table. If he couldn't make an instant diagnosis, the patient was asked to come to the office. Some doctors brought their appointment books to the coffeehouse. Later the patient would get a bill for the coffeehouse consultation and pay it without protest. The doctor had earned his money, and the patient had saved some valuable time that was better spent at the Palace. Come to think of it, the Palace was a very civilized place.

❖   ❖

The Palace had many faces. In the morning it was often frequented by newspapermen who wanted to read the papers without being bothered by telephone calls and visitors; by traveling salesmen in need of instant rest and a cup of strong coffee; and by pensioners who were always sure to find peace and a few fellow pensioners there and were glad to listen to one another's complaints. The coffeehouse was conveniently located in the very heart of town, at the corner of Main Street and Railroad Station Street. Both the Czech and the German theaters were within easy walking distance, as were the important streetcar lines, banks, shops, markets, and the main fire station. If you stepped out of the Palace and turned right, you were on Main Street, which at six in the evening became the *Korso*, the alfresco promenade where you were certain to meet anybody you were looking for. The Gronners took a dim view of the *Korso* because it kept some people out of the coffeehouse. They said the *Korso* was for *schnorrer* since it cost nothing to walk there. If you belonged to the "better people," you would meet your friends at the coffeehouse. They overlooked the fact that we promenaded in Main Street during the *Korso* hour to see the pretty Ostravian girls who wouldn't risk their reputations by being seen at the Palace.

And if you left the coffeehouse and turned left, you came to the end of Main Street and soon passed the coke braziers and steel furnaces of the Solomon mine. In Ostrava the pits were close to the center of town. Coke and steel were produced right where the black coal came out of the ground. In wintertime darkness came early, and I would often walk past the Palace.

The curtains were drawn but from behind the windows came a soft hum of voices and a breath of warm air and the scent of fresh coffee and women's perfumes. The lights were bright inside but I resisted the temptation and walked on. Soon I would see the furnaces, and a glowing mass that came out of the braziers. Dark, helmeted figures with blackened faces would direct jets of water against the glowing lava, and clouds of vapor would rise into the cold air. People from elsewhere said it was a sight out of Dante's *Inferno,* but for us who had grown up in the coal town the dearly familiar sight held no terrors. Without its coal pits and steel mills, Ostrava would have been another dull, undernourished, anonymous town. There were quite a few of them in the vicinity, with no prosperity, coffeehouses, theaters, cinemas, crooks, girls. Our town certainly would have had no "American" flavor.

❖   ❖

Around noontime there was a lull at the Palace. Almost everybody went home for lunch, except the bachelors who went to small restaurants where elderly women gave them *Hausmannskost,* plain home cooking. Then the Gronners, those brilliant cynics with flair for the whims of popular taste, with an instinct for anticipating future trends, introduced another "American" habit: lunch at the coffeehouse. They were truly the one-eyed ones in the land of the blind. They knew they were right because no one would dare tell them that they were wrong. Of course there was a widespread local prejudice against eating warm food at the coffeehouse. As the name implied, a coffeehouse was for coffee, period. It was also for cake, in the afternoon—another Viennese habit, cherished by the women. Coffeehouse purists claimed that the smell of freshly made coffee was incompatible with the aroma of cooked food. A ham sandwich or a pair of *Würstel* might be tolerated if one was very hungry. But in principle "a coffeehouse was not a restaurant." Again, *period*.

The Gronners made certain concessions to the purists. In the beginning when they started their "experiment," only a relatively small section of the place was turned around noon into a part-time restaurant. Near the revolving door, not a desirable location, white tablecloths were spread over some of the marble tables for the poor souls who might want to eat lunch there. Everybody felt sorry for them, including they themselves. While they sat there having their lunch they were outcasts even though they might be Palace regulars. And as a further concession, the Gronners served only dishes that would not spoil the hallowed coffeehouse aroma. Goulash was taboo. The stale smell of warmed-over *Gulasch* was a symbol of a Viennese *Beisl,* a sort of joint whose habitués, brought up on stale goulash and fresh beer, would not feel comfortable in the sophisticated atmosphere of the Café Palace. Boiled beef and roast chicken were served at the Palace on the theory that they "didn't smell," and on Sundays *Wiener Schnitzel* was offered to local connoisseurs, but that was as far as the "cynics" would go. They also ruled that the restaurant would have to "disappear" at two in the afternoon. Then the white tablecloths were removed even if some latecomers were still eating lunch. They had to finish eating on the marble tables and they were told to hurry up: the sight of them having a plate of boiled beef might offend some habitués who came only for coffee. The impertinent headwaiter would suggest that they take their dessert, a chocolate cake, "over there." Then the revolving door was left open for a while, no matter how cold it was outside. Only when the treacherous scent of food had been "aired out" was the door closed again. At five minutes past 2 P.M. the Palace was again what it was supposed to be—a coffeehouse.

By that time it was crowded with people on their way "back

to work," who always seemed to have an extra hour for good talk and playing cards. There was also a lot of business which people around the Europe called "Palace business." Stock exchange prices were discussed, the "Palace lawyers" opened their brief-cases, the first conferences began, some deals were made. The early afternoon "black coffee"—it was called that even when it wasn't black—was the equivalent of the American ritual of the business lunch. Some people came to the coffeehouse only at that time of the day, to carry on their business negotiations.

By four in the afternoon the clientele and the atmosphere had completely changed. The "Palace lawyers" and their clients were gone, and so were the "characters," as they were called, who came only for business reasons. Now the women arrived and soon were in control. The holy ritual of the *Jause* was about to begin. The *Jause*, strictly a Viennese invention, was the mid-afternoon break, usually coffee with plenty of whipped cream, pastry, cakes, pieces of *Torte*, the more the merrier, and extra portions of gossip. My mother said she would rather have a good *Jause* than lunch and dinner. The caloric intake was consid-erable. The first piece of cake might be followed by a second. And there would be more *Schlagobers*, which was synonymous with Vienna.

The greatest attraction, though, was the almost legitimate chance to tell tales about those not present. Women who hadn't appeared perhaps didn't care whether they were talked about by their friends. Or they didn't dare show their faces. Non-appearance was taken as a sign of guilt. Around five in the after-noon most tables at the Palace were occupied by groups of women, old, middle-aged, and not so young any more, who talked, often at the same time. There had been almost no women at the Palace at two o'clock. Now the male element was invisible, except for the gallerists upstairs who didn't care about the people downstairs, who cared only for their card games. If the Gronners had ever heard of an instrument measuring the decibel level (which I doubt) they would have discovered that the sound volume was the highest of the day at that time. Sometimes a sensitive habitué who was early came in through the revolving door, heard the sounds and saw the women, closed his eyes, turned and walked out again, telling the waiter, "I'll be back later." The waiter understood. He was a man, after all. Soon it would be six o'clock and the women would be gone.

The "six o'clock crowd" gave the Palace its glamorous ambiance and our town its "bad" name, which we cherished. All the people were there who loved to be where the action is, who wanted to see and be seen, who believed that fashions are values: the self-appointed insiders, the gamblers, the drivers of fast cars, the experts who thought they knew America though they had never been there, the fast men who could have any woman they liked, the fast women with the supercharged hips who claimed that men were nice toys, something to play with. We had no gossip columnists in our town, the profession developed later, but if they had existed they would have observed the Palace crowd from the vantage point of a good table. They would have seen who was with whom, who had left whom. Often why somebody hadn't shown up was more interesting than why somebody was there.

We *Chacharen* were there too, singly or in small groups, or with the fast-living crowd whose members we secretly admired. They wore the right clothes, had just returned from "chic" places, spoke almost a secret language of their own. Anything to be different from the hoi polloi. The critics said they were not "serious." Of course, they might *be* serious, but they tried hard not to *appear* so to the hoi polloi.

Some of the men were said to be dangerous for the reputation of any woman seen in their company. They had the doubtful attraction of being irresistible. Any woman seen with them was said to be their prey, which meant (we thought) that she had to sleep with them. Even if it wasn't true, the men involved in such speculations did nothing to dispel such rumors. They were not gentlemen; they failed to understand the meaning of the word. But a *Lebemann*—a man about town—was not expected to be a gentleman. He would discuss his alleged love affairs though they might exist only in his imagination. He enjoyed being known as a *Lebemann*—literally, a "living" or "fast-living" man, which wasn't bad; how many of us are really living and alive?— because he knew the expression bestowed a nobility of sorts on its bearer. A *Lebemann* was not born. He had to work hard to become one.

Among the *Lebemänner* were specialists, as there were among lawyers and surgeons. Some specialized in respectable married women and others preferred actresses, no matter how untalented they were. In my juvenile circles it was rumored that these *Lebemänner* specialists could physically possess—the strange word was really used fifty years ago—a woman only when they were strengthened by the knowledge that many other men in the darkened auditorium also wanted to "possess" her.

If an actress came only for a few months there wasn't much time, but the *Lebemänner* efficiently organized the conditions of her career. As soon as a new "target" appeared in town she was informed by a member of the *Lebemänner* guild that she needed influential connections, or connections with influential people. It was no secret that some *Lebemänner* had had no formal school-ing after public school and were not able to write a letter with-out grammatical mistakes. It was not explained to the poor woman exactly who the "influential" people were. The general managers of banks and factories? The producers at the theater who chose the actresses for important parts? Critics and impor-tant editors?

I couldn't answer these questions today but strange things did

happen in town. I knew two members of the *Lebemänner* guild
who were getting tired in their middle forties. They didn't really
like getting involved with actresses, but their reputations re-
quired it of them. Some people said, "He 'seduced' her"; that
was another strange expression used in those innocent days. The
Lebemann had to become involved with the actress assigned to
him, whether he liked it or not. All this sounds pretty foolish,
but a while ago a world-famous movie actress was in Vienna,
getting "engaged" for the seventh time in her life. Later she got
married. Perhaps she believed it was love. At any rate, she acted
as though she believed it. Years later the *Lebemann* admitted to
me that the whole thing had been a bore; he hadn't really cared
about the actress and all she had cared about was her career.

"Did you really care about *any* woman?" I asked him.

"Yes. Once or twice. I fell in love with a woman who might
give me warmth and affection, and wasn't thinking of career and
success. But . . ."

I waited.

He said, "She didn't care about me."

❖   ❖

All this went on at the Palace, vanity fair and silliness fair,
where some people were always watching to see whether they
were still being watched. It was a baroque situation. The coffeehouse was one large stage, and the people there were at the same
time performers, critics, and spectators. That too, I suppose, was
the powerful influence of the baroque city of Vienna, which is a
large stage where everybody is performing a part and at the same
time watching his own performance. But unlike the sidewalk
cafés in France and Italy where people go before they do something more important or after they have done it, the Palace was
the reason itself, with nothing before and nothing after.

The show at the Palace was the best in town. No premiere at
a theater could equal it. The *fluidum* of the Palace was so strong

that it was almost palpable: erotic tensions, a touch of decadence, love-hate thy neighbor. Some people who came there had
lived through strange experiences, through war and hunger and
boom and bust, through poverty and wealth and poverty again
and new wealth. The only thing they had in common was survival. To do justice to their life stories a writer would have
needed the genius of a Balzac, a Dickens, a Tolstoy.

Some had come from what were called "good" families, once
wealthy and solid. But the big break after the end of the First
World War had respected no values, no rules, no pillars of society or any other pillars. All these people liked being on the stage
of the Café Palace. They enjoyed their short, glorious appearances there. It proved to them that they had learned to swim
without taking any lessons. They had been thrown into the cold
water and had not drowned. They had survived and were the
winners. They didn't know yet that they were only short-range
winners. The next test was already looming ahead of them and
that was a test that few survivors of the First World War and its
aftermath were able to pass.

Those were the winners. There were also the losers, but they
wouldn't come to the Palace. They stayed in their cold, lonely
homes. They were bitter and talked endlessly about the wonderful past. Or they complained about the terrible present. Life was
either white or black for them. They didn't want to learn that it
was mostly gray.

❖   ❖

The Palace was a fascinating phenomenon, but phenomena
are short-lived. Their attractiveness is always limited; that is
their essence. At the Palace the handwriting could have been
seen on the mirrors, but people were too busy watching themselves to look. For a few happy, hectic years during the late
1920s and early 1930s the Palace seems to have had a genuine
function as a bridge of tolerance, a structure of compromise, and

perhaps even a way of pseudo life which some believed to be real life. They looked the other way while national and social pressures were building up around them. When the destructive forces of Nazism were building in neighboring Germany and Austria, the Palace, with its glitter, its chandeliers, its mirrors, its chrome fixtures, was unable to sustain itself.

I don't know how the collapse occurred; more exactly, I don't know how it began. First, it was said, some German (Sudeten German) habitués stopped coming to the coffeehouse. They had had no fights; they just stayed away. German managers, architects, lawyers, doctors. The intelligentsia. The actors and editors and musicians still came, but after a while they too left the scene. When we met them in the street and asked them why they no longer came, some of them, the nice ones, seemed embarrassed. We must have been very stupid, we Jews and Czechs. Perhaps we didn't want to know what was happening all around us. Then one heard rumors and incredible stories. A former habitué of the Palace, a German architect who had been there every day, was said to have called the place "a pool of sin." We refused to believe it, since he had been quite happy wading in the pool. Other German ex-habitués were more explicit, avoiding all ambiguity. They said the Café Palace was a "Jewish Sodom."

After that no one could plead naïveté any longer. Strangely, the first to react were not the Jews but the Czechs. The Czech actors, officials, lawyers, and journalists stayed away. Not because they agreed with the Germans: they stayed away in order to protest. The Germans were said to have secret meetings. They now called themselves Sudeten Germans, giving their group a national identity. It seems pretty obvious now, but there were some innocents among the Jews who cautioned patience. The whole thing would blow over and in no time they—the Germans —would be back. There had been similar arguments before, dur-

ing the Habsburg era. Of course, then it was the Czechs who
had suffered from a national minority complex. Once I spoke
about all this to Dr. Spira, the wise Talmudist. He still walked
up and down the western side of the *Rynek*, the main square. I
asked him what he thought of the new "situation." He raised
both hands in a dramatic gesture and let them fall. He looked at
me but spoke no word. Then he nodded and resumed his walk. I
understood his silence; I was shocked by his feeling of resignation.

We Jews still went to the Palace, but after a while some of us
stayed away too. The Depression had finally reached the con-
fines of daily life in my home town. People had no money
for "luxuries," and some said the Palace was too expensive. It
had been axiomatic that no matter how broke you were "you always had money for a black coffee" at the Palace. You might
even tell the headwaiter to write it down, you would pay next
week. But the headwaiter, more impertinent than ever, seemed
to have forgotten the many tips he had received in the past. He
said he could no longer extend credit. He said it with no regret,
implying that there were other coffeehouses in town.

I wasn't at home in March 1939, when the Wehrmacht arrived in Ostrava. I was later told that the Café Palace was one of
the first places they took over. Members of the Gestapo arrived,
accompanied by some former patrons who suddenly wore uniforms. They questioned the headwaiter, the waiters, everybody.
I don't know what happened to the Gronners, but I heard some
ugly stories. Somebody had walked into the Palace, asked for a
"cup of gold," and been arrested. Why? No sense asking. The
man had disappeared; no one pretended to know where he was
or why he had been taken away. A few weeks later his wife had
received a bundle containing the clothes he had worn when he
stepped into the place. She was already a widow but didn't
know it yet.

❖ ❖

I went to the Palace once more in the early 1950s, on my last visit to my home town. This was the dark Stalinist era in Czechoslovakia, when fear was widespread. The Palace was still there. I was surprised. Other citadels of what was now called "the rotten capitalistic bourgeoisie" had been turned into recreation halls for workers or were used for "socially useful functions," such as indoctrination and re-education. It was a great time for semantic nonsense; it still is.

I walked through the revolving door into the coffeehouse. The walls and mirrors were still there, the marble tables and the green plush banquettes. The large place was almost empty. A few people sat around and stared out into the street. They seemed to have been forgotten, or they were waiting for something; it was hard to say. Instinctively I looked up at the gallery. The attractive women had gone, and the card players who had always been there had also disappeared.

I sat down at the table where I had always been with my cousin Fritz. He had been "lucky." He had managed to get away and had lived in Israel for a few years, a tired, sick man, and had died a normal, peaceful death. Had we really been sitting at this table, the one that was always reserved, but with no RESERVED sign on it? The banquette was shabby and should have been redone a long time ago, and the mirror behind me was cracked. The large chandelier was still there but quite a few bulbs were missing. The place was sadly run down. A waiter stood in the corner, reading a newspaper. His tuxedo was as shabby as everything else. He must have seen me but he didn't come over. He was not interested. He got paid very little—waiters are not considered "productive" members of the Communist society. (They can be quite productive in the capitalistic world which, as everybody knows, is headed for eventual oblivion.)

I waited for a while and finally called for service. He came over nonchalantly; he wanted to show me that he didn't care. He brought me a cup with some brownish liquid in it. The cup was slightly cracked and some of the liquid had spilled into the saucer; a small piece of sugar was disintegrating in it. It was hard to remember that the country had once exported a lot of sugar; now it was rationed.

The waiter remained standing next to me. I looked up: he had his right hand extended. He wanted to be paid at once. Now I was really shocked. It had been an unwritten rule of coffeehouse life that the waiter who happened to be nearby would instantly disappear when one called *"Zahlen!"* or *"Platit!"* which means "Check, please," in German or Czech. Even if he had nothing else to do, the waiter tried hard to postpone the ordeal of taking money from you. Some people in a hurry would rise from their table, hoping the waiter might notice their imminent departure, but he still avoided them. Ruthless people would walk toward the revolving door, and naturally the waiter would be standing there, holding his wallet in his hand and staring at the guest regretfully, as if he wanted to ask, "Does it have to be?" The guest paid and was complimented to the door and respectfully asked to come back soon, sir, and give us the honor again.

And now this waiter had violated the sacred rule. Perhaps he wasn't a waiter but only played the part of one. I paid and gave him a tip, which was "officially" forbidden. He took the extra money but did not thank me. That would have been an admission of having accepted a tip. Instead he walked away and resumed reading.

I tasted the brownish liquid, but it didn't taste of coffee. I closed my eyes and tried to recapture the smell of strong coffee that had always enveloped me like a soft blanket the moment I came in through the revolving doors. But it didn't work, my memory didn't function, though I usually remember smells better than faces. The smell didn't return, and I opened my eyes again.

It had been a mistake to come here, searching for something that no longer existed. Only the walls, the tables, the chairs had remained. But the sounds and sights were gone, the voices, the laughter, the faces. I looked around desperately, trying to find *some*thing to lead me back into the past, only twenty years before, and suddenly I felt terribly alone and full of guilt. Why was I sitting here, just I, a former Ostravian *Chachar?* Because I had been lucky, some would say who had been less lucky. But I wasn't lucky to be here. I was conscious of my intense loneliness. And I was afraid to be here, surrounded by ghosts. I got up and walked toward the door. I knew I would never come back to the Palace, never. And I haven't.

14

AMONG THE FEW memorabilia that have survived my past fifty years, the wanderings and dislocations, the wars and revolutions, the hasty departures and moving operations, the luggage and the crates, there is a document I care little about. I have no idea how it did remain among my belongings. In the past thirty years I have never lived in a house of my own, never had my own furniture. Possessions create complications. I often wonder whether my mother would not have been able to leave our home town, after "they" had arrived, if she hadn't cared too much about her possessions. She refused to leave without her china, her rugs, her silver, the many small things she kept in vitrines that had sentimental value only to her. By the time she had resigned herself to leaving everything there it was too late. Ever since, I have kept as little as possible. A few of Poppy's paintings, my violin, my books, the carved wooden statue of St. Sebastian, a few odds and ends. The less the better. But certainly not that "document" which is still here.

It is an impressive roll made of parchmentlike paper, beautifully printed, embroidered with a lace seal. My academic degree, or diploma, from Prague University. The roll is still in the original container. It never occurred to me to have it framed and hung on the wall behind my desk. The document states that on March 8, 1930, I became *doctor juris* under the auspices of Professor Augustinus Naegle, then the Chancellor, of Professor

Marianus San Nicolò, the Ordinarius, much feared during his examinations in Roman law, and of Professor Oscarus Engländer, the Promotor. *"In virum clarissimum, Josephum Wechsberg, e Mähr. Ostrau oriundum, postquam examinibus legitimis laudabilem in universo iure doctrinam probavit."*

I won't attempt to translate it. It sounds better in the original Latin, like the ancient ceremonial of the mass. I am still surprised, though, that I was promoted to doctor of law by my venerable alma mater, founded in 1348, one of the oldest universities in the world.

Prague had rarely been mentioned when I lived at home. Prior to 1918, I knew people who regularly went to Vienna but I remember no one who went to Prague. Some would go *through* Prague on their way to the Bohemian spas, Karlsbad (Karlovy Vary) or Marienbad (Mariánské Lázně), but that was different. Goethe made seventeen well-documented journeys to the Bohemian spas but he never bothered to go to Prague though he called it, with poetic license, "a truly royal and classical city . . . unlike Berlin, which one sees only when one is inside, one sees Prague only from the outside or from above." No wonder he called his autobiography *Dichtung und Wahrheit*. My mother went to Marienbad twice, "to lose weight," as she said. She had to change trains in Prague but didn't bother to walk out of the railroad station to look at the city. She mentioned this after her return as though she were proud of it.

When the family decided, in 1925, that I would study law—I don't remember having been consulted—it had to be Prague University. I was a citizen of Czechoslovakia, and a future lawyer *had* to be a citizen. And in a proper Jewish family in Ostrau the oldest son was expected to be a "Herr Doktor." I dutifully went to Prague, enrolled at the German University—the venerable institution had a Czech and a German branch—and spent a couple of days there, getting acquainted with Herr Wand, the efficient and greedy proctor's man. Fortunately my diploma doesn't say that I rarely attended the professors' lectures and that I was rarely in Prague. Once in a while I returned there from wherever I was for a few weeks of hard study. I always passed the prescribed examinations. My physical presence in Prague during the lectures was "proved" by my inscription book with the signatures of the professors. The book didn't say that the signatures had been obtained through the good services of Herr Wand, who for payment of five Czech crowns, then the price of a tolerable meal, would slip my book among the documents which the professors signed as a matter of daily routine. Then Herr Wand would affix the stamp of the university, making it official.

After enrolling at the university I took a train to Vienna. There was no need to live in Prague, since the first examinations took place only after the end of the third semester and this was still my Viennese period, owing to my mother's reminiscences and to my infatuation with music and opera. In Vienna, I studied music at the Academy, for myself, and went to the Opera and eventually became a member of the celebrated claque there. For the family, I studied at the Hochschule für Welthandel (University for World Trade). My uncles thought the Hochschule "sounded well" and the studies there would help me "to get into industry" if I should really be a failure at law, as I had indicated. I hated every moment of it. It was a complicated life, keeping up with all these institutions of higher learning, and sometimes I didn't know where I was. No wonder I finally dropped everything and escaped to Paris to play the fiddle.

Among the events I remember in Vienna, aside from spending almost every night in the Fourth Gallery at the Opera, was my short meeting with Arthur Schnitzler. The governess in Schnitzler's house in Sternwartestrasse was the sister of my uncle Heinrich in Olmütz (Olomouc), the one who had sponsored my poor mother's unfortunate adventure, the elegant stationer's shop that later went broke. Possibly to atone for his sin, Uncle Heinrich had asked the governess, his sister, to introduce me to the great poet and playwright. Schnitzler, then in his middle sixties, benevolently talked to me for a while. He was an impressive man with a carefully trimmed beard and deep, penetrating eyes. We didn't talk about his plays, which I really didn't understand at that time. Only much later did I admire Schnitzler's amazing knowledge of people and his obsession with the eternal themes of life, love, and death. I don't remember what he told me that day, but I now feel I understand his writings better because I "met" him.

In Vienna, Schnitzler was widely admired as a writer's writer, but I was no writer yet. Personally I revered him for his fantastic foresight. He had accurately sensed the breakdown of the Habsburg monarchy and its society. He had known the future as only a true poet knows it, but there was nothing he could have done about it. He wrote his plays and went to the coffeehouse and was much maligned and often misunderstood. I did not go to the coffeehouses where the writers of Vienna made daily appearances; I was too busy with my music and my claque activities. On the rare evenings when the claque wasn't busy at the Opera —when *Parsifal* was given, since a mysterious tradition did not permit applause during and after that opera—I would attend a Schnitzler performance at one of Vienna's theaters. I also began to read about the conservative rebels of the various Viennese schools. Peter Altenberg, poet and raconteur—a typical Viennese combination—who began as a member of the literary group known as "Young Vienna" and later became almost a professional anarchist, in a mild, Viennese way, to be sure. And Karl Kraus, poet and essayist, playwright and moralist, whom we admired for his courage, waging his personal war against "the morally corrupt society of Vienna." After a slight acquaintance with this segment of Vienna, during my week in Uncle Alfred's house, I had had the strange feeling that Kraus had been hiding behind the curtains in Aunt Anna's drawing room with the free-standing staircase, taking down some conversations verbatim. I didn't understand that a good writer doesn't have to be there. He *knows*.

❖   ❖

Eventually I did receive my diploma. There I was, a *doctor juris*, twenty-three and called upon to go into a profession which I disliked, as soon as I had passed my eighteen-month military service in the Czechoslovak army. I would have to begin as a *Konzipient*, an apprentice-at-law, before I was permitted to prac-tice law on my own. In a law office the youngest *Konzipient* had to do the dirty work. Naturally. Getting up at six in the morn-ing, on a cold winter day, to be in court before eight, while sen-ior partners were having a leisurely breakfast and reading the morning paper. It was no consolation to know that they too had started out as *Konzipients*. Another distasteful duty was the de-fense of petty criminals who were entitled to a lawyer but couldn't afford one. The Lawyers' Chamber would assign an *ex officio* lawyer to them, with no payment. When it was the turn of our office the criminal wouldn't get the experienced senior partner but the struggling *Konzipient*. Naturally.

❖   ❖

Actually, I was lucky in my first job. I became *Konzipient* at the feudal law office of Dr. Fajfrlik, the most distinguished Czech law firm in my home town. There were also German and Jewish firms and other Czech law offices, but none could com-pete with Dr. Fajfrlik's patina and noblesse. The rooms had the forbiddingly formidable appearance that I later saw again in some celebrated law offices in London and Boston. Old wood paneling, old leather chairs, dim lights, everything quiet, the smell of old leather bindings. No one ever raised his voice. No one used the brutal indicative verb form if he could employ the conciliatory subjective, which is tricky in Czech—but that was the only concession made to legalistic necessities. At the office of Dr. Fajfrlik a fact was a fact, not the reason for finding a loophole around it. If the fact was confirmed, it became part of the record. No one assured a client he was innocent on the mere presumption that he just couldn't be guilty because he had a name or money or an alibi. The standard of professional ethics was high. It was that kind of office.

I got the job because my friends predicted I would never get it. It was a successful protest action. They said I was a Jew and had gone to German schools, the exact opposite of what they needed at Dr. Fajfrlik's. I had no letter of recommendation, I was not introduced by anyone, I simply went. I was interviewed by Dr. Fajfrlik, Jr., the son of the firm's owner, who had the build of a strong fullback. As we talked we both remembered having played soccer on opposite teams, during Gymnasium tournaments. Junior had of course gone to the Czech Gymnasium. We didn't remember having met but it was agreed we might have shaken hands at the end of a game, as was customary. It was a pleasant talk.

After a while Fajfrlik, Jr., remembered why I was there and took me into his father's office. The older Fajfrlik was a venerable patriarch whom I had often admired when I saw him in the street. He had a white beard, wore black clothes and a golden watch chain over his waistcoat, and he had a pince-nez. This gave him a faint resemblance to President Masaryk, which was perhaps no coincidence. Dr. Fajfrlik had been a personal friend of Professor Masaryk in the final years of the Habsburg monarchy, when both had been considered potential "traitors" in Vienna. It had taken *Zivilcourage* to remain a friend of Masaryk in those days. No wonder that professional ethics was a way of life at the Fajfrlik law firm.

The old gentleman talked to me for a few minutes while Junior kept a deferential silence. Not about law and the university. He knew, of course, that I knew nothing about the practice of law. He asked me whether I had done my military service in the Czechoslovak army and seemed pleased when I told him that I was now a lieutenant in the reserve, infantry. He nodded and talked about my family. He had known my father and Grandfather Wechsberg.

Dr. Fajfrlik chuckled.

"Your grandfather was a smart man but a decent man," he said. "An unusual combination for a modern banker."

He chuckled once more, and nodded to his son, the soccer fullback, and that was that. I was hired. I would remain there until the son of a partner who was now studying law in Prague was ready to join the firm. I agreed with the understanding and left the office proudly. My friends in Ostrava thought I was kidding when I told them I was on the staff of the celebrated law firm.

The older Fajfrlik had founded it at a time when the expanding mining firms and large corporations began needing legal advice. The firm was mostly involved in the tricky problems of corporate law. Our clients, the general managers and presidents of the large, old companies, came to us for Interpretation of the Law and for Advice—and not because they were in a jam. They might have problems but they rarely had trouble. Cheats, crooks, and experts in repeated bankruptcy certainly did exist—but not within the refined sphere of our law firm. They went elsewhere. Anyway, they wouldn't have liked the ambiance of the Fajfrlik offices, where elderly women, dressed in black and looking like court councilors' widows, acted as secretaries. They treated files with reverence and carried briefs around like gold certificates.

Sometimes I was asked to study a complex legal problem for days and write an opinion on it. Quite a challenge for a young man of twenty-five whose past included a stretch of playing the fiddle in disreputable brothels in Montmartre. They knew it and couldn't have cared less. As the only staff member who spoke German and French, I was soon promoted as a sort of diplomatic attaché. I was asked to join meetings when board members from France and other faraway countries visited the corporate head-quarters in Ostrava. At the law office of Dr. Fajfrlik I might have become a real lawyer, a jurist of prominence, perhaps even a luminary of legalistic wisdom. It wasn't in my cards, though. Eventually the partner's son finished his studies in Prague and was ready to join the firm. I shook hands with the Fajfrliks, father and son. They wished me luck and meant it. I left them with real regret.

Having worked at the most prominent law firm in Ostrava, there was no way for me to go up locally, and I didn't like the idea of going down. Also, I was becoming aware of the limited range of possibilities in the "provinces." We were not "provincial" in Ostrava, certainly not; but it was a city in the provinces. I decided to try the capital. Prague in 1934 was not a bad place to be. The country was in serious trouble. In neighboring Germany Hitler had come to power in 1933 and now threatened the very independence of Czechoslovakia. When one is young and unafraid, the capital of a troubled country is an interesting place. Some people said it was high time to get out, that we were all living on borrowed time. I thought they were crazy. But in 1934 I wouldn't have cared even if I had *known* they were going to be right.

❖   ❖

Many fast trains leaving Ostrava consisted of two parts. One went to Vienna, the other to Prague. At the railroad junction of Přerov the train was divided. The forward coaches went on the western branch of the line to Prague, and the rear coaches followed the southern route to Vienna. Since 1930, when I graduated from Prague University, I had no longer ridden a coach in the rear, marked with the sign "Wien." Vienna had lost much of its attraction. It was still a good place to enjoy music and opera, but it was a dying city, almost an artificial city. Perhaps I was no longer young, *really* young. Instead I would board a coach in the front part of the train marked "Praha." The main railroad station was named after President Wilson. Most people approved. They said the least one could do for Woodrow Wilson, who had helped to establish the Czechoslovak Republic, was to name the station after him.

By that time I had been all over the world. I had learned history the hard way, at first hand. I might spend an occasional week in Vienna when the State Opera had an especially tempting program. But gradually I began to feel more at home in Prague. It's hard to explain. Everybody was alive and the peculiar border situation—Czechs living next to Germans and Jews—reflected the situation in my home town. I preferred the polemical life in Prague to the decadent elegance of Vienna.

❖   ❖

In Prague I found a job with the law firm of Dr. A. and Dr. P. There I was introduced to the less distinguished but perhaps much more common practice of law. It was an active firm but not an eminent one, like Dr. Fajfrlik's. Our clients didn't come for Expert Opinion or Legal Advice. They needed help because they were in trouble, and please don't ask too many questions. They did not belong to what was then somewhat euphemistically known as the privileged classes. They had cheated on their taxes and been caught, they beat their wives and forgot to pay their alimony, they double-crossed their partners and defrauded their bosses. Many of them lived in the dim border zone between felony and crime.

The best one could do for them, I was taught in my new job, was to turn their delicts "into something less serious." At the law offices of Dr. A. and Dr. P. there was no respect for facts. Facts were either ignored or circumvented; there were always "ways and means." There were "mistakes" and "mistaken identities," witnesses who conveniently didn't remember and psychiatrists who made people remember only certain things. It was quite a shock for the former *Konzipient* at Dr. Fajfrlik's, and not a healthy one.

The first rule in my new job was, "The client is never wrong." Disappointed and finally desperate, I began writing, mostly at night. I sensed that my days as a lawyer were numbered. I was having arguments with my bosses, who were irritated by what they called "my ethical excesses." Eventually I was ordered to leave my ethics at home.

"You'll have to learn a lot," said Dr. A., the older partner. "First, an able lawyer does nothing in a simple manner that can be done in a complicated way. Second, there is no so-called unlawful action that cannot be explained and excused, if a lawyer has knowledge and skill and knows his way around."

Dr. P., the younger partner, agreed. "To err is human, and lawmakers are human. They make errors when they write their laws. They leave some things unsaid. We exploit their omissions. We are optimists. We know that there is always a way out. Most people don't know it, of course, and that's why they ask us for help."

Dr. A. compared a law to a net made of meshes. "One tries to open a mesh here and another one there. It would help you if you would presume the client to be innocent."

I said, perhaps foolishly, "Even if I am convinced that he is not innocent?"

Dr. A. pushed his glasses up from the tip of his nose, where he wore them when he was reading, to the customary position in front of his eyes. He gave me a penetrating glance. I felt like a medieval cardinal who has expressed doubts about doctrine and is called before the Inquisition.

"Such opinions," he said, "will not get you far in our profession. Also, you show no imagination when writing out bills."

"A little fantasy is a good thing, *Herr Kollege*," said the younger partner.

Again I was foolish and told them about a lawyer in my home town who was well known for the bizarre imagination shown in his bills. He was said to invent improbable lines of action and claimed to have rendered professional services under hazardous circumstances. I once saw one of his bills, which said, "Woke up at night and worried for one hour about case: 100 crowns."

My bosses saw no humor in this story. Dr. P. thought it was a brilliant idea and he might occasionally "borrow" it. Dr. A. concluded sadly that I was probably in the wrong profession.

Oddly, it was a client named Zabloudil who brought my law career to a sudden end. Many people in Prague who believed in the mysticism of nomenclature were not surprised. The Czech word *zabloudil* means "he went astray." Zabloudil had gone astray and admitted it. His candor was refreshing. He didn't deny it, he was no victim of circumstance. He had played around with the firm's balance sheets and said he ought to be punished. He had done it for years and now the tax people knew it. What they didn't know, not yet anyway, was that Zabloudil's boss, the manager, had known for years about his bookkeeper's activities, and thus was an accomplice.

"The tax people still think I was doing it on my own," Zabloudil said. "But of course it's bound to come out."

"Nothing is bound to come out," Dr. A. said with quiet dignity. "You will deny the accusations. You made a few mistakes. We shall prove it. Maybe you acted under irresistible compulsion."

Zabloudil shook his head. "There was no compulsion at all, *pane doktore*. I knew what I was doing. I also embezzled funds of the firm, at least half a million crowns. I made false statements under oath. For the past eight months I have paid no alimony to my divorced wife, and now she is after me. And—"

"Pane Zabloudil," interrupted Dr. A., "you've come to the wrong place. Why don't you go to a priest and make a confession?"

"Exactly what I told my boss, the manager. But he insisted that I come and see you. For the sake of the firm. He says the firm always had a good name."

"He is right," said Dr. A. "We have represented your firm for years. And we are going to preserve its good name."

If all this sounds like a chapter from *The Good Soldier Schweik*, the illusion was strengthened by Zabloudil's appearance. He had a certain resemblance to Jaroslav Hašek's immortal anti-hero, as drawn by Josef Lada. Zabloudil had a round face, a turned-up nose, and his eyes reflected the innocence of a happy childhood. He looked honest and trustful.

"Everybody makes mistakes," Dr. A. said sententiously. "From this moment on, Mr. Zabloudil, you'll talk to no one. You'll remember nothing. *We* are going to do the talking for you. You are in capable hands."

Zabloudil looked surprised. "Do you really think you can fix it? But they *know* what I have done. The only thing they don't know is that the manager—"

"Pane Zabloudil!" Dr. A. got up, dramatically raising both hands. "I don't want to hear anything. Go back and do your work. We will confer about the situation and then we shall decide on our strategy."

Zabloudil seemed dazed. He wanted to say something, shook his head, and walked out.

Eventually he was charged with half a dozen crimes and was

going to be tried. Dr. A. didn't worry. He would personally defend our client. He and his junior partner had designed a complex scenario of what they called "the lines of conduct." They had almost convinced Zabloudil that the manager was innocent, that Zabloudil himself was almost innocent.

And then Fate intervened on my behalf. Or the Good Lord who didn't want me to become a lawyer. Dr. A. got sick and Dr. P. was called out of the country. We tried to postpone Zabloudil's trial but failed. Dr. A. called me from his sickbed and told me to take over for him.

"You've been in on this case from the beginning, *Herr Kollege.* You've talked to Zabloudil repeatedly when you went to see him in jail. He is ready for all contingencies. He studied his instructions. And you know yours."

I did. My bosses had built a fine house of cards, blending certain facts with confusing excuses. They had drilled Zabloudil, who would claim that he was innocent. He had "only" misunderstood his instructions. He had committed a few errors, no more.

I went to see him the day before the trial. He radiated honesty. He was confident that he would get away with it.

But the next morning, when two uniformed guards escorted him into the courtroom, he looked pale and shaken. His confidence was gone.

I asked him what had happened. *Every*thing had happened. Late in the afternoon, after I had gone, he had been visited by a lady named Vlasta. She had told him it was all over between them.

Zabloudil had never mentioned to me a lady named Vlasta.

"Excuse me, *pane doktore,* but a man has a right to his private life, hasn't he? I didn't want Vlasta to get involved. She had agreed to wait for me even if there should be—a certain delay.

Then the two of us would go to South America. To start a new life. I love her. And now—" He buried his face in his hands.

"And now what?"

"Yesterday she told me it's finished. She is going to marry another fellow who is not involved with lawyers and crooks and the courts."

It was too late to do anything. The judge entered, the bill of indictment was read. Zabloudil seemed apathetic. He didn't seem to care about anything. The judge asked him whether he pleaded guilty or not guilty.

I wanted to intervene but Zabloudil jumped up. Yes, he was guilty on all counts, and he wanted to go to prison. He sat down, looking relieved.

There was some confusion in the courtroom. The judge seemed perplexed. The public prosecutor, whom I had known when we both studied at the university, came over to me.

"You may claim sudden irresponsibility for your client," he whispered to me. "We may agree to postpone the trial. Otherwise you may have trouble with your bosses." He was a nice guy.

I thanked him and asked Zabloudil to claim sudden confusion. We might obtain a postponement. The medical experts would be asked for their opinion.

He shook his head. He didn't look confused. "No," he said aloud so everybody could hear him. "I want to go to prison. And I hope the manager goes to prison too, where he belongs."

Zabloudil got two years, owing to extenuating circumstances. The manager was arrested and later got three years, despite the active efforts of Dr. A. and Dr. P. But that was long after I'd worked for them. Dr. A. had fired me, by telephone, when I came back from court. My legal career had come to an end.

❖   ❖

The first thing I did after losing my job in Prague was to take a train to Vienna. I felt like going home, or at least back. When

I got into the ópera house and sensed the smell of cold marble, my heart was beating. I bought a standing-room ticket in the Fourth Gallery and ran up the hundred and twenty-six stairs. Some of the people I had known were there and were glad to see me. A little surprised, perhaps, but I didn't understand their surprise.

I don't remember the performance, I don't even know what opera was performed that night. But I was there, I was back. For a while it was like old times.

It didn't last. This was 1935, and it wasn't like the old days. There were people in uniforms at the Opera. My friends in the Fourth Gallery claque told me they had been "ordered" to applaud for certain artists with impeccable Aryan ancestry. I looked at them, speechless.

"It no longer matters how they sing," one man said. "But they must be all right."

"All right?" I asked stupidly.

"Not musically but politically." And he told me he had traveled to a small place in Carinthia where his family had lived for generations, to get an *Ahnenpass* (genealogical passport) proving beyond doubt that he had been of Aryan ancestry for generations.

"But the Germans are not here," I said desperately.

"Not yet," he said.

I soon found out that he had not exaggerated. In the theaters of Vienna there had been a change. Not on the stage, the actors were still as good as ever. But the audience was different. At the Theater in der Josefstadt, which Max Reinhardt had created, an actor explained to me that they had to change their timing.

"It's hard to explain," he said wonderingly. "People used to react faster. The laughs would come more quickly. There were so many Jews in the audience and they would laugh first, and the others would follow. These people are no longer there. Some have gone away, and those who stay don't feel like coming to the theater."

He gave a helpless shrug. "So we have to adjust. We have to wait longer until the laugh comes—and sometimes it doesn't come at all."

I was walking all over Vienna, trying (as Brahms had said) to retrace my steps. The houses where Beethoven, Mozart, Brahms, and Bruckner had lived were still there. The memorial tablets were there. But these were just houses—walls and roofs and windows and marble plates. It wasn't the same any more. I went to the Opera once more, but I didn't enjoy the evening, and I went back to Prague.

The following year I went around the world. I was writing, and I had hoped that the combined income from some newspapers in Prague, Vienna, and Switzerland would finance my trip. This time I arrived in America from Hawaii and landed in San Francisco. I crossed the United States by Greyhound bus. An exhausting experience but an interesting one, and I was young.

After my return to Prague, I went to Vienna once more. It must have been late in 1937, and some people were very nervous. They said "it" was bound to happen very soon. Schostal, the head of the claque, and my friends from the Fourth Gallery had disappeared. No one knew where they were. When I asked, people shrugged their shoulders. I became accustomed to the meaningful shrug. It was by way of an answer.

The next time I saw Vienna it was on the screen of a Prague movie theater. I saw the Heldenplatz, crowded with enthusiastic people; the Führer, also an Austrian, spoke to them from the balcony of the new Hofburg. It was depressing.

Life in Prague was not dull in these months. People were still under the illusion that they would be spared the nightmare but they didn't really believe it, and they spent their money recklessly. "You cannot take it with you," they said. "Might as well spend it."

Everybody said the end of the world, as we had known it, was close; but no one knew *how* close it was, and no one did anything about it. Hadn't there always been catastrophes? We would survive the next one too, or wouldn't we?

In September 1938 my wife and I went to America. As tourists, for three months, that was the idea. The Czechoslovak government had partly financed the trip. I was to address American audiences about the Sudeten German problem. I spoke no English, but the lectures were written for me and I would learn them by heart, phonetically.

We were in the middle of the Atlantic, on the French Line ship *Champlain*, when the ship's radio reported that the Munich agreement had been signed on September 30 and that the Sudetenland had been occupied the following day. When we arrived in New York and I went to report to the Czechoslovak Consulate General at 1440 Broadway there was a white spot on the wall in the room of the consul general, where the picture of President Eduard Beneš had hung. It was all over. I would have to start a new life. In America.

✥ 15. ✥

I HAD MY father's cuff links with me when I went to America, and I often wore them, even on occasions when more elegant cuff links were called for. Instinctively I preferred the plain ones with my mother's portrait, the ones my father had ordered and had liked so much. I owned some gold cuff links, but I rarely wore them. Once a woman in Hollywood—it would be Hollywood—asked me why I didn't wear "the gold things." I told her the story of how my father had gone to a gifted silversmith in Vienna with a photograph of my mother and had the cuff links made to order.

She listened and nodded, as though she were apologizing.

"Of course," she said. "Of course."

Not long ago I noticed here in Vienna that the subtle mechanism that holds the cuffs together didn't function properly any more. The tiny lever, shaped like a miniature boat and fixed by a thin metal thread to the stem of the links, seemed precariously low, on the verge of breaking off. Once I did lose the left cuff link—fortunately at home where I later found it on the rug. Had this happened outside in the street, the cuff link would truly have been lost. Someone might have found it but would he take an old silver cuff link—worthless, so to speak—to the nearest police station?

I wrapped the cuff links in soft tissue paper. I would take

them to the small, old jeweler's shop in Vienna's Operngasse. From the entrance one can see the southwest corner of the State Opera. The small shop is only a few years younger than the Opera; it has been there since 1891. It cannot compete with a fashionable modern jeweler not far away who usually exhibits only one large diamond in his window. An impressive stone, lying in a small box lined with blue velvet, illuminated at night by two powerful lights from above. No alarm mechanism is visible but it's quite obvious that a modern alarm was installed. Vienna, like so many other big cities, is no longer a safe place.

The smaller shop exhibits some old things that cannot compare with the commercial value of the large diamond. They have had great sentimental value to their owners, though. The store window facing the street is filled with an odd profusion of medallions, old bracelets, brooches, gems, and chains made of semi-precious stones. There are small and large watches, among them a Schaffhausen pocket watch exactly like the one my father had worn on a chain and which later "disappeared." The store specializes in old pieces. The owner buys them from elderly people who need the money, or from younger people who do not care about silly heirlooms—people who think they need the money so they can spend it quickly. Lately there has been much demand for old things, and the owner of the store ordered some pieces reproduced. But she is a decent woman and tells you the truth: some things are not really old, they only look old.

Inside there are vitrines filled with an assortment of old glasses, china, ivory, jade. The finest piece—it is not for sale—is the ancient regulation clock, over two hundred years old, whose round pendulum ticks off the seconds with imperturbable calm. The clock is run by a bronze weight hanging from a chain. Once a year the clock is wound with a special key and the bronze weight is lifted up. The clock is said to be as accurate as the modern electronic clocks.

I had discovered the lovely old store a while ago when it was necessary to have my old alarm clock repaired. That is another heirloom dear to me: as long as I can remember, it stood on my mother's bedside table. It was made around the turn of the century—at the same time as the cuff links—in the Swiss Jura, and survived despite improbable dislocations. The clock is housed in a rectangular glass case held together by a brass frame, displaying proudly its inner secrets. On top, visible under the glass, is the small wheel that watchmakers call the balance, swinging back and forth. When you press a small button on top, the chimes will tell you the time, very pleasant at night when you lie in bed and don't want to turn on the light. The dial has Roman numerals—once fashionable, later outdated, and nowadays again fashionable.

The clockwork's sound is pleasant and melodious, unlike modern alarms that are often shrill and make an awful racket. The old alarm clock will wake you, but gently. The chimes ring every quarter of an hour, and they are sweet and soft and don't disturb your sleep. On the contrary, one would miss their absence.

Whether my mother bought the clock or my father gave it to her, I cannot say. But after my father had gone and we were "suddenly" poor, and my brother and I slept in my mother's bedroom because she had to rent the children's room, the alarm clock was always on her bedside table. On school days, when I had to get up in the morning, she would set the alarm for seven-fifteen. It always worked and woke me, and I slipped effortlessly from morning slumber into consciousness. The clock was on my mother's bedside table when I left my home town and went to Prague and, in the summer of 1938, to America.

For a while I missed the sweet sound of the chimes. But when one is young one doesn't miss possessions for very long; more important things came up, and the sound of the chimes was forgot-

ten. We were immigrants in New York, concerned with the little important problems of survival, and later we went to
Southern California because people said it was less expensive to
live there. It was, and it also was a very strange life, and I don't
like to think of it. But I remember the day when we were
notified that a large wooden box had arrived from Ostrava. It
was late in 1940. My mother had packed some things that she
wanted us to have, "before it is too late." Perhaps she already
knew that she wouldn't be able to keep them. Fine old linen, tablecloths and napkins, embroidered with her initials, some of the
old silver she had loved so much, and a few pieces of Meissen
china. And the dear old alarm clock, in its original black leather
case, with the key in a special compartment. You pressed the top
of the case at a certain spot, the top opened, and the clock could
be taken out.

I pressed the top and took out the clock and the key. I had no
hope it would be running after that long journey. Much of the
Meissen china was broken. My mother had been unable to get
expert packers; how she managed at all to get the wooden box
out of German-occupied Czechoslovakia I cannot say. She must
have fought a stubborn battle against some minor Nazi bureaucrats and must have filled out innumerable documents. Perhaps
she had had the secret help of some Czechs who hated the
Nazis. She never wrote about it, she didn't dare. Somehow the
box had reached a German port—I believe it was Hamburg—
and started its long, slow voyage across the Atlantic, through
the Panama Canal, along the west coast of the United States,
until it arrived at the port of Los Angeles.

I remember well how I slowly wound the clock, with no hope,
and suddenly the small wheel started running back and forth.
The clock was all right! The chimes too were working, the familiar sound. We placed the clock on the mantel above the fireplace. The fireplace didn't work but the clock did, its chimes

marking each quarter hour. When we had company, people were delighted with it. It was no longer an alarm clock but a minor work of art in the living room.

Later the clock accompanied us as we drove from the west coast to Connecticut, and as we took the boat back to Europe. We didn't dare ship it, it had become too precious; we carried it in our luggage. Here in Vienna, I again keep it in the living room. Not above the fireplace, because in Vienna there are no fireplaces, but on top of a baroque chest, next to a wooden Madonna. The Madonna and the old alarm clock seem to like one another.

Eventually time caught up with the clock, as it does with us. Clocks have much in common with human hearts. Someday both stop running. The alarm didn't stop suddenly. I suppose it was too well brought up to quit overnight. But it had to be wound more frequently and it badly needed cleaning. I had never taken it to a watchmaker, afraid he might repair it so thoroughly that it would never run again. But now there was no alternative. I took it to the small jeweler's store. I had seen two similar old pieces in the shopwindow. Perhaps they had a skilled watchmaker to whom we might entrust our old clock. I wouldn't take it to one of these modern stores selling quartz crystal watches that look like small computers, and tiny computers looking like wristwatches. Nothing looks like itself any more; appearances are intentionally deceiving. I believe that an alarm clock should look like one. At the old store they might understand the clock. They might have patience with it.

❖   ❖

I had never been inside. When I opened the door I expected a bell would ring—it was that kind of door. But it didn't. Two old, fragile ladies sat behind the counter. They reminded me of the nice women murderers of *Arsenic and Old Lace,* though of course they wouldn't have murdered anyone. When I came in they seemed worried rather than pleased. I understood. They had heard all these stories of jewelers being held up. A man coming in alone was suspicious.

The smaller one—later I found out she had been the owner since the death of her husband, who had been an expert watchmaker—had asked her cousin to stay with her. She admitted there was little they could do if a determined would-be burglar came in. They couldn't afford a modern alarm system.

Apparently I convinced them that I wanted to take nothing. On the contrary, I wanted to leave something there. The ladies relaxed. They admired the old alarm clock. So much more beautiful than the new ones now made in Germany and elsewhere. Some had rich, gold-plated frames; the old ladies, though, liked the bronze frame better. Did I know that such a genuine old clock was now worth at least seventeen thousand schillings (more than fifteen hundred dollars)? No, that wasn't the point, certainly not, the cousin said. But these clocks went back to the generation of our grandparents, and someday they would all be gone. Both ladies sighed. I liked the way they looked at my clock, as though it were an old person.

I had been right. They still had an old artisan—one "should really call him an artist," said the smaller one—who understood these clocks. He was probably the only real expert in the city. They spoke of him with respect, almost with awe. They didn't mention his name; he was to remain a nebulous figure. Right now he was busy and could not be bothered. But eventually he would get around to my alarm, would take it apart—"very, very carefully, do not worry"—and clean it. The job would take a long time and—here they coughed apologetically—it would be expensive. Such repairs were no longer made commercially, routinely. The artist was getting two hundred and fifty schillings an hour, almost fifteen dollars, and he worked only a few hours a day because his eyes were getting bad.

In fact, said the owner, it might almost be less expensive to buy a new imitation, with a one-year guarantee and a sturdy, noisy alarm that would wake up even the soundest sleeper.

"Of course, you wouldn't want a new clock," said the cousin. She pronounced the word "new" with distaste.

Of course not, I said. I understood also about the expense, as long as it was treated gently by a man who understood it. The two ladies were delighted. Just then a hard-boiled woman came in and, without bothering to wait her turn, said she had a little extra money, "over ten thousand schillings," and wanted to buy something that had value and would look nice on her. She turned and looked at herself in the mirror but I don't think she liked what she saw there. Well, she said to the two old ladies, how about showing her some things?

The small woman seemed flustered and looked at me. I said it was all right and left my name and telephone number, and asked them to call me when the clock was ready. They looked at me gratefully and I walked out. Turning left, I stood in front of the State Opera. Some things at least didn't seem to change—or did they? Now it wouldn't occur to me to climb up to the Fourth Gallery, though the acoustics there are still the best. How many times had I run up the stairs, arriving with my heart beating fast, to get a good place in the first row of standees. Later, my heart might beat again when somebody sang especially well and we members of the claque started the well-deserved applause.

Nowadays I sit downstairs in the stalls. Very comfortable, and I am surrounded by substantial-looking people who can afford the prices. But their hearts don't seem to beat faster when somebody sings exceptionally well, and the claque in the rear and upstairs is noisy and shouts and protracts the applause—something we would never have done—until the people around me start to get annoyed and hiss "Sh." In such moments I look up. I almost wish one could turn the clock back, but one cannot.

❖   ❖

The ladies called to tell me that the old alarm clock had been repaired. When I went there they told me the clock was almost as good as new. The soft chimes still tell the quarter hour. The alarm doesn't function properly, but I said I no longer needed the alarm. No more school, no more early trains and planes.

A little later, when I lost and luckily recovered the left cuff link, I naturally took the cuff links there. They might have an old silversmith who would be able to fix the mechanism. The old ladies nodded understandingly. When I told them the little angel was really my mother, they both had tears in their eyes.

"Your mother when she was very young?" the smaller woman asked.

"Yes. I wasn't even born yet."

"And you still have them," said the cousin, nodding, stating a simple fact. "And you are afraid to lose them."

They looked at the mechanism, which was still working but seemed fragile. The owner said yes, they had a silversmith. Even older than the watchmaker, and he didn't work much any more, only if a special job appealed to him.

"He might do it," she said. "Or he might not. It's hard to say. Goodness, he may even be the man who originally made these cuff links. It's fine Viennese workmanship."

I said that would be too much of a coincidence, and besides, I no longer believed in coincidences.

She said, "He's a decent man. When he thinks the repair will be too expensive he suggests that the customer buy something new instead. But I suppose in your case—"

"Yes. I'm not going to buy a new pair of cuff links."

Two weeks later they called and asked me to come by. When I stepped in, the owner of the store went to the small safe in the rear and opened it. She took out the cuff links as though they were jewels of great value.

She said the old silversmith couldn't remember having made these cuff links, but he'd had a couple of friends when he was young who had specialized in that kind of work. They had died long ago.

I looked at the cuff links. They didn't seem to have been touched.

"He explained to us he would be afraid to repair them," said the owner. "He would have to use a soldering lamp and might hurt the silver profile. The dark color might go. And the lovely profile might disappear entirely. You would have a sturdy clasp but no longer the cuff links you like so much."

She looked at me. "I am sure you wouldn't want that to happen."

I shook my head.

"Take them with you," she said. "Wear them at home where you are sure to find them if you lose one or both links. Actually, the mechanism is still working well though it looks brittle. But don't take any chances, don't wear them outside. You wouldn't want to lose your beautiful cuff links, would you?"

No, I don't want to lose them. I put them in my pocket, and I thanked the two old ladies and left.

I still have my father's cuff links.